S0-BDL-378

BISON
BOOKS

OUTPOST OF THE SIOUX WARS
A History of Fort Robinson

Frank N. Schubert

University of Nebraska Press
Lincoln and London

♾ The paper in this book meets the minimum requirements of American
National Standard for Information Sciences—Permanence of Paper for Printed
Library Materials, ANSI Z39.48-1984.

First Bison Book printing: 1995
Most recent printing indicated by the last digit below:
10   9   8   7   6   5   4   3   2   1

Library of Congress Cataloging-in-Publication Data
Schubert, Frank N.
[Buffalo soldiers, braves, and the brass]
Outpost of the Sioux Wars: a history of Fort Robinson / by Frank N. Schubert.
p.   cm.
Originally published as: Buffalo soldiers, braves, and the brass, by White Mane
Pub. Co., 1993.
Includes bibliographical references and index.
ISBN 0-8032-9226-0 (pbk.: alk. paper)
1. Fort Robinson (Neb.)—History.   I. Title.
F674.F7S35   1995
978.2'93—dc20
94-45252   CIP

Reprinted by arrangement with the White Mane Publishing Company. The
original title was *Buffalo Soldiers, Braves, and the Brass: The Story of Fort
Robinson, Nebraska*.

To Irene

TABLE OF CONTENTS

AUTHOR'S PREFACE

The individual military post has been a popular focal point for the study of the Army's functions in the trans-Mississippi West. While fort histories vary in quality, they all reflect an ongoing concern with the role of the Army in the spread of Anglo-American society over the continent. Although most of the authors of such works understand that the military had an impact beyond the subjugation of tenacious Indian foes, their publications frequently mention the diverse functions of the Army only in passing and concentrate on the battles and campaigns of the Indian wars.[1] So many areas of inquiry are left unexplored or only briefly mentioned.

The fort was a community with problems of housing, sanitation, education, and social services. It had its own class structure and complex relations with neighboring civilian communities. Enlisted men and officers, blacks and whites, and soldiers and civilians established a web of interdependencies. Soldiers sought recreation and entertainment, officers looked for investment opportunities, and civilians sought markets for their goods and services. The post offered important facilities and aid to early settlers and a source of income for growing communities. The town, on the other hand, served the military community in a number of ways, from real estate investments to prostitution. These and other relationships bound the military and civilian communities together.

So the history of Fort Robinson, like that of other military posts, is much more than a record of battles. This book attempts to delineate the development of the post as a community whose three main components—officers with their wives and children, married enlisted men and their families, and the single men in the barracks—lived in close physical proximity but under substantially different conditions. Divided by military rank and traditions and sometimes by race, these parts of the community had their own social lives and problems as well as different relations with the nearby town of Crawford.

vii

Because Fort Robinson housed black troops for many years, race relations formed a significant part of the post's history. The black Ninth and Tenth Cavalry regiments, both of which earned reputations for skill and reliability in the Indian wars before coming to Robinson, spent several years on post.[2] Portions of the Ninth garrisoned the fort from 1885 to 1898. The Tenth came later, from 1902 to 1907. The discrimination practiced by post authorities and the response of townspeople to the black garrisons are only part of the matter. The African-American men and their families also had to come to terms with the situation, while maintaining their ties with the African-American community at large.

In many respects, Fort Robinson resembled a company town in which decisions regarding the nature and distribution of services emanated from a central authority. The Army provided a whole range of social services in schools and library, church and hospital. Although very important to the enlisted community, these services sometimes proved inadequate. In these cases the men pooled their resources and leadership to meet their needs, whether for a Sunday school or a forum for the discussion of race issues. The enlisted soldiers several times filled voids left by official negligence and indifference.

While discussing these services and the military community itself, this book also examines the impact of the fort on the neighboring town of Crawford. The civilian community depended on military spending in various ways. War Department expenditures for contracts stimulated business and brought some residents power and profit while the money spent by soldiers on whisky and sex helped support municipal government through taxation of saloons and prostitutes. For the town as a whole, dependence on the post brought a steady source of income and ultimately a well-deserved reputation as a regional center of vice, "the stink pot of Northwest Nebraska."[3]

Evolving in conjunction with the town for which it provided important services and opportunities, the post was itself a community with many of the needs, problems, and complexities of other western settlements. While it shared many characteristics with other kinds of communities, most notably company towns, Fort Robinson was above all part of a huge public investment in the spread of Anglo-American society throughout the trans-Mississippi West, an outpost that protected and nurtured civilian settlement in the Pine Ridge country. It was a community with a public purpose.

ACKNOWLEDGEMENTS

This book has been in the making for a long time. It began just about twenty years ago as a doctoral dissertation at the University of Toledo. Since then many librarians, archivists, and fellow historians have helped me find my way through the literature and the documentation. Some have also helped me hone my ideas about the role of the Army in the West. Some have been good friends too.

I would like to thank Don Bell, Thomas R. Buecker, Tony Burroughs, Roger Daniels, Leigh DeLay, John Dwyer, Frederick A. Eiserman, Maureen Endress, Elaine Everly, Judith Gardner, Diane R. Gordon, Martin K. Gordon, James A. Hanson, Grace Hardin, June Hedburg, Opal Jacobson, Karen Jefferson, Michael L. M. Kay, David Keough, Lola Kuehl, William H. Leckie, Mildred Mason, Chris Nelson, Vance E. Nelson, Gordon L. Olson, Eli Paul, James E. Potter, Dorothy Rapp, Paul Riley, Michael C. Robinson, Max E. Schubert, Louise Smalls, Donald Snoddy, Richard Sommers, Margery Stoner, Earl F. Stover, Thomas W. Sweeney, Michael Tate, Martha Vestecka-Miller, James D. Walker, and Michael J. Winey. All of these people helped me get some things right. For what is missing or wrong or even wrong-headed, I am responsible.

When this project started, Irene and I had been married a little over two years. An excellent reference librarian and thoughtful critic, she has taught and helped me in many ways over the last two decades. More important, she has been my best friend. That is why this book is dedicated to her.

Frank N. Schubert
Fairfax County, Virginia
July 1992

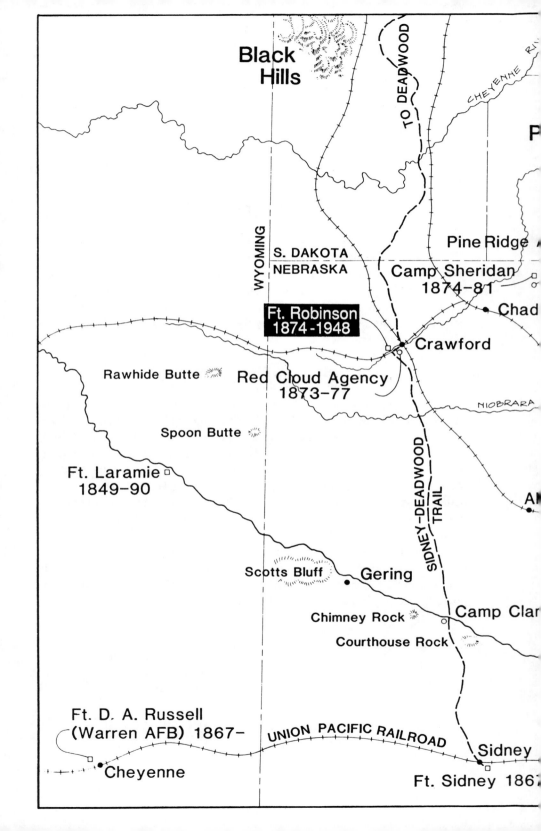

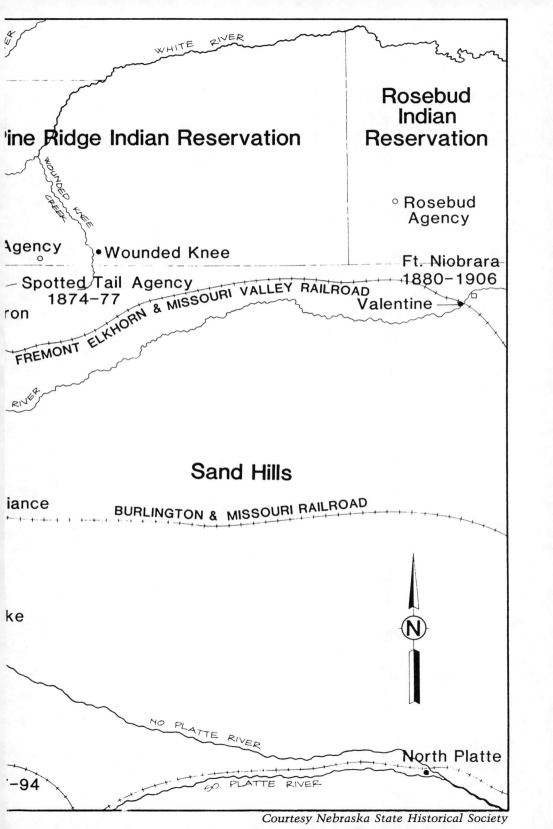

White River

Pine Ridge Indian Reservation

Rosebud
Indian
Reservation

Wounded Knee Creek

○ Rosebud
Agency

Agency
○

• Wounded Knee

Ft. Niobrara
1880–1906

Spotted Tail Agency
1874–77

FREMONT ELKHORN & MISSOURI VALLEY RAILROAD

Valentine →

ron

River

Sand Hills

iance

BURLINGTON & MISSOURI RAILROAD

ke

N

No. PLATTE RIVER

North Platte

–94

So. PLATTE RIVER

Part I

MILITARY
OPERATIONS

Chapter 1

THE SIOUX WARS, 1874-1878

THE WHITE RIVER flows clear and shallow from its source in the northwest corner of Nebraska into the Missouri. About fifteen miles from its beginnings, the river winds through a broad valley, as much as seven miles wide, between the nearly perpendicular White Cliffs on the west and the less stark Pine Ridge to the east. The Oglala tribe of the Teton Sioux, the people of Red Cloud and Crazy Horse, called the stream White Earth; the river valley was part of the tribal hunting ground.

When Red Cloud and the Oglalas yielded to government pressures to leave their agency near the Platte River road and Fort Laramie in 1873, they chose to go to the valley of the White Earth between the cliffs and the Pine Ridge. Wood, water, and pasturage were ample there. The land around the low, grassy hill on which the buildings of Red Cloud agency were constructed showed little agricultural potential, but the Oglalas were not a farming people and had no interest in planting.

The Sioux who moved to White River in 1873 put about seventy miles between themselves and Fort Laramie, the nearest military post. Perhaps the government, in its eagerness to remove the Indians from Platte River trails and towns, failed to consider the implications this distance might have. The Sioux had not resigned themselves to the increasingly rapid encroachments of whites. Efforts to ransack the Black Hills of its gold, which

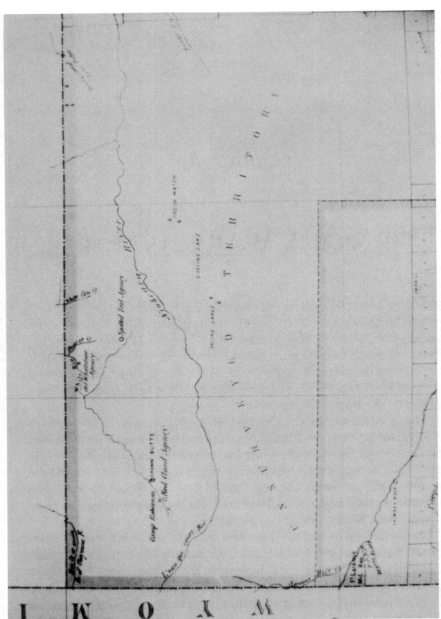

Lieutenant Gouverneur K. Warren had led a survey party into the valley of the White River in 1855. Still, only the Sioux and Cheyenne knew very much about the area around Camp Robinson. This 1876 map, prepared by the General Land Office of the Department of the Interior, reflects the state of knowledge at the time.

helped bring on the great war of 1876, had not begun, but there were whites enough to provoke the Indians.

The government's representative at the new Red Cloud agency, Dr. J. J. Saville, quickly became alarmed by Sioux militancy and the distance between him and the garrison at Fort Laramie. Saville called for troops to protect his agency in January 1874, and the Interior Department supported his plea. Lieutenant General Philip Sheridan, who commanded the vast Military Division of the Missouri, resisted at first. Sheridan, hoping to have Red Cloud's agency and another set aside for Spotted Tail's Brule Sioux forty miles downstream on the White moved east to the Missouri River, claimed he could not comply during the winter.[1]

A series of depredations in February forced Sheridan and the War Department to reconsider. On February 6, Indians from Red Cloud killed an agency-bound teamster. Three days later, while Saville conferred at Spotted Tail with agent E. A. Howard, the clerk at Red Cloud was killed. On the same day a large war party from Saville's agency ambushed three members of a wood-gathering party near Laramie Peak and killed two of them, including Lieutenant Levi Robinson. Before the end of the month, General Sheridan sent Colonel John E. Smith with a force of nearly one thousand soldiers known as the Sioux Expedition to protect the two agencies on White River.[2]

Smith received his orders from Brigadier General Edward O. C. Ord, commander of the Department of the Platte, whose department included Iowa and Nebraska as well as the territories of Utah and Wyoming. So the new and already troublesome Sioux agencies were his responsibility. Ord, who took no joy in ordering the departure of the Sioux Expedition, found it "somewhat provoking" that the Indian Bureau delayed its requests for help until the winter season.[3]

While the timing of Smith's expedition was rooted in the situation at Red Cloud, the establishment of a camp on White River was part of General Sheridan's overall approach to the problem posed by the Sioux and their allies. Sheridan planned a ring of posts around the great Sioux reservation that had been established by treaty in 1868. This ring included forts Abraham Lincoln and Rice to the north and Sully and Randall to the east as well as Smith's camp. Later, there would also be posts to the west in the Yellowstone valley and one in the Black Hills, the heart of Sioux country.[4]

The thermometer registered thirty-eight below zero when Smith's column assembled at Fort Laramie on February 26. Hard-drinking Major Eugene M. Baker commanded a battalion of seven companies of the Second and Third Cavalry. Captain Henry Lazelle led nine infantry companies. Before the expedition left on March 2, Smith warned his men against both communication with Indians and the danger of straggling. Major Baker received a special admonition: no spirits. The cavalry reached Red Cloud agency three frigid days later, and the slower infantry caught up on March 7. Temperatures on the trek dipped to twenty-five below zero, and some men lost a hand or foot to the icy weather.[5]

Colonel Smith stationed four companies of infantry, a cavalry troop, and a Gatling gun at the "Camp at Red Cloud Agency" under Captain James J. Van Horn. After leaving a similar force at the Spotted Tail agency, Smith took the rest of the expedition back to warm quarters and trader whisky at Fort Laramie. The troops at the two new camps had no trouble maintaining quiet at the adjoining agencies because, when they arrived, hostile Indians fled north into Dakota and Montana. However, the agencies remained potentially troublesome as refuges for unfriendly Indians, and in Omaha Ord wondered aloud why they had been placed so far from troops in the first place.[6]

Besides, the Army's presence only subdued the expression of hostility by the Sioux who stayed. Officers at the new camps felt this muted anger from the outset, the commander at Spotted Tail noting that the Indians viewed the military presence "with prejudice and mistrust." Colonel Smith observed "a sullen feeling" at Red Cloud, and reported that Indians at both agencies "do not hesitate to express a desire that the troops leave their country." The Indians' attitude had a very practical impact on life at the new posts. Through the spring of 1874, soldiers carried weapons at all times, and the daily wood train from the camp at Red Cloud went out only with a large escort.[7]

The day-to-day tension prompted Colonel Smith to consider moving his camp away from the agency. After advising the distraught Saville of his decision, he moved his troops on May 2, to a site up White River about 1.5 miles and practically in the shadow of the cliffs. The new camp, nestled in the angle formed by the confluence of the White with Soldiers Creek, was close to water, grass, and wood, as well as far enough from the agency. It was also the very definition of an isolated frontier post, about 125 miles from the railroad and over 80 miles from the nearest telegraph, and more than a year would pass before definitive surveys connected the camp by road to Cheyenne and Sidney, whence came mail and supplies. Smith had named the original site Camp Robinson, after the officer killed near Laramie Peak in February, and the name was transferred to the new location. A month after the camp moved, Congress appropriated $30,000 for construction of winter quarters at Robinson and the camp at Spotted Tail, which had been named for Philip Sheridan. The troops began an urgent effort to build their barracks and stables before winter, and Robinson was on its way to becoming a permanent post.[8]

The decision to move was probably wise. Several difficulties arose over the next few months, and the distance between Camp Robinson and the agency permitted anger to subside before a dispute became serious. A number of incidents threatened to touch off major conflicts. The most dangerous of these took place in October, when agent Saville tried to erect a flagpole. He never got a chance to run up the colors, because his charges smashed the pole into kindling. Saville asked for troops without explaining the gravity of the situation, and only the quick action of Sioux elders prevented gunfire when Lieutenant Emmet Crawford and twenty-two men of the Third Cavalry rode into the agency compound.[9]

More serious problems developed from Lieutenant Colonel George A. Custer's summer expedition into the Black Hills. Custer's mission called for a reconnaissance of this region, which was largely unknown to whites, and location of a site for a post in this heart of the Sioux country. Custer's men carried out their survey and identified a place near which Fort Meade was built four years later. But whatever else their duties required, members of the expedition used every spare minute to prospect for gold. When discoveries were made, Custer dramatized them by sending scout Charlie Reynolds racing to Fort Laramie to telegraph the news. Word of the gold strikes caused great excitement in the Missouri River towns. Prospective miners tried to hire Reynolds as a guide into the hills, and the Army received warnings of parties organizing in Sioux City and Yankton. Officers and men at Robinson and Sheridan were about to take on the onerous assignment of enforcing the Indian title to the Black Hills, which had been acknowledged in the 1868 treaty.[10]

The Army's plan to insure respect for the treaty with a well-coordinated effort by small patrols proved difficult to implement. In October, for example, Brigadier General Alfred H. Terry, commander of the Department of Dakota from his St. Paul headquarters, told Sheridan in Chicago of two parties approaching the hills from the southeast. Sheridan passed the information to Ord, who sent troops from Camp Sheridan in pursuit. Finally, after two weeks, the patrols located one party: it was Indian Commissioner S. D. Hinman and an escort, rather than gold seekers. The other, if it existed, was never found.[11]

John Gordon of Sioux City led one of the parties that set out for Black Hills gold that fall. The Gordon party marked "O'Neil's Colony" on their wagons, as if headed for the new settlement at O'Neil, Nebraska. After the deception was discovered, Captain Guy Henry with thirty-eight men of his own troop of the Third Cavalry and twelve Ninth infantrymen left Camp

Robinson in pursuit. Robinson was "a mere shelter for its garrison," according to Captain Henry, but at least a fire could be kept aglow in the little dwelling, part log hut and part tent, that he shared with his wife. And outside it was frigid, perhaps even too bone-chilling for the gold-crazed. The patrol spent the last week of December and first days of January combing the hills, barely escaping a dreadful blizzard. They bent and broke their tent pins in the rock-hard ground trying to make camp, hacked through the ice to find water for themselves and their horses, and warmed their bits before putting them in their horses' mouths, but for all the hardship the march was fruitless. Henry charitably suggested that "if the proper authority had known as well as we of the character of the service required, it is probable that the orders would never have been issued." But they had been issued, and Guy Henry was a soldier. When he returned, he was so badly frozen that he lost several fingers, and his wife failed to recognize his black swollen face.[12]

Captain Henry was still in the field when the Army tried a new tactic. The idea belonged to Lieutenant Colonel Luther P. Bradley, a stern clear-eyed campaigner whose moustache and goatee pulled his unsmiling face downward. With experience in the Sioux wars dating back to his command of Fort C. F. Smith on the Bozeman Trail in 1867, Bradley was now in charge of the District of the Black Hills. He told the commanders at Robinson and Sheridan to recruit "competent and discreet" Sioux guides to find the miners and report their location to his District of the Black Hills headquarters at Fort Laramie. Troops could then go after the trespassers. Three months later, Bradley tried a variation on this theme. He ordered the commander at Sheridan to enlist fifty Indians as scouts with the pay of cavalry soldiers. Again, the Indians were to detect parties of miners going to the hills.[13]

Though Bradley's efforts complied with President Grant's directive to keep prospectors out of the region, the autumn of 1875 saw the government trying to buy the Black Hills. Senator William Allison of Iowa led a group of commissioners out to Camp Robinson to deal with the Sioux owners of the hills. Very few Indians attended the Sioux Commission sessions, and those who did were in an ugly mood. Therefore, no treaty could be completed. Brigadier General George Crook, who had replaced Ord at Omaha, knew the miners would return in the spring of 1876 and that serious trouble would probably follow.[14]

While many Robinson troops escorted the commissioners from conference to post and even into the Black Hills, other soldiers continued the effort to exclude the miners. Captain Anson Mills and a detachment from Camp Sheridan had captured the elusive Gordon in May 1875, but other parties still dodged the patrols. The doubly difficult duty of chasing whites

Colonel Guy V. Henry, Sr., who first came to Camp Robinson in 1874 and returned later with the Ninth Cavalry.
Massachusetts Commandery, Military Order of the Loyal Legion, and the USAMHI

Luther P. Bradley.
USAMHI

William H. Jordan, Camp Robinson's commander for much of 1874, was a captain in the Ninth Infantry for nearly twenty years.
NSHS

in lands belonging to potentially hostile Indians was absurd as well as hazardous. Every officer concerned expected the United States to take possession of the hills within a short time. Directions from higher headquarters, as they were passed down by Colonel Bradley to Captain Mills at Sheridan and Captain William H. Jordan at Robinson, always specified that captured miners would be held until the government authorized entry. A week's restraint may have seemed a year to frontiersmen lusting for gold, but the officers on the perimeter of the Black Hills were just as eager for release from the obnoxious task of policing the hills.[15]

During July tensions mounted over the incursions of miners. Two days after General William Sherman reiterated Grant's order to expel trespassers, Captain Mills reported that a gold-seeker had killed a Sioux warrior. Colonel Bradley then established a base camp in the Black Hills near Harney Peak, named significantly for Brigadier General William S. Harney, whose expeditionary force had devastated Little Thunder's Brule Sioux band at Ash Hollow in 1855. The temporary outpost, garrisoned by an infantry company and two cavalry troops under Captain Edwin Pollock of the Ninth Infantry, remained active as a base for patrols until November, when the Dakota winter threw up its own barrier against all but the hardiest and greediest.[16]

Captain Jordan and his small Camp Robinson garrison also faced other problems, including Sioux horse-thieves and Cheyenne escapees from Department of the Missouri reservations. Between May 21 and July 5, 1875, Captain James Egan, Second Cavalry, and K Troop spent twenty days in the saddle. They covered over 600 miles, but found only tracks. Futile pursuit of horse-thieves still occupied Robinson cavalry troops in December when Lieutenant Oscar Elting and twenty men of K Troop, Third Cavalry, tracked a raiding party fifty miles down the White River, to be thwarted by a severe snow storm.[17] While Jordan's troops chased bandits, the Indians at Red Cloud agency raided their Ponca and Pawnee enemies to the east, and William Rowland, the Cheyenne interpreter at Red Cloud, killed an agency Indian. The Cheyenne in the vicinity destroyed Rowland's cabin, but he and his family escaped to Camp Robinson. In the midst of all this, the harried Jordan had to plead with his superiors not to reduce his command of 250 officers and men.[18]

1875 had not been a good year for the Army at Robinson or elsewhere on the northern plains. The Black Hills, which had acquired a reputation as a new El Dorado, still belonged to the Indians. Meanwhile, the Sioux raided settlements for cattle and mail stations for horses. The Army could not stop these forays or the whites panting for Black Hills gold. In December the commissioner of Indian affairs demanded that all Sioux and Cheyenne surrender at their agencies by the end of January 1876. The Indians failed to comply, and the Bureau of Indian Affairs gave up control of non-reservation Indians to the Army.[19] If 1875 had been a bad year for the military, 1876 would be even worse, for both the Indians and the Army.

The year began with General Crook wondering how he would protect the settlers in the Department of the Platte without more men. The Indian Bureau eased his problem by ending the issue of passes to Indians wishing to hunt south of the North Platte. Crook, a veteran of the Apache wars who stressed knowledge of his foes and their environment and believed in relentless pursuit, had already carved out a distinguished career by combining the use of pack trains and Indian scouts with a willingness to attack in winter. Now he ordered post commanders to "attack and destroy" all violators. The main problems were elsewhere, however. Bands of Sioux and Northern Cheyenne still roamed the hunting grounds of Dakota and Wyoming after the January 31 deadline, and General Sheridan had his long-awaited opportunity to punish and subdue them.[20]

The Camp Robinson garrison did not participate in the campaigns of the spring and summer of 1876. The troops continued their round of patrols on the road south to Sidney. However, the Indians at Red Cloud probably did take part in the battles to the north. Crook and Colonel Wesley Merritt, commander of the Fifth Cavalry, surely thought they had. Merritt intercepted 800 Indians along Warbonnet Creek on July 17, and drove them back toward Red Cloud. Crook saw many Cheyenne warriors from the agency with the Indians he chased unsuccessfully through Wyoming and Montana. Sheridan, who was at Robinson in June with an old friend, scout and stage star William "Bill" Cody, agreed. The hangs-around-the-fort Indians were few, and it was plain that many winter residents had gone north. The Indian Bureau disputed this claim but let the Army take over the agencies at Red Cloud and Spotted Tail and disarm the residents.[21]

Lieutenant Elting, the new agent at Red Cloud, and the Robinson garrison faced a nearly impossible task. The Indians outnumbered the bluecoats by almost seven to one and grew more belligerent after Custer's defeat on the Little Big Horn. Captain Jordan, with fewer than 200 men, barraged headquarters with pleas for reinforcements. Tension was even greater at Camp Sheridan, and Major George A. Gordon and two companies of Merritt's regiment were sent there from Fort Fetterman. On August 4, as soon as trouble subsided at Sheridan, Major Gordon was rushed to Robinson.[22]

Just before Gordon arrived, civilian thieves ran off eight head of cattle which had been set aside for issue to Indians. Jordan sent a detachment in pursuit but was worried about depleting his strength. Major Gordon reached Robinson, took one look at the situation, and concluded that only a lack of inclination prevented an Oglala attack on the post. He said it was "out of the question to carry out instructions regarding disarming and counting with the present force." Jordan agreed and recommended a delay until the Fourth Cavalry arrived.[23] The agency Indians obviously intimidated the officers on post. Perhaps only the Indians' failure to recognize an opportunity or their genuine unwillingness to fight saved the garrison from Custer's fate.

In mid-August Captain Jordan received his long-awaited reinforcements. Tough and competent Colonel Ranald S. Mackenzie, the new commander of the District of the Black Hills, arrived with his Fourth Cavalry, units of the Fourth and Fourteenth Infantry regiments, and a battalion of artillery. Considered by some the frontier Army's premier Indian-fighter, Mackenzie had graduated at the top of his West Point class in 1862. Civil War promotions came fast for many, but his rise had been meteoric by any standard. A second lieutenant of Engineers in 1862, he was a brigadier general in command of a cavalry division before the war ended. Like Crook, he could be counted on to take the fight to the enemy. Over 600 men now occupied Robinson and two temporary sites nearby, Camps Canby and Custer.[24]

The very presence of this force had a stabilizing effect. Only one incident marred the quiet of Mackenzie's first two weeks at Robinson. His effort to arrest Little Big Man and his three sons, whom Mackenzie labeled "murderers and robbers of a very bad description," caused some excitement. But the attempt itself was an index of changed power relationships. Only a month before, Jordan had refused even to count Elting's Indians. Now Mackenzie was arresting them. More important, on September 26, with 800 soldiers at Robinson, the Indians at Red Cloud agency signed a treaty and gave up their rights to the Black Hills.[25]

Before the treaty was signed, Mackenzie counted 4,700 Indians, over 1,000 of whom were adult males, still in possession of their arms and mounts, and still a significant threat. To eliminate this menace General Crook, just back from a disastrous campaign that came to be known variously as the mud march and the horsemeat march, ordered "a general surround" at Red Cloud, which he intended to supervise personally. The surround was part of Sheridan's overall approach to ending the Sioux problem, by occupying the game country to the north, harassing the Indians into submission through constant pursuit, and controlling the agencies from which their reinforcements came. Crook told only Merritt and Mackenzie of the plan to surround, dismount, and disarm the Indians. Mackenzie would provide reliable Indians as scouts for Merritt, whose cavalry would conduct the actual encirclement.[26]

Two of the Army's premier Indian-fighters, George Crook (left) and Ranald Mackenzie (right).

Colonel Wesley Merritt in 1885.

The department commander had to modify his plans because the Indians at Red Cloud refused to aid Merritt. Crook, who preferred hiring scouts from the tribes he fought, would get no help here. So he sent three of the most skilled white and mixed-blood scouts available instead—California Joe Milner, Baptiste "Bat" Garnier, and Baptiste "Bat" Pourier—and hastily recruited a company of Pawnees under Frank and Luther North. Merritt moved steadily southward and kept Crook's secret well. Lieutenant Charles King of Merritt's staff, though unsure of the destination, mapped the country around Red Cloud for his commander. According to King, "none knew behind the silent horseman at the head of the column . . . ." Merritt's caution successfully screened his approach, but when he arrived, he found that Mackenzie had already done his job.[27]

Red Cloud and Red Leaf had moved their bands about thirty miles down river from the agency. Crook and Mackenzie became fearful that they would join northern hostiles or provide them with aid and comfort. So, early in the morning of October 23, Mackenzie accomplished the surround with his force divided into two battalions under Major Gordon and Captain Eugene Mauch. The Sioux slept while Gordon and Mauch ringed their camp. By the time the Indians realized the soldiers' presence, resistance was useless. The maneuver was completed without violence.[28]

After confiscating the Indians' weapons and horses, Crook "deposed" Red Cloud and appointed Spotted Tail, whom he called "the only important leader who has had the nerve to be our friend," head chief at both agencies. Crook probably spoke for Mackenzie as well as himself when he predicted that "we shall have our enemies in the front only in future." But Mackenzie had little time to gloat. Before October ended, he left for Fort Fetterman, to command the expedition which would eliminate Dull Knife's Cheyenne band as an effective foe. The successful surround, which reduced Dull Knife's prospects for supplies and support on the White River, was a vital prelude to Mackenzie's forthcoming campaign.[29]

Closing the sanctuary at Red Cloud did not end the futile resistance of the Cheyenne and Sioux. In February 1877, panic spread among residents of the new Black Hills settlement of Deadwood when Sioux raiding parties killed a few careless whites and stole some livestock. Mayor E. B. Farnum begged help from Crook at Fort Laramie and Sheridan in Chicago: "We are attacked by Indians. All our stock captured. Can you send us some immediate relief." Lieutenant Joseph F. Cummings of the Third Cavalry and sixty-one men of C Troop rode out from Robinson on the same day, arrived on February 20, and immediately attacked an Indian village on the Belle Fourche to the north. Three days later he recovered a great deal of the lost stock in a surprise attack. Cummings halted his pursuit when he noticed that Sioux signal fires marked his path until he turned back to Deadwood.

Three days later the feisty young officer told Crook he would "start on a little raid tomorrow."[30]

Colonel Mackenzie, fresh from his victory over Dull Knife, returned to Robinson as post commander in mid-March. He found civilian rustlers added to his problems, and sent troopers of the Fourth Cavalry and scouts in pursuit. Mackenzie decided to withdraw the troops in the Black Hills, and Mayor Farnum again warmed the telegraph line with pleas to Crook. Farnum insisted the soldiers were "absolutely necessary," and convinced Crook to countermand the order. Troops remained in the hills through April, when Farnum's telegrams stopped. Although the depredations presumably ceased, Lieutenant Colonel Bradley, who replaced Mackenzie in May, sent patrols into the hills through the summer as a precaution.[31]

While bellicose tribes harassed Black Hills towns, mass surrenders took place at Camp Robinson. Crook reported that over 250 Cheyenne and Sioux gave up at Red Cloud on March 13 and 14. Poor weather slowed other Indians on their way in to the agency. Spotted Tail spent the month in the north urging hostiles to surrender. The chief of Crook's rump Sioux government probably convinced many of the Indians to return to the White River agencies. By mid-April the number of capitulations exceeded 900.[32]

General Crook went to Camp Robinson in April to witness the surrenders. He and Mackenzie spent five days at Spotted Tail agency watching troopers disarm new arrivals. The situation pleased Crook, who wired Sheridan that the northern Indians there were in a good—presumably docile—frame of mind, and that they spoke of others on their way south. Indeed, before the month ended, another 500 Cheyenne gave up at Red Cloud. When these came in, hungry and cold, there were already hundreds of lodges near the agency, Arapaho and Oglala as well as Cheyenne. Over 2,200 miserable Indians succumbed that spring to the combination of military pressure and Spotted Tail's diplomacy.[33]

While thousands surrendered at Robinson and Sheridan, the bands of the Oglala Crazy Horse and Sitting Bull of the Huncpapas remained free. The Army avidly sought control of these defiant and able war chiefs. Even General Sheridan, always well informed of events in Crook's department, found newspaper rumors of Crazy Horse irresistible. As early as January, Sheridan asked Crook to verify a story that the Oglala wanted to surrender. As winter turned to spring and Sitting Bull fled to Canada, even more attention focused on Crazy Horse, and Sheridan's single rumor of January grew to be many. Crook wryly commented from Robinson that, "there is some difference of opinion here as to whether Crazy Horse and the Indians with him will come in or not."[34]

Three days later Crook reported the arrival of two parties from Crazy Horse's camp. The newcomers convinced him that the chief was coming, but Crook decided not to assert it officially without further verification. Additional couriers reported the approach of Crazy Horse on April 27, and Crook sent an officer out with a wagon load of food for the new arrivals, then eight or nine days away. Crook left Robinson on the following day and was at his office in Omaha on May 6, when Mackenzie reported the arrival of Crazy Horse's band at Robinson. The 889 people, including 217 fighting men, surrendered 2,000 horses and 117 stand of arms. The Sioux wars were over. Relentless pursuit through the winter of 1876-1877 had exhausted the Sioux rather than decisively defeated them on the battlefield, but they were still beaten. Crook wrote that "hostilities of the extensive character they assumed during several years past are closed."[35] He was right.

This was the situation Luther Bradley faced when he took over at Camp Robinson on May 26 after a numbing all-night stagecoach ride from Sidney. The veteran Bradley was Crook's choice to finish the job, arrange for the last surrenders, and bring a definitive end to the Sioux problem on the Pine Ridge. His letters to his wife at Fort Sanders, near Laramie, Wyoming, made it plain that he expected to stay at Robinson only until the matter of the Sioux was resolved. When he arrived, these Indians were waiting for him. Immediately, he assumed command and met "the principal men among the Indians." That morning he had his first look at Crazy Horse, as well as a handshake. Bradley found the Oglala to be "a young slender and mild mannered fellow" who nevertheless was "evidently the leader of his band."[36]

Bradley faced two irresistible forces. One was the hot, dry wind that blew for days on end. When it came from the west, it seemed to carry half the territory of Wyoming with it. Bradley called the Pine Ridge "the windiest country I have every seen," but was unsure that Wyoming was in fact swirling by, because the wind blew "from all points of the compass in the same day, and the dust [was] kept flying all the time." Equally implacable was the wave of white settlement that swept over the region from the east. The thousands of Indians camped near his garrison and, dependent on the government for rations and supplies, testified to the power of the tide. Unlike the Indians he had dealt with during his last tour of duty in the Black Hills, these people were "quiet and friendly." Bradley hoped this behavior bespoke "the beginning of a new era."[37]

The tranquil summer ended in a few days of chaos. At the end of August, Crazy Horse and Touch-the-Clouds told Lieutenant William P. Clark of their plans to leave Red Cloud agency with their bands. Colonel Bradley had visions of all the hostiles of 1876 going north, and made up his mind that they would not. He hurriedly asked Crook to augment his force of 300. General Crook decided the forces at Robinson and Sheridan were adequate. He expected the troops at Sheridan—with the help of Spotted Tail—to restrain Touch-the-Clouds, while Bradley dealt with Crazy Horse. The movements were to be conducted simultaneously and in secret.[38]

A stealthily executed encirclement had worked against Red Cloud a year earlier, but this one proved more difficult. Crazy Horse left the agency before Bradley could surround his camp. As the troops approached the fleeing Indians early in the morning of September 4, they scattered like "a frightened covey of quail." Crazy Horse and his family fled down river, with troops and scouts under agency head man No Water in pursuit. The entire operation was handled with great care, almost circumspection. Neither Bradley on the scene nor Crook, who directed the operation from Fort Laramie, wanted a general conflict.[39]

Crazy Horse was captured at Spotted Tail agency by troops from Camp Sheridan on the night of September 4. By the next morning Bradley had the situation in hand. Soldiers escorted the Oglala leader to Robinson while scouts hunted stragglers. Lieutenant Clark wired Crook that Crazy Horse would be jailed at Robinson and recommended that the chief "be started for Ft. Laramie tonight and should be kept going as far as Omaha . . . ." In a congratulatory telegram to Bradley and Clark, Crook accepted Clark's suggestion and ordered Crazy Horse taken to department headquarters. On the same day General Sheridan also put in a bid for possession of the captive.[40]

Events of the evening of September 5 at Camp Robinson rendered discussion of Crazy Horse's ultimate destination academic. The chief never got beyond the guardhouse door. When he saw that he was being jailed, Crazy Horse bolted. Several agency Indians restrained him, while an Army sentry bayoneted him in the stomach. Before morning Crazy Horse, "the strange man of the Oglalas," was dead.[41] "So ends a troubled life," Bradley wrote his wife before the long night was over, but "his death is a good thing for his own people as well as for us."[42]

Although Colonel Bradley had a few anxious days after the killing, he remained confident that the agency Indians would stay quiet. Some of the chiefs confided to him that they were glad for the end of Crazy Horse. The Oglala Little Wound told Bradley, "We had a fire-brand among us, and we've got rid of it," and others apparently agreed. The chiefs helped Bradley and Captain Daniel W. Burke at Camp Sheridan, with whom Bradley kept in close touch, calm the agitated northern tribes. Only three days after the slaying, Bradley reported that the excitement had declined and that he expected no further trouble. He was relieved. He had enough of Indian troubles and wanted to go home to his wife and sons.[43]

In spite of his eagerness to put the episode behind him, Bradley feared he was leaving a situation that would not end well. He expected that the Indian Bureau would move the hapless Sioux from the White River. He did not add his voice to the formal protest of the move by Lieutenant Jesse M. Lee, the agent at Spotted Tail, but he did feel sorry for them. He also thought more trouble was ahead. The Indians opposed the move and some were likely to slip away, forcing the Army to hunt them down again. "I wish the people east," he wrote, "would take interest enough in the Indian question to understand it, and try to make the Government settle upon a policy that would ensure peace, instead of continually stirring up the Indians to revolt."[44]

But while much unhappiness lay ahead for the Sioux, the death of Crazy Horse marked the end of the Army's troubles with them. The sole exception was the Ghost Dance enthusiasm of 1890. Before the end of 1878, the defeated Sioux meekly accepted two moves from Red Cloud. First they went to a new agency on the Missouri River. In the following year, they accepted a second removal, this time west to the Pine Ridge agency in southwestern Dakota, about sixty miles northeast of Robinson.[45]

Chapter 2

CHEYENNE AUTUMN TO GHOST DANCE WINTER, 1878-1891

THE SUBJUGATION of the Sioux did not bring the Robinson garrison permanent relief from Indian troubles. Almost at the same time that Crazy Horse's capture marked the end of the Sioux war, the seeds of a new and bitter conflict were sown. Nearly a thousand Northern Cheyenne were removed from Red Cloud agency to a reservation in Indian Territory in May 1877. Although Colonel Mackenzie convinced himself that a Cheyenne majority desired the move, the Indians assented only after threatened with starvation and promised that they could return if they found their new location unsatisfactory. Their rations were restored when they decided to go. Then they set out for the reserve they would share with the already hungry Southern Cheyenne.[1]

The Cheyenne returned to Camp Robinson in the autumn of 1878. Rather than starve in the south, they undertook an incredible journey of about 1,500 miles back to their beloved Montana. Nearly 300 left the reservation at Fort Reno, Indian Territory, in September, almost on the first anniversary of Crazy Horse's death. They eluded troops from posts in Kansas and Nebraska as they made their way northward. When they got into the Nebraska sandhills, they split into two groups. One under Little Wolf spent the winter undetected in Little Chokecherry valley; the other under Dull Knife collided with a large patrol from Robinson during a storm and was captured. Five companies of the Third Cavalry had combed the hills and valleys east of Robinson for nearly a week before they stumbled on Dull Knife. One hundred and forty-nine boneweary but defiant Cheyenne were taken back to post and confined in an old barrack at the southeastern corner of the parade ground.[2]

Major Caleb Carlton, who had led the pursuit of Dull Knife, did his best to squelch any illusions about easily returning the Cheyenne to Indian Territory. They had told him they would rather die than go back. General Crook believed Major Carlton and the Indians. He told Sheridan: "If prisoners are to go south it will be necessary to tie and haul them."[3]

Major Carlton made a thorough, diligent search for Little Wolf and the remaining Cheyenne. He spent eighteen hard November and December days in pursuit of the well-hidden Indians. After the long patrol, Crook removed Carlton and reduced the Robinson garrison to two troops of the Third Cavalry, hoping to convince Little Wolf to be less vigilant, even careless. Then the Robinson troops might find and capture him and his band.[4]

Carlton's advice concerning Cheyenne adamancy proved no more successful than his patrols. Commissioner of Indian Affairs Ezra Hayt wanted them taken to Kansas, where those guilty of depredations could be sifted out. He recommended that the innocent be returned to Indian Territory. Secretary of the Interior Carl Schurz concurred, and so did the War Department.[5] To implement this policy, Captain Henry Wessells at Robinson tried to starve Dull Knife's band into submission. He starved them into rebellion instead. Late at night, on January 9, 1879, the prisoners burst out of their makeshift jail, fatally wounded two troopers, and dashed east across the White River bridge at the post sawmill.[6] Then they turned south, crossed the river again farther upstream, and set out for the white cliffs. A rear guard of about five heroically slowed pursuers and bought with their blood the time for the main body to escape.[7]

Wessells heard the firing, dressed hastily, and sent C Troop out in pursuit. Captain Peter Vroom, camped nearby with three troops of the Third Cavalry, also heard the shots. He sent A Troop to aid Wessells and placed E Troop astride the road to Sidney. Wessells and Vroom chased the Cheyenne in what amounted to a brutal game of cat and mouse. Wessells stayed close to the Indians when he could but at least three times held back from an attack because he was confident that he could wear them down.[8]

Wessell's tactics inflicted a severe toll on the Cheyenne. They were compelled to fight a two-week war of attrition in spite of hunger and severe cold. Finally, when they could run and fight no longer, they turned to face the troops in a six-foot deep trench on the western side of the white cliffs northwest of Robinson. The hole near Warbonnet Creek amounted to a pre-dug mass grave. At about 2:30 p.m., on January 22, one hundred troopers charged the pit, overran it, and killed twenty-three of the occupants. They were buried where they fell.[9]

Wessells chose his cautious tactics shrewdly. Eight soldiers died in the various fights, including four on January 22. And the Army plainly con-sidered the affair as serious as any Indian campaign for the Adjutant General authorized participants to wear a war chevron.[10] Had Wessells been more aggressive, his losses might have been substantially higher.

On the day before the slaughter on Warbonnet Creek, General Sher-man ordered Sheridan to investigate the outbreak. President Rutherford B. Hayes had expressed annoyance at reports of "unnecessary cruelty" by Army officers. A three-officer board of inquiry found no such brutality and absolved everyone of everything. The board acknowledged, albeit belated-ly, that the outbreak and the events that followed showed that "the statements of the Indians were not brag, and that they literally went out to die."[11] The Cheyenne had walked over a thousand miles from Indian Territory with the same message but had not been heard. Before they could convince the government that they would rather die than return, many of them had to perish.[12]

While the Army solved the Cheyenne problem the only way it knew how, white ranchers began to take up grazing lands in the White River valley. The return of the Oglala Sioux to the Pine Ridge in 1878, added to the garrisons at Robinson and Sheridan, promised a large market. In addi-tion, the end of the Sioux wars assured secure conditions for cattlemen. Beef prices were high and remained lucrative for another decade. E. W. and H. L. Newman established a ranch twelve miles south of the site of the town of Gordon in 1877, the Hunter ranch came months later, and New Yorker Edgar Beecher Bronson occupied land only four miles from Robin-son the following year.[13]

The arrival of these first cattlemen gave a new significance to the gar-rison's regular patrols along the White and the Niobrara. Now the troops protected whites and Indians from each other. In December 1878, General Crook reported the theft of over 2,000 horses from the Pine Ridge and Rosebud Sioux agencies by citizens of northern and central Nebraska. In turn, Indians raided ranches for new mounts, and frequently law-abiding whites paid with their livestock for the crimes of others.[14]

As whites moved into the area and the Indian threat declined, Robin-son's status changed. The post had initially been established as a "camp," a temporary installation for the protection of Indian Bureau employees at

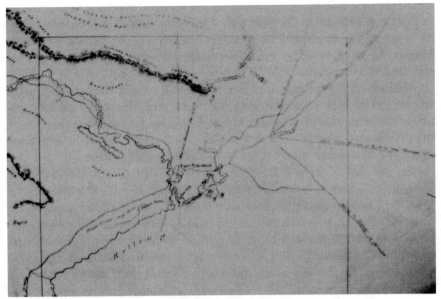

This 1879 Army map, made shortly after Robinson was designated a fort, shows the confluence of Soldiers Creek, from the northwest, and White River from the southwest.

Fortifications Map File, #140-15, RG 77, NA

Red Cloud. The Indian tenure on White River had been temporary, but the cattlemen came to stay. Robinson also became a permanent post—a "fort"—by order of General Sheridan at the end of 1878.[15] General Crook had argued against such an installation on the White River. He believed Camp Sheridan, which was closer to the agencies at Pine Ridge and Rosebud, strategically better suited. Crook changed his mind in 1880, because the facilities at Robinson were better, and Sheridan was abandoned a little later.[16]

Meanwhile an overall strategy evolved for the defense of the northern plains. Although the overall number of Army garrisons was declining throughout the 1870s and 1880s, Fort Niobrara was established in 1880 south of the Rosebud agency in Cherry County, Nebraska, to protect local settlers and ranchers. In the early 1880s Niobrara and Robinson came to be regarded as Department of the Platte "picket posts," along with Forts Laramie and McKinney in Wyoming. As an Omaha paper put it, these and similar posts in the Department of Dakota would "hem in the great Sioux nation with a circle of bayonets." Robinson and Laramie in particular acted as sentinels over the Pine Ridge Sioux. The Union Pacific track across the plains to the south formed a base line for logistical support, while posts at Omaha, Sidney, Cheyenne, and Salt Lake City acted as depots. With the other rail lines that were forming a network across the West, the tracks also allowed the Army to achieve economies of scale, stationing larger forces at fewer posts while expanding their operational range and improving their access to supplies and communications.[17]

These elaborate defense preparations came years too late for the major Indian wars. In fact, the strategy reflected the very subjection of the northern tribes. It was designed to protect influxes of whites who had waited for the government to clear the region. The declining need for troops did not deter the Army. Colonel John Gibbon, the new commander of the Department of the Platte, asserted in 1884 that the troops at Niobrara and Robinson watched the "most powerful and warlike tribe of Indians on the continent." Railroad track was about to cross northern Nebraska from Iowa, and Gibbon wanted the garrisons increased. By his logic, the more heavily populated Nebraska and Dakota became and the weaker the Indians grew, the more troops were required. Four years later Major General John Schofield, who replaced Sheridan in Chicago, may even have been somewhat embarrassed by the complex system. He explained in his 1888 report that the growing clusters of civilians near reservations made Indian raids more dangerous—if they occurred. Schofield acknowledged that the level of conflict declined steadily.[18]

For a brief period in the spring of 1885, the Sioux frightened settlers and soldiers on the line of the new Fremont, Elkhorn, and Missouri Valley Railroad. When hunting parties from the Dakota reservations visited the country between Robinson and Niobrara, citizens armed themselves for war, and troops from Niobrara patrolled westward to the town of Gordon. Meanwhile the Ninth Cavalry, which was slated to move north from Kansas anyway, hastened into Nebraska. Nothing came of the scare, however. Autumn came and the patrols continued, but the marches "failed to disclose any depredations."[19]

After the Elkhorn and Burlington lines crossed at Robinson in 1886, the post's role in the defense of the northern plains expanded. While Robinson grew, troop strength at Fort Laramie dwindled until the post was dismantled in the spring of 1890. Robinson became headquarters in 1887 for Colonel Edward Hatch's Ninth Cavalry, one of four regiments in the Army of the time made up of black enlisted men, and the size of the garrison increased significantly. Up to that time troop strength had hovered around 200 men. By mid-1889 the number of men fluctuated near 450.[20] The outpost on the Pine Ridge had become a major installation.

Along with the railroad and the growth of the post came civilian settlement. A town named for Emmet Crawford, the officer who had dashed

Crawford, about two years after it was founded.

into the agency with his troopers during the flag-raising incident of 1874 and who was later killed in the Apache wars, began in 1886 as a collection of tents at the end of track. At that time rumors already flew regarding transfer of the Ninth's headquarters to Robinson. Businessmen in Buffalo near Fort McKinney, Wyoming, fretted over the impending removal of most of the troops to Nebraska in 1887. Then in 1890 Fort Laramie closed, reflecting a trend that ended the active lives of nearly one-fourth of all posts in 1890 and 1891. McKinney followed in 1894. Residents of the new town east of Robinson appreciated the situation. Crawford was barely a year old when a local newspaper commented on the possibilities ahead. If troops were concentrated at Robinson, "What a town it would make of Crawford, and what a time it would be to start a building boom." Down the road at Chadron, the seat of new Dawes County, similar appraisals were made. A town editor said "much money would find its way into circulation in this county." Like Crawford, Chadron envisioned a bright future.[21]

The only military operation of 1887 had nothing to do with Indians. Captain Charles Parker's K Troop, Ninth Cavalry, spent nearly six months near Cheyenne, Wyoming, protecting Interior Department agents as they removed illegal fences placed on government land by cattle barons.[22] However, residents of Dawes County soon had one more reminder of their proximity to large groups of potentially hostile Indians. A brief scare in

1888 disturbed only the most easily frightened, but the Ghost Dance enthusiasm in 1890 brought a full-fledged panic to northwestern Nebraska.

The anxiety of 1888 had its origins in the optimism of the previous year. Congress reduced the Pine Ridge Reservation in response to the demands for land for the many new settlers in the vicinity. White residents became concerned that Indians might resist the encroachments on their reservation. The rumors of war centered in Oelrichs, northeast of Robinson in Dakota, where an unknown warrior told an anonymous settler that the Crow, Sioux, and Shoshoni were on the verge of a grand alliance which would wipe out the small communities and even Fort Robinson. Many families fled to the post, and some officers, including Captain Augustus W. Corliss of the Eighth Infantry, foresaw "a long and bloody war." Events proved Corliss wrong, but he understood the cause of Indian conflicts well enough. He observed that war would come "on account of the infernal greed of the white men for the lands now held by the Indians, while millions of acres of other land just as good outside the reservation are open for their occupation."[23]

Captain Martin B. Hughes, with two troops of the Ninth Cavalry, investigated the rumors at Oelrichs. At the same time, infantrymen from Fort Meade, a picket post in Dakota, also closed on the town. Hughes immediately saw that soldiers were needed only to restore confidence among the whites. He left a lieutenant and four troopers there to show the flag and returned to Robinson a day later.[24]

The trouble at Oelrichs proved imaginary, but the Indians' grievances still awaited resolution. Colonel Hatch held a council with Sioux leaders from Pine Ridge, less than a month before a March 1889, carriage accident ended his life. The Oglala chiefs complained anew of encroachments on their reserve and, later in the spring, repeated their dissatisfaction to Lieutenant Colonel James Brisbin. The chiefs wanted "white soldiers" to aid in driving away squatters, and Brisbin promised assistance. After scouts confirmed the presence of squatters, Brisbin ordered Lieutenant Matthias W. Day to verify their report. These investigations dragged the affair into June. Perhaps the Sioux despaired of Army help by then. They apparently dropped the issue, and no more action was taken.[25]

The grievances persisted and new troubles came in the spring of 1890. In April a group of unhappy Cheyenne sought to go from Pine Ridge to the Tongue River home of their relatives. Colonel Joseph Tilford, who assumed command at Robinson just in time to face this problem, seized the Cheyenne and jailed them briefly on post. Then, in June, settlers north of Chadron reported that Indians menaced their homesteads. Tilford sent a troop of the Ninth Cavalry under Captain Clarence Stedman, who learned

An unidentified first sergeant with a portion of his troop of the Ninth Cavalry at Fort McKinney, Wyoming, where parts of the regiment were stationed between 1885 and 1890.

American Heritage Center, Univ. of Wyoming

only that Indians had been seen in the vicinity. Tilford reported that he found no substance to any reports of Indian troubles, but nervous settlers still looked over their shoulders for signs of Sioux hostility, and Pine Ridge Indians still insisted that whites encroached on their reservation. In addition, another problem became apparent over the summer of 1890: the Indians were desperately hungry. Several times, the Robinson commissary officer issued rations to famished bands from Pine Ridge.[26]

This witch's brew of fear, mistrust, and now hunger received a substantial stir from the new Ghost Dance theology, spread from a Nevada Paiute named Wovoka. The new faith seemed to promise the rebirth of Indian dominance on the plains, facilitated by the bullet-proof Ghost Shirts and the ritual of the Ghost Dance. In the midst of these developments, a new and inexperienced agent, Daniel Royer, replaced veteran Hugh Gallagher on the Pine Ridge reservation.[27]

Colonel Tilford had developed an effective working relationship with Gallagher. They had kept each other abreast of developments during the abortive flight of the Cheyenne in April and Red Cloud's attempt to visit the Shoshoni on Wind River in July. Tilford, seeking to maintain regular contact with the agency, sent Royer a courteous and informative telegram. The colonel advised that scouts had warned him of "a dance of some magnitude" at Pine Ridge. They had told him "that any interference . . . might result in trouble," and Tilford wished "to be kept informed of affairs" at the agency. He also asked Royer to open regular communication, because any troops needed at Pine Ridge would come from Robinson. In addition, Tilford offered some friendly advice. "Let these Indians dance," he said, "so long as they harm no one. I am told that if any means are taken to stop them summarily there will be trouble. If at any time you deem the presence of troops necessary telegraph me the circumstances as I am justified in ordering out the troops of my command should the condition of affairs warrant it."[28]

Tilford's letter probably reinforced Royer's worst fears. He had already alerted the Commissioner of Indian Affairs to the possible need for troops. Now the commander of the nearest garrison warned him that interference with the dancers would be dangerous and offered military support. The Ghost Dancers defied Royer when he tried to arrest one of them on November 11. It is more remarkable that he screwed up his courage to act at all. Royer may indeed have stood in terror of his charges, but the words of the experienced frontier officer Tilford could hardly have helped.[29]

Three days after the confrontation of November 11, Royer visited Tilford at Robinson. He reported that the dancers openly defied his police, resisted arrest, and threatened those who remained at the agency. Royer

Colonel Joseph Tilford
had been in the Army
almost forty years
when the Ghost Dance
crisis occurred.
He retired six
months later.

NSHS

K Troop of the Ninth Cavalry on the Pine Ridge. The troop's three officers stand on the left.
The soldier seated third from the left, with the chevrons and medal, may be First Sergeant
George Jordan.

NSHS

believed only a military force large enough to awe the Indians could restore order. Tilford concluded that the situation was indeed grave. Royer, he said, "is no alarmist"; the Sioux could muster "a vast horde of good fighters." The troops at Robinson, Niobrara, and Meade would be required. The Indians boasted that they could easily defeat a force the size of Tilford's, and the commander apparently thought so too. Only after Tilford sent this pessimistic appraisal to Omaha did Royer ask him for military support.[30]

Tilford alerted his command for field duty on November 17, and the garrison marched for Rushville, south of the Pine Ridge agency, on the following day. Because Tilford was ill, Captain Corliss commanded the expedition. The maneuver came too late to fend off a general panic. The same issue of the Chadron *Democrat* that advised people that the Army had matters well in hand ran a scare story with a Dakota dateline: "Indians who do their trading in town always invest their supplies change in cartridges which, it is said, they take home and lay away for future reference." Before November passed, many settlers from adjacent Sioux County congregated in Harrison or went to Fort Robinson for protection. From Harrison to Valentine, towns along the Fremont, Elkhorn, and Missouri Valley line filled with refugees. The terror also spread to Lusk, Wyoming, whose citizens unsuccessfully petitioned Tilford for arms.[31]

During the first week of December the expedition from Rushville moved north to Pine Ridge. Major Guy Henry assumed command and drilled his cavalrymen to respond to whistle instructions, so that high winds and other noises would not create confusion. Meanwhile troops poured onto the reservation. By mid-month over 1,400 soldiers occupied the Pine Ridge and Rosebud reservations, and the Ghost Dancers had fled into the Bad Lands. On December 13, Brigadier General John R. Brooke, up from Omaha to supervise operations from Pine Ridge agency, cautioned commanders at Oelrichs and Rapid City outposts: friendly Indians searched for fugitives, whose return Brooke expected shortly. Within a day he altered his view. A fight with civilians had convinced the Indians in the Bad Lands to resist, and Sitting Bull had been killed at Standing Rock agency. A troubled Brooke informed an Oglala council, and was relieved that the news "produced no excitement of any kind."[32]

Indians who sat in council at the agency did not constitute Brooke's problem, however. While not perfectly tranquil, the agency was calm enough for Ninth Cavalry troopers to dance with Sioux women. The real difficulty, out in the hills, became more serious as growing numbers of Sioux left Standing Rock after Sitting Bull's death. The Ninth Cavalry battalion, three troops from Robinson and one from McKinney, rode west to Harney Springs in pursuit of the fugitives.[33]

December 29 found the Ninth fifty miles north of the Pine Ridge agency. Word of the massacre of Big Foot's Miniconjou band by the Seventh Cavalry earlier in the day at Wounded Knee Creek threw the agency into chaos. Brooke said the Indians there were "terribly frightened" and "excited but not hostile." A few shots were fired in the early afternoon, and more Sioux escaped to the Bad Lands. Brooke ordered Lieutenant Colonel George B. Sanford to sweep the country between his post at Oelrichs and the agency. He also pulled Henry back from the north. He and his cavalrymen made what became known as "one of the most wonderful forced marches on record," to get back, eighty-six miles in twenty-four hours. Henry's slower wagons came under Sioux fire near the agency. Lieutenant Philip Bettens hastily formed a defensive circle, and sent volunteer Corporal William O. Wilson for help. Wilson eluded the Sioux and reached Captain John S. Loud with news of the attack. Loud's troops eased the pressure until the Seventh Cavalry drove off the Sioux. Private Charles Haywood of D Troop, Ninth Cavalry, was killed by an Indian in a cavalry uniform. Corporal Wilson won a Medal of Honor for his dash for help.[34]

Later in the day Colonel James Forsyth and the Seventh Cavalry let the Sioux trap them in a valley. Henry and his exhausted troopers chased the Indians away, returning the favor of that morning. Colonel Forsyth, already under fire for the actions of his regiment at Wounded Knee, lost his command after this farce at Drexel Mission. However, he later won restoration and even promotion to brigadier.[35]

The Drexel Mission fight was the last clash of any magnitude. It had been the third major skirmish in two days and touched off a second wave of panic in northwestern Nebraska. Fort Robinson, which supported troops in the field with ammunition, rations, and medical services, now sustained several hundred terrified civilians as well. In the few days after the fights at Wounded Knee, the agency, and Drexel Mission, settlers poured onto post. An incredulous Tilford asked Brooke if the fears had any basis in fact. His fort became a center for refugees, who had to be fed and housed. In addition, Tilford had to provide rations for the large number of rural settlers who flocked to the towns along the railroad.[36]

When the Nebraska National Guard arrived on January 5, General L. W. Colby also noticed the chaos along the Elkhorn line. Colby's troops had been sent by Governor John Thayer in response to a telegram from Sheriff James Dahlman in Chadron. The part-time soldiers occupied towns from Harrison to Valentine and, according to Colby, restored confidence among the populace. To Tilford, who had to support them as well as civilians and regulars in the field with rations, they probably meant little except several hundred more mouths to feed.[37]

Military operations persisted into mid-January when the last Sioux returned to the reservation. After Major General Nelson A. Miles reviewed the troops at the agency on January 24, all units withdrew except four troops of the Ninth Cavalry. The last men of the regiment remained on the reservation until late March, enduring a winter "terrible in its severity," with only canvas shelters.[38] Private W. H. Prather asked bitterly why "the Ninth, the willing Ninth," which had been "first to come, will be the last to leave." He could not understand why "we poor devils and the Sioux are left to freeze."[39]

Snow fell and piled up through March. The cavalrymen on Pine Ridge could not be relieved for ten days because of the storm. When they finally left the agency on March 24, they had to fight through a new blizzard with drifts as high as five feet. Most of the men arrived back at Robinson snow-blind and exhausted.[40]

Fort Robinson had taken on an aspect of gloom during the campaign. Only three officers and a few soldiers remained behind with the wives and children. After the men returned and both soldiers and officers had toasted the safe return of comrades, the routine reverted to patrols and scouts. The toughest winter the Ninth Cavalry had seen for many years was finally over.[41]

Chapter 3

YEARS OF TRANSITION, 1892-1916

IN THE YEARS AFTER the Pine Ridge campaign, Robinson grew in significance. The post had served well as a base of operations during the winter of 1890-1891. So, when the number of installations was reduced during the following decade, and regiments were consolidated at single posts, Fort Robinson became even more important as both a depot and a regimental headquarters.[1]

Along with changes in the post's size and stature came new functions. As the decade progressed and the high plains economy responded to national changes, the Robinson garrison took part in a number of civil disputes, primarily strikes, as protector of large business interests. The growing importance of civil disturbances was accompanied by a decline in Indian scares, which still took place but inevitably proved illusory. This trend to an increased involvement in labor disputes, interrupted at the turn of the century by the wars in Cuba and the Philippines, continued in the next two decades. During the years after the Pine Ridge campaign, the role of Fort Robinson troops changed dramatically, from involvement in local Indian wars to participation in far-flung industrial disputes and foreign wars.

When the Ninth Cavalry units at Robinson were sent into the field in June 1892, their assignment reflected the garrison's changing mission. The cavalrymen went to northern Wyoming to restore order in the wake of the Johnson County cattle war, which pitted the large and powerful Wyoming Stock Growers Association against the small ranchers of the northern part of the state. The big growers, unhappy about the cordial relations between its northern foes and white troops at Fort McKinney, asked for the black cavalrymen of the Ninth, and the Army obliged by sending Major Charles Ilsley and the regiment to Wyoming on June 7. Five Indian scouts, including veterans Little Bat Garnier and Woman's Dress, accompanied the command; Colonel James Biddle and the regimental staff followed two weeks later. Only the unit gardeners remained behind with the Eighth Infantry.[2]

Within a few days after the establishment of Camp Bettens on Powder River, local whites goaded the black cavalrymen to violence. The soldiers attacked the tiny settlement of Suggs, and what the Crawford *Tribune* called a "free-for-all" erupted. Private Willis Johnson of I Troop was killed in the brawl, which abruptly ended the regiment's role in the cattle war. The soldiers spent the rest of the summer in their camp, while local civilians blustered about prosecution and conviction of the men involved. In late September most of the regiment returned to Robinson. The last two troops, D and E, returned in mid-November and the episode ended.[3]

Robinson troops were called out again during the railway strike of 1894, which began as a response to the layoffs and wage cuts of the Pullman Company. In weeks the unrest spread through the plains region to Wyoming and Montana. The government called out troops to break the strike under the pretext of protecting the mails. All Army garrisons were alerted to the possibility of insurrection against state governments. Therefore, Robinson was ready when a Department of Platte telegram of July 6 directed the command to prepare for immediate field service.[4]

Units of the garrison began to depart on the following day. Captain Corliss and C Company went—by railroad, of course—to Evanston, Wyoming. Lieutenant Edgar Hubert and D Company left on July 8 for Rawlins, another Union Pacific town in Wyoming. A week later most of the cavalry troops entrained for duty at Butte, Montana. In all these places the soldiers protected the property of railroad companies and guarded trains operated by non-union workers.[5]

All units returned to Robinson before the middle of August. They and other Department of the Platte garrisons received the commendation of Brigadier General Brooke for their performance. Some of the towns to which the troops went also reacted favorably. Both officers and men of the Ninth were reported to "speak in glowing terms of the treatment they received at the hands of the people of Butte." Lieutenant Hubert's infantry, on the other hand, faced a community united in hostility toward the uniformed strikebreakers. The citizens imposed a "rigorous boycott" on sales to both soldiers and United States marshals. Several prominent residents of Rawlins were arrested, but no violence erupted.[6]

In the following summer, Ninth Cavalry troops again took the field, this time in response to rumors of a Bannock uprising in the Jackson Hole country of Wyoming and Idaho. The Bannocks insisted that treaty rights made them immune to state restrictions on hunting. Governor William A. Richards of Wyoming sensed trouble and called for Federal troops rather than impose any risks on the state militia.[7]

On July 24 Colonel Biddle received orders to send a field grade officer and four troops of cavalry to Market Lake in southeastern Idaho. This expedition under Major Adna R. Chaffee was joined by five companies of the Eighth Infantry from Fort D. A. Russell. Then the combined force of over 400 encircled the Jackson Hole area. The Indian threat never materialized, and Brigadier General John Coppinger, the department commander, commented that the menace never really existed. The Bannocks, he said, were in more danger than the whites.[8]

Two of the four troops remained at Market Lake, southwest of the Teton Mountains, until late October. In August the rest of the men were reassigned to Fort Washakie, adjacent to the Wind River reservation. This sudden change of station surprised and disappointed wives and children in Nebraska but pleased the white civilians near the Shoshoni reservation, who were always glad to see even black troops.[9] The Bannock scare faded quickly into memory and became just another case in which groundless fears caused an excessive military reaction.

Two summers later the Ninth Cavalry prepared to return to the same part of Idaho, this time after news of a threatened uprising on the Fort Hall Blackfoot reservation. Fort Robinson was alerted to equip troops for lengthy field operations. Three days later Lieutenant Colonel John Hamilton and 240 troopers loaded a train for the expedition. By the next day, department headquarters concluded that Idaho's Governor Frank Steunenberg had exaggerated the menace. A hastily sent telegram reached Fort Robinson barely in time to halt the movement. The troops, who had already boarded railroad cars for Idaho, detrained and unloaded their animals and equipment. Then the empty coaches and freight cars returned to the depot at Chadron.[10]

Unlike the Bannock scare of 1895, this panic was accurately assessed in time. The aborted movement merely provided the garrison with an expensive exercise in mobilization. While both of the Idaho "uprisings" were largely imaginary, the cattle war and railroad strike which preceded them had no illusory qualities. This difference defines the 1890s for Fort Robinson's garrisons and many other frontier posts. The nation was moving into the modern industrial era and the Army's mission reflected the transition.

The accidental practice exercise of July 1897, was well timed. Late in the following winter, the flag in front of post headquarters dipped to half staff in memory of men who died on the battleship *Maine*. Two months later the troops began to pack. The United States had declared war on Spain, and the cavalry units of the Sixth and Ninth departed for Chickamauga four days after the alert. Over sixty railroad cars took the men, animals, and gear from Crawford to America's first foreign war in fifty years.[11]

The Crawford depot teemed with civilians as the town bid the men "God speed on their mission to whip the Spaniards." Some of the older wellwishers recalled similar scenes from Civil War days. All seemed confident that the Ninth Cavalry, "a well-disciplined, fighting regiment," would play a prominent part in the upcoming conflict.[12]

The departure of the Ninth marked the end of an era in the regiment's history. Old heroes were left behind. Some, like First Sergeant George Jordan and Sergeant John Denny, both of whom won Medals of Honor in the Apache campaigns, had retired and taken up residence in Crawford. Others, like Medal of Honor holder Emanuel Stance, were long dead. New heroes would be made in Cuba. Some of the men who served for so long at Robinson, like Trumpeter Lewis Fort of H Troop who bid farewell to his wife Bertie before boarding the train, would be brought down by Spanish Mauser bullets on San Juan Hill. Those who survived found the white man's burden a heavy load, as they carried it from Cuba across the Pacific to the Philippines.

After the transfer of the troops to Georgia, practically all Department of the Platte posts were staffed by only enough men to protect public buildings. Because of their proximity to the Sioux reservations, Niobrara and Robinson retained token forces of cavalry. Company I of the Eighth regiment, commanded by Captain Argalus G. Hennisee, arrived at Robinson on April 18.[13] They maintained and policed the fort while the wives and children of Ninth Cavalry soldiers anxiously awaited word of their men.

The brief Cuban campaign and the much longer and more brutal Philippine campaign which followed kept many western posts undermanned until 1902. Therefore, when the Western Federation of Miners led a walkout from the Coeur d'Alene mines in the spring of 1899, the corporations and the government brought in troops from Robinson and other distant posts. Soldiers were appropriate strikebreakers: the Idaho strike of 1899 was a battle in an armed war between the miners and their capitalist adversaries.[14]

Preparations to send troops to the Idaho mines began in February, when the post commander, Lieutenant Colonel Charles Viele of the First Cavalry, received a coded message from department headquarters. Two of Viele's four troops were ordered to Wardner, Idaho, on May 19. No one was

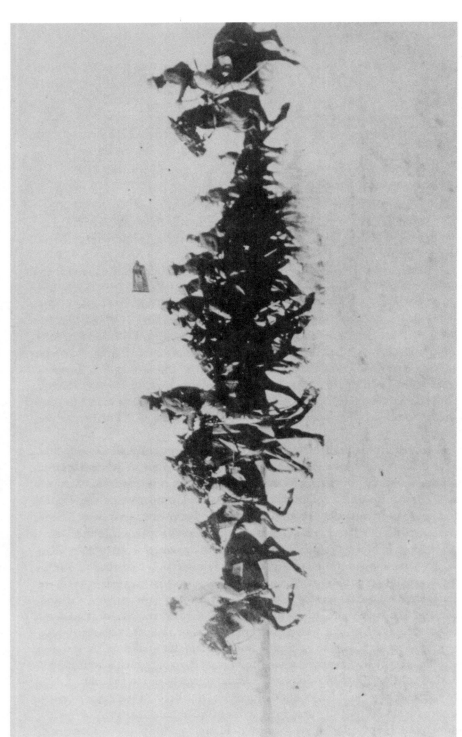

Charge! Guidon snapping in the breeze, a troop of the Tenth Cavalry dashes into action during a training exercise at Fort Robinson.
NSHS

Elements of the Tenth Cavalry marching onto guard duty. The 1905 post headquarters building is at the left.

A company dining room around 1898. The white Company I, Eighth Cavalry, was on post that year; troops of another white regiment, the First Cavalry, came in 1899.

Colonel Jacob Augur, who commanded the Tenth Cavalry and the post during the furor over the Ute migration.

NSHS

Bandsman Albert S. Lowe of the Tenth Cavalry, mounted on his horse Eagle. Copied from The Colored American Magazine, vol. 7, January 1905.

The Moorland-Spingarn Research Center, Howard Univ.

surprised: the Crawford *Tribune* had guessed their destination two weeks before the order came. A and L troops spent six months in Idaho, guarding railroad shops, rolling stock, and bridges, as well as prisoners detained in Wardner.[15]

From the time of this strike until 1906, Fort Robinson troops were not called into the field. The problem in the latter year fit well into the pattern established before the turn of the century. An abject band of White River Utes left the Uintah reservation in northeastern Utah to join northern tribes of Sioux, Crow, and Cheyenne Indians. The Utes either expected better hunting in the northern mountains or sought a defensive alliance against further white encroachments.[16] Their northeastward migration through Wyoming had the desperate quality of the Ghost Dance enthusiasm. Wyoming Governor Bryant B. Brooks, responding with all the acumen shown by Idaho's Steunenberg in 1897 and Wyoming's Richards in 1895, panicked and barraged the government with pleas for military help.[17]

The government exercised more caution than it had in response to earlier rumors of Indian wars. After all, Brooks's list of verified "depredations" included nothing more serious than the related crimes of grazing Ute ponies on winter feed reserved for livestock and killing cattle for food. Rather than ask for troops, the Interior Department sent veteran agent James McLaughlin to talk with the Indians. He convinced about fifty to return to Utah, but the rest remained adamant. Some told McLaughlin they were going north into the Big Horn Mountains; others claimed their destination was the Sioux reservation at Pine Ridge.[18]

Meanwhile the Wyoming press adopted Brooks's view of the situation. Newspapers cataloged a large number of Ute atrocities, most of which involved food gathering.[19] The far-off New York *Times* joined the chorus and reported an imaginary battle with cowboys, in which two of the whites were allegedly killed while defending cattle from the starving Indians. The Crawford *Tribune*, with nothing intelligent to add to the Ute-infamy refrain, solemnly reported that the Indians had obtained "fire water" and were "raising the devil."[20]

Indian Commissioner Francis E. Leupp wrote that the atrocity stories were "absolutely false," and intended "to arouse the citizens" against the Utes. The author of the only scholarly study of the episode concluded that even "the losses to cattle and sheep were extremely small," and the only violence was verbal. By early November even some Wyoming newspapers began to realize that the Utes had neither the will nor the ability to cause large-scale destruction. The papers then began to shift blame for the incendiary stories of October to eastern newspaper correspondents.[21]

The more sensible evaluation of the problem came too late to halt troop movements. On October 21, department headquarters in Omaha directed Major Charles H. Grierson, the son of the Tenth Cavalry's first commander, and two troops of the Tenth's First Squadron to Gillette, Wyoming, from Fort Robinson. Four days later the other half of the squadron followed. One squadron of the white Sixth Cavalry at Fort Meade left for Wyoming at the same time.[22]

Major Grierson first sent Captains Robert Paxton and Carter Johnson to convince the Utes to turn back. Johnson, a veteran of almost thirty years on the frontier who had been stationed at Robinson three times previously as enlisted man and officer, reported that the Indians were determined to reach Montana and that only a vastly superior force could convince them to return. Brigadier General Edward S. Godfrey then sent out Colonel Jacob Augur and the Third Squadron, Tenth Cavalry, leaving only about forty men at Robinson. Godfrey also alerted the rest of the Sixth Cavalry.[23] Over 800 soldiers were now in the field against perhaps half as many hapless Ute men, women, and children.

The cavalry troops moved into position around the Utes. The Tenth blocked routes north into Montana, and the Sixth straddled paths east into Dakota. At the end of October, both regiments conducted patrols before closing in on the Indians, who were camped on the Powder near Arvada, about fifty miles northwest of Gillette.[24]

On October 29, the two squadrons of black cavalrymen camped in clear sight of the Utes. On the next night a Ute warrior nearly caused an armed clash when he jostled a sentry near the Tenth's bivouac. Several of the guard's companions quickly intervened and prevented the pushing and shoving match from becoming serious.[25]

Another incident on the following morning almost erupted into a major battle. Troopers captured about fifty horses from five scared Ute herders and led the animals back toward their camp. About one hundred armed Ute warriors overtook the detachment, stampeded the herd, and harassed the outnumbered soldiers, who held their ground and their tempers. After a few minutes the Utes broke the tension by riding off.[26]

During these last days of October, the Tenth patrolled the vicinity of the Indian camp to prevent Crow and Cheyenne warriors from Montana agencies from joining the Utes. On October 30, detachments turned two hunting parties back toward Montana. On the next day Captain Johnson again conferred with the Utes. The best he could do was convince the chiefs to accept an escort to Fort Meade. The Utes would winter there, while two of their leaders, Red Cap and Black Whiskers, lodged their complaints with President Theodore Roosevelt. On November 4, the entire band and a cavalry escort arrived at Meade.[27]

Troopers of the Tenth patrolled the Wyoming-Montana border until the middle of November, probably as a precaution against trouble on nearby reservations. Then the men returned to Fort Robinson.[28] The regiment won no battles, but its achievements were still substantial. The troopers' level-headed and restrained conduct kept the tense situation under control and prevented needless casualties.

Early in the next year, the Tenth Cavalry packed its baggage for shipment to the Philippines. Most of the regiment boarded train coaches for their San Francisco embarkation point on February 28. Three troops stayed behind until the Eighth Cavalry, fresh from Philippine duty, arrived in May. The transfer ended almost twenty consecutive years of black garrisons at Robinson. M Troop of the Tenth, among the last units to depart, boarded a Burlington train for Fort Riley, Kansas, on May 19. Private Sidney Kirtley, hospitalized with a broken leg, watched from a ward window as his comrades boarded the cars. Kirtley convalesced at Robinson until October, when he asked to join his fellows: "I am a colored man and belong to Troop M, 10th Cavalry and, as my troop is at Ft. Riley, feel I would be much better satisfied there." Surgeon Paul Shillock approved, and the last cavalryman of the Tenth departed.[29]

The change of regiments did not alter Robinson's importance to the Army. The post remained a regimental headquarters, and the department commander praised Robinson's physical condition and environment as the best in the department. The location of the military reservation, its size, and the nature of the terrain all made the post well suited for cavalry. In spite of fulsome praise from various officers, most large training exercises took place near Fort D. A. Russell, Wyoming. The selection of this site was due more to the influence of Wyoming Senator Francis E. Warren than any military advantage.[30]

The Eighth Cavalry remained until late 1910, when the regiment returned to the Philippines. The troops saw no action during their three years on the Pine Ridge. Their Twelfth Cavalry replacements, arriving in the United States on the Philippine shuttle, also settled into a calm routine. Field maneuvers mixed occasionally with the game of county-fair soldier to break the monotony until 1913. In November the first squadron left for the Southwest, in response to rumors of a Navaho rebellion. The soldiers moved to El Paso, Texas, in early December, as part of the large force on the Mexican border. The rest of the regiment went to Colorado as strikebreakers in the coal fields west and north of Denver and near Pueblo. Only sixty men remained on post.[31] Indian-fighting days were definitely over: half the garrison protected a distant border from foreign revolution, while the rest defended Rockefeller property in Colorado.

Some of the troops returned from Colorado in early 1915. Through that year and the early months of 1916, all but twenty men left for Columbus, New Mexico, and duty on the border. Carter Johnson, who had led the Utes from Wyoming in 1906, came out of retirement to command the post and a small housekeeping detachment. Johnson stayed on duty until his heart failed on December 23.[32] After he died only the few oldtimers who stayed in Dawes County provided a living connection with the Indian wars of the post's early years.

Part II

THE
MILITARY COMMUNITY

Chapter 4

OFFICERS AND THEIR FAMILIES

THE EARLIEST OFFICERS' quarters on post were "board and canvas" shacks, little better than the tents of the enlisted men. These conditions improved before the end of 1875, with the completion of six adobe brick duplexes. The new line of residences faced the adjutant's office and the guardhouse across the parade ground. Each building had a common doorway, hall, and porch, under a steep, shingled roof. At the west end of the line stood the post commander's home, which was palatial by comparison to the two-room homes of his subordinates. It contained a sitting room, parlor, dining room, and kitchen on the ground floor as well as four upstairs bedrooms and a bathroom.[1]

Barely ten years after the adobes were constructed, Lieutenant Colonel James Brisbin described them as being "in wretched condition." By the time a new set of adobes went up in 1887, the condition of the old buildings had indeed become deplorable. Moreover, the sewer system that was installed in 1889 was never extended to the old quarters. The yards around them remained honeycombed with privy vaults and saturated with kitchen and laundry slops. Even after the dwellings were converted to single family units in 1893, they remained surrounded by filth.[2]

The six newer duplexes were considerably more spacious than the original ones. Each family enjoyed a parlor, two bedrooms, kitchen, dining room, bath, and servant's room. The homes were still adobe, however, and

Colonel Edward Hatch, who commanded the Ninth Cavalry for twenty-three years.
Massachusetts Commandery, Military Order of the Loyal Legion, and the USAMHI

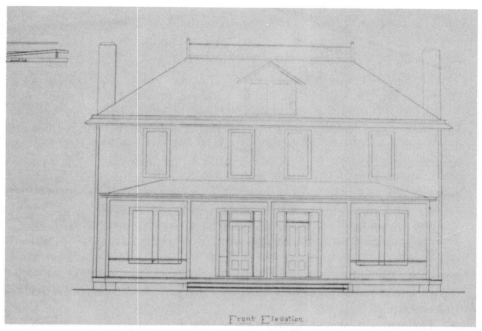

Front Elevation of the 1887 adobe duplexes, drawn in the office of the chief quartermaster, Department of the Platte.

Misc. Fortifications File, Fort Robinson, #14, RG 77, NA

The 1889 officers' duplexes, such as the one shown here, were based on a design similar to the one used for the 1887 buildings. The roofline and attic were different.

NSHS

Colonel Edward Hatch warned that this type of construction in north-western Nebraska was "a grand mistake." During a forty-hour driving rain the next year, the walls of one house collapsed, proving Hatch's point.[3]

In 1891 five double sets of "light, airy, and cheerful" captains' quarters were built. These two-story habitations with four bedrooms per family faced across a new parade ground to the flagstaff. A new home for the post commander contained an additional bedroom and sitting room. Ellen McGowen Biddle enjoyed life in this house while her husband commanded the fort between 1892 and 1896. In later years she recalled that this excellent dwelling had the best plumbing she had seen in military housing.[4]

The plumbing in the post commander's quarters must have been the exception. Surgeon Henry McElderry attributed the illnesses of two of Captain Charles Taylor's children in April 1896 to sewer gas leaking into his home through faulty pipes. In the years that followed, the drain pipes from the wash tubs and water closets frequently clogged, and the wood-encased sinks crumbled.[5]

The seniority system by which quarters were assigned exacerbated housing problems. When residences were in short supply, the arrival of a new officer threatened to leave the junior lieutenant and his family homeless. In 1890, for example, Lieutenant Charles Young was forced out of his home and almost into the cold by a series of moves. Fortunately, Major James Randlett's transfer from post enabled the post commander, Colonel Joseph Tilford, to divide Randlett's former quarters into residences for two lieutenants and their families. In spite of such expedients, officers' families still occupied the 1875 adobes through the 1890s.[6]

Captain William H. Jordan and Lieutenant Jesse M. Lee, of the Ninth Infantry, were the first to bring their wives to Camp Robinson. Major Henry's pregnant spouse also arrived in 1874. In addition to wives and children, an officer's household included servants, who were frequently recruited among the enlisted men or their wives. Women from nearby Crawford and other towns also worked as domestics. Captain Corliss, for example, employed a white woman from Crawford as a cook and a black maid from on post. Post officers also made use of a soldier to do their marketing in Crawford. During 1891 Private William Jenkins drove a daily wagon to town to purchase meat and vegetables, and then delivered the orders to the appropriate homes.[7]

Occasionally, an officer's wife expected more of enlisted men than a commander would allow. Mrs. Mary Garrard, whose husband Captain Joseph Garrard was in Cuba with the Ninth Cavalry, rained abuse on Lieutenant George Stockle for his refusal to allow Private Thomas Polk to work for her. Polk failed to cut her lawn because he had to repair water pipes.

In addition, Stockle had refused her request to send a soldier with harness and buckboard to take her visiting. Stockle said Mrs. Garrard "should not live in any military post unless her husband is present to be responsible for her rude conduct."[8]

Servants seem to have been a generally unmixed blessing for post officers. However, the turnover in the Corliss household suggests that relations were not entirely harmonious. In 1887-1890, Corliss had five different cooks and four maids, but there is no evidence of any serious complaints or problems in his or other households. A few Tenth Cavalry women, including Mary McCown, wife of the regiment's quartermaster sergeant, went on "a binge" in early 1904. Overindulgence in "Hunter Rye Whisky" and locally purchased cocaine and laudanum left three servants stupefied. After the episode Captain Robert J. Fleming's maid was hospitalized because of the combined effects of bad whisky and cocaine.[9]

Many households included animals as well as servants. Privately owned chickens, cows, and pigs roamed the post and added their own odors to the aroma that came from the cavalry stables. Yelping dogs frightened horses and contributed generally to the menagerie atmosphere. The problems created by domestic pets became so great that ordinarily amiable Colonel Guy Henry even threatened to shoot stray dogs and cats. His warning prompted the *Army and Navy Journal* to suggest that the Colonel would obtain better results with similar threats to the owners.[10] An unknown person had tried an informal variant of Henry's plan three years previously. In the spring of 1888 this culprit poisoned five officers' dogs.[11]

The problem survived all efforts at a solution. Shortly after Henry's threat, Lieutenant Colonel George Sanford complained that the dogs terrorized horses and mules. In turn, runaways endangered both riders and pedestrians. Sanford renewed Henry's warning, probably with similar results. Six years later, Colonel David Perry faced the same problem. Lieutenant Frank Armstrong's dog Billy followed the second squadron on mounted maneuvers and drove the horses to distraction. Perry demanded that Armstrong lock up or tie down his pet.[12]

Not all off-duty hours were spent in pursuit of stray pets. Officers and their families found many ways to enjoy their leisure, though some did not adjust easily to the isolation of Fort Robinson. Fanny McGillycuddy, wife of Post Surgeon Valentine McGillycuddy, authored the earliest and best known comment on Fort Robinson social life. After less than two weeks on the White River, she noted in her journal: "Commenced enjoying the camp. Finished." Over the next few months, however, she allowed her contempt to slacken somewhat. Horseback riding, dinner and card parties, walks, and chess all brightened her stay at Robinson.[13]

Many of Fanny McGillycuddy's amusements became regular features of officers' society on post. Card parties, which usually featured casino, euchre, or keno, were frequent sources of entertainment. Forty-eight guests attended such an affair given by Lieutenant and Mrs. John F. McBlain in the summer of 1895. Dances also remained popular. Weddings, birthdays, anniversaries, and the arrival or departure of officers all provoked these "grand balls" or "grand dances." Less formal dances, known as hops or germans also broke up the monotony of post life. Ellen Biddle remembered that the commissioned community still had "the old-time Friday Night Hop, always so enjoyable." These gatherings usually took place in the inelegant amusement hall, frequently with music by the regimental band.[14]

Some seasons were marked by little or no social activity. In the winter of 1889-1890, several members of the "society element," as officers and their families were known, went east to visit, and at least one resident complained that "everything is dull." At other times, parties occurred in flurries. In one week of February 1893, officers and their wives attended two card parties and a german with a Valentine motif given by Captains John Guilfoyle and Charles Taylor. In addition, the women enjoyed "ladies night" at the officers club with cards, dancing, and an oyster and champagne feast.[15]

The officers club operated at least from 1888 to 1895. Aside from Wednesday evenings, the two-room facility provided the officers with a haven where they could relax away from their families. The club offered meals, bar, library, and camaraderie. It also gave Captain Corliss, who was secretary-treasurer for several years, a way to spend many unhappy Sundays after his wife's death in early 1890. A civilian steward who served as manager occasionally had the assistance of soldiers detailed for duty there.[16]

The *Army and Navy Journal*, which had a correspondent among the Robinson officers or their wives, frequently reported festivities on post. The reporter, who was occasionally swept away by the subject matter, may have been Ellen Biddle. The company at Robinson did indeed impress her as delightful. She later recalled that "Fort Robinson was remarkable for its society," and that "in no city would you have found a more charming coterie than there was there when I arrived." The *Army and Navy Journal* stories may have been intended to impress urban readers with the sophistication of Robinson society or to feed the vanity of the writer's companions on post. Captain John Loud's wife, for example, may have enjoyed skimming remarks about her "silver gray silk [dress] trimmed in chiffon, diamond ornaments." Such attire surely impressed local civilian women. One Sioux County pioneer, Mabel Stewart Newell, recalled that "the officers' wives wore fancy dresses and their hair-dos and hats were very exciting to us."[17]

Officers engaged in several outdoor activities, in addition to their dances and parties. Riding, which Fanny McGillycuddy had enjoyed, remained a popular pastime. Surgeon Samuel McPheeters, briefly on post during the winter of 1906-1907, rode the horses belonging to his friend, Captain Robert Paxton, at every opportunity. Even in November, McPheeters went out without overcoat for "a glorious ride" of ten miles. Riding, like hunting, was not without its dangers. And among the greatest perils was Colonel Edward Hatch, who careened about post almost daily in his own four-horse carriage. In the spring of 1889, he turned the rig over, throwing three ladies from the carriage and breaking his own thigh. Hatch died of apoplexy four weeks later.[18]

Other outdoor amusements included hiking and picnics. Captain Corliss, who also hunted small game with his son Bob, liked to tramp the bluffs north and west of the post. Corliss also started a minor athletic fad at Robinson. He taught small-sword fencing to Bob, and later to his wife and Colonel Hatch's daughter Bessie. Then his enlisted men and other officers received instructions. Corliss called the sport "the craze of the post," and had more than enough students to keep busy.[19]

Polo, which came to the United States from England in the 1880s, was very popular at Fort Robinson during the Tenth Cavalry's tour of duty. Post officers played before local audiences, and a regimental squad clashed with other Army teams and civilian opponents. In 1905, the team invited opponents from Denver and elsewhere to compete for the "Tenth Cavalry Challenge Cup," which the Tenth won and kept. Two players, Lieutenant Seth Cook and Captain Ephraim Graham, qualified for a national team which defeated a team of British poloists in a Denver exhibition. Eighth Cavalry officers also played the game, but their fame never extended far beyond the Pine Ridge, where they seem to have been known as easy marks.[20]

In the 1890s late summer maneuvers in South Dakota also brought one of the highlights of the social season. The proprietor of a Hot Springs, South Dakota, hotel hosted the officers and ladies of Forts Robinson and Meade at an elegant ball. Ellen Biddle described the ballroom of the Evans Hotel as "beautifully dressed with flags and candles ready for lighting." In 1895, Carl Gung'l and the Ninth Cavalry's band gave two concerts and supplied music for the ball—waltzes, polkas, lancers, yorks, two-steps, and schottisches. The next annual gala was cancelled when Lieutenant James W. Benton died immediately beforehand while swimming at Hot Springs.[21]

Three months after Benton's death, Colonel Biddle retired from the Army. The officers of the Ninth Cavalry surprised him with "a very beautiful loving cup" at a dance given in his honor. The Biddles departed on the following day, after a serenade by Gung'l and his band. In her

The Ninth Cavalry band at Hot Springs in 1895.

NA

reminiscence of the occasion, Mrs. Biddle made it seem a military version of a master-class antebellum plantation dream. She said all the black soldiers came to bid her husband farewell, "tears rolling down their cheeks." Then as the train pulled out, "the cry of the men . . . was like the wail of the wind through a pine forest."[22] In fairness to Ellen Biddle, it should be noted that the Crawford *Tribune* observed that Biddle had many friends on post and in town, some of whom showed their disappointment at his departure.[23] However, it is not likely that the enlisted men cried and moaned a great deal at the departure of the officer who had so rigidly circumscribed their own lives.[24]

Ellen McGowen Biddle had relished social life at Fort Robinson. Elizabeth Burt, whose husband served on post during the late 1880s, agreed that "social gatherings of various kinds made the months pass pleasantly." Surgeon McPheeters also liked post society.[25] Only Fanny McGillycuddy dissented from this view, and even she found ample activity after her initial dissatisfaction.

Black officers who served on post enjoyed the society of their white peers much less. The three black chaplains—Henry Plummer, George

Charles Young and John Alexander as West Point cadets.

USMA and NSHS

Lieutenant Colonel Andrew S. Burt, who served at Robinson with the Eighth Infantry. His forty-year career started with his enlistment as a private in the Sixth Ohio Infantry in 1861 and ended with his retirement as a brigadier general in 1902.
USAMHI

54

Prioleau, and William Anderson—and as many line officers—Lieutenants John Alexander, Charles Young, and Benjamin O. Davis—appear to have been systematically excluded from the gatherings which enchanted and amused others. The very presence of Alexander and Young, the second and third black graduates of West Point, respectively, vexed many officers. In a strange twist, the whites felt the Army discriminated against them by assigning the only two black officers to the Ninth at Robinson.[26]

These few African-American officers adjusted to the situation in a variety of ways. Alexander, described by former post trader W. E. Annin as a "brainy, soldierly-looking mulatto," kept to himself and received the praise of the regimental adjutant for his self-imposed isolation. Plummer sought the company of enlisted men, while Prioleau defined his place in the military caste system as apart from both officers and men. Davis was at Robinson for less than six months of 1905 before he departed for Wilberforce University to serve as military instructor.[27] Lieutenant Young was perhaps too busy trying to satisfy superiors with his abilities as an officer to worry much about dances and parties. Colonel Joseph Tilford reprimanded him for several "tactical errors" committed as officer of the guard. Tilford, who never scrutinized the performance of white subordinates with such care, later reported these infractions as well as habitual tardiness and carelessness to the Adjutant General.[28]

The numerous reports of social events that appeared in the *Army and Navy Journal* never mentioned Young or Alexander. Neither did Captain Corliss in his diary, where he also frequently gave the names of all guests at a dance or dinner party. However, Corliss did keep in his scrapbook Lieutenant Alexander's note designating Corliss as his proxy in officers club elections, which essentially formalized the ostracism of the black officer. Regimental orders mourning Alexander's untimely death in 1894 suggested that his acceptance of his isolation was one of his most laudatory traits. The orders praised him for "appreciating the delicate distinctions of social intercourse which the peculiar and oft-times trying position of his office thrust upon him."[29] The distinctions Lieutenant Grote Hutcheson spoke of were, of course, far from delicate. Alexander knew that his racist colleagues wanted nothing to do with him, so he stayed away and spent his off-duty hours alone.

Post officers were less reluctant to share their leisure activities with officers at nearby forts. In 1879 Surgeon William Corbusier and his wife celebrated Independence Day at their Camp Sheridan station with a dinner party for Sheridan and Robinson officers, Pine Ridge missionaries, and even some Sioux chiefs. In later years, Robinson and Niobrara officers exchanged sporadic visits. In June 1887, Colonel August Kautz and a group of Eighth Infantry officers visited Robinson for a dance and local officers returned the favor the following week. At another time, Niobrara officers and ladies treated their visitors from Robinson to a play.[30]

Officers on post also had the company of relatives and friends from the East. The number of guests tended to increase as the Indian threat faded and included officers who had served on post in earlier years. Despite these occasional visits of relatives and trips to Niobrara, the officers and their families relied mainly on each other for entertainment. The intimacy of their relationships, due to their isolation at Robinson as well as class and occupational cohesion, resulted in several marriages between officers on post and the daughters of their colleagues. The fact that no lieutenant ever injured his career by marrying the colonel's daughter probably encouraged such alliances. Lieutenants Edgar Hubert and Joseph Beardsley, both of the Eighth Infantry, married the daughters of Colonels Hatch and Brisbin, respectively. Lieutenant George F. Hamilton of the Ninth also married Kate Chaffee, daughter of future chief of staff Adna Chaffee.[31]

Very few civilians were invited to participate in the activities of this group. Benjamin Paddock, post trader and son of a Nebraska senator, was apparently part of the officers' social circle, and rancher James Cook had many friends among Ninth Cavalry officers. Relations between the officers and the elite of Crawford rarely went beyond necessary formalities, however. Leroy Hall, a prominent local resident, dined once with the Corliss family, and one Tenth Cavalry officer, Lieutenant Herman Dilworth, married the daughter of Morgan J. Williams, the leading local contractor.[32] The paucity of social contacts may have been due to class distinctions between the officers and their wives—called "Crawford society" by one civilian observer— and local residents, whom the same person called "the people."[33]

Secret societies provided the only ground on which officers and civilians regularly met as equals. Even white enlisted men participated in the rituals of these fraternities with no apparent distinction based on military rank. As early as 1889, post officers and non-coms visited the Crawford Masonic Lodge together. Captain Corliss and several others participated in the activities of local Masons. Captain and Mrs. Charles Parker and Veterinarian John Tempany of the Ninth and his wife belonged to the local chapter of the Eastern Star. Nestor Lodge of the Knights of Pythias and the local Eagles group had members among post officers. Both societies invited Eighth Cavalry members to banquets before the regiment left for the Philippines in 1911.[34]

Officers and their wives participated in other local organizations as well. Mary Tempany served the small Crawford Woman's Suffrage Association as vice president in 1899. But neither this group nor the secret societies involved as many officers as the Grand Army of the Republic, the organization of Union veterans of the Civil War. Membership in the grand army declined over time, of course, as eligible veterans died. What marked this organization as unusual, more than the level of officer participation, was the inclusion of black enlisted men and retirees among the membership. Other fraternities were notorious for racial segregation. Locally, black troopers had to establish their own lodge of the Knights of Pythias, because of this organization's exclusionist policy.[35]

With the exception of membership in fraternal organizations, officers routinely excluded enlisted men from their social activities. On rare occasions, a commander might give a dance for his men, which some officers and their wives also attended. Captain Clarence Stedman's ball for his troop of the Ninth Cavalry in 1887 may have been the last such affair. Colonel Hatch, Major Andrew Burt, and some others attended. Captain Corliss, who did not go to the dance, wrote that Major Burt behaved scandalously there. Corliss did not state what Burt did that caused "a great deal of gossip in the post today," but said he was sure of Burt's excessive drinking though not his sanity.[36]

Most kinds of misbehavior brought little more than such private censure to officers. The case of Captain James A. Hutton of the Eighth Infantry provided the only exception in which the cohesiveness of the officers on post was significantly disrupted. Hutton's troubles began in an argument with trader Paddock at the officers club. Hutton, a sixteen-year veteran, struck Paddock in the face several times and knocked him down. Lieutenant Gonzales Bingham, the officer of the day, rushed in to arrest Hutton, who answered Bingham's demand for his sword with "Go to hell, God damn you, I won't obey your orders." Club Secretary Corliss finally took the blade after Hutton had gestured menacingly with it. Hutton was then placed under arrest in his quarters. He was convicted of conduct unbecoming an officer and disobedience of Lieutenant Bingham's orders, and sentenced to suspension from rank and confinement on post for four months.[37]

After his restoration to command, he faced an investigation at Fort McKinney for alleged mishandling of funds while Exchange Officer. In addition, Colonel James J. Van Horn, commander of the Eighth Infantry, expressed displeasure with Hutton's failure to master drill regulations. Then, in 1894, Colonel Biddle had to order Hutton to pay the large post exchange bill he had accumulated at Robinson. Around the same time, Hutton began to drink heavily, and left his family penniless at Robinson while he ran up bar bills in Omaha on an unauthorized vacation. Finally this catalog of misdemeanors overcame the almost infinitely elastic tolerance of officers at Robinson for their fellows, and Hutton was cashiered on July 31, 1894.[38]

Chapter 5

ENLISTED MEN AND THEIR FAMILIES

WHILE REASONABLY commodious housing became available for officers and their dependents at an early date, enlisted families lived in near squalor for decades. Army policy permitted only wives who served as laundresses to reside in government housing, so appointments to the positions were eagerly sought. Still, the quarters allotted to the washerwomen were scarcely better than the shacks built from discarded materials or the abandoned military buildings other families occupied without official sanction. After 1878, even laundresses no longer had official approval to reside on military posts, and enjoyed only the informal tolerance with which officialdom looked on other enlisted families.[1] All soldiers' households existed under conditions that severely tested the viability of even the closest families.

Laundresses Row at Fort Robinson resembled stables more than homes. A single building, which measured 144 by 35 feet, stood behind the first post hospital and too near the ice pond on Soldiers Creek to do anybody any good. The structure was divided into twelve sets of quarters. Each twelve by thirty-five unit was partitioned into three rooms, front to back. A window in front and another in the rear let in the only light. The center room had neither light nor adequate ventilation. Each kitchen had a hydrant but no water removal system. A back-yard privy near the ice pond completed each home. In 1893, twenty-seven adults and eleven children resided there,

58

in what Surgeon George Adair called "an undue aggregation of sanitary evils." The row represented a constant threat to the post water supply.[2]

The post commander authorized a maximum of three laundresses for each company. Unit commanders designated those who would get the privilege of residence on the row, and the supplies—stove, cooking utensils, and table—which went with the quarters.[3] In June 1891, Captain Jerould Olmsted of E Troop, Ninth Cavalry, selected the wives of Sergeants William Howard and Allen Cragg, and Corporal Charles Grayson as occupants. So, even though the Army had withdrawn official approval from the laundress system, it persisted under the management of post officers at Robinson well after the ban.[4]

The passage of time did not substantially change conditions on soap suds row. In 1903, Sergeant Eli Dolby and his wife Maria still had no sewer connections. Slop water from their kitchen ran out over the ground and flooded the adjoining yard, where the two Dolby children played with their friends.[5]

While housing on Laundresses Row was bad, other quarters were even worse. Surgeon Jefferson Kean cited the case of a corporal who resided with his wife and child in a one-room shack, about twelve feet square. The hovel was made of waste timber, had one door and no windows. The door provided more than ample ventilation, however. It admitted "light and dust in equal abundance."[6]

In the 1890s families occupied abandoned log barracks as well as individual cabins. These did not even have the advantage of privacy. One old dormitory on the lower post, known as "the Bee Hive," had been the site of the escape of the Cheyennes in January 1879. The squad room was used as a quartermaster storeroom, but the rest was occupied by men of the Ninth and their families. What had been the orderly room, kitchen, mess room, and an enclosed porch, was partitioned into a total of fifteen small rooms. Eight wives and ten children resided there.[7] Another unused barrack housed the post school in its squad room and four families in the smaller rooms. Three black wives lived with a total of six children in the log building. The white wife of a soldier also had quarters in the same tenement.[8]

Surgeon Adair deplored these conditions, but wanted any substitute housing to be at least as far from the residences of officers as Laundresses Row on Soldiers Creek.[9] Doctor Kean and the Department of the Platte's medical director thought that the lack of provisions for the health, comfort, and decency of the enlisted men's families menaced the health of the entire garrison. Kean suggested that small cottages be built for those of good character, who were at least on their third enlistments. Though only twenty-seven married men fell into the category, he guessed that as many as sixty would want such cottages. Presumably the squalid conditions at Robinson kept many from marriage or from bringing families on post. Kean's proposals were not adopted. Enlisted quarters remained a threat to sanitation and soldiers' families remained a "pariah class."[10]

Fire, which Surgeon Kean did not mention in his otherwise thorough report, was an obvious menace in the old log buildings, where several cooking and heating fires burned simultaneously. No conflagration occurred for nearly a decade after the Bee Hive was first occupied, but when it came the building was gutted. On the afternoon of March 23, 1898, Sergeant Harry Wallace's wife left the tenement to visit friends. Before she departed, she locked two of her children, four-year-old Gertrude and two-year-old Mattie, in a room. The oldest of her three children was in school. Around three o'clock, smoke was spotted and the alarm sounded. Soldiers who rushed to the building made several heroic but futile efforts to rescue the trapped children before the aged structure collapsed in flames. The two girls were found together on a bed, "burned to a crisp."[11] The blaze also left six families homeless. The Crawford *Tribune* commented sympathetically that the fire was "one of the saddest affairs . . . in this section of the country for many a long time."[12]

Fire did not present the only possibility for sudden death. On an evening in January 1892, Private Jerome Patton of E Troop, Ninth Cavalry, asked Sergeant Allen Cragg's wife for a drink of water. He entered her Laundresses Row apartment and bent over the washstand to quench his thirst, while Mrs. Cragg sat nearby. Suddenly, he struck out at her with a chunk of coal, leaving a large gash on her forehead. She screamed and Patton fled toward Crawford. Her husband chased him all the way to the house of "a colored Cyprian." The enraged sergeant fired at Patton but missed. Patton fled and an all-night chase began. Around daylight, Cragg again found his adversary, this time in a saloon. He shot twice and missed. City Marshal Morrison joined the pursuit and trapped Patton in a livery stable. The lawman managed to restrain the still seething Cragg and delivered Patton to the post guardhouse.[13]

Some few enlisted men lived in homes less dangerous and more commodious than the Bee Hive and Laundresses Row. Members of the post and regimental non-commissioned staff lived in detached houses. These fortunate men included the hospital steward, ordnance sergeant, commissary sergeant, and chief musician, as well as the regimental sergeant-major, saddler sergeant, and quartermaster sergeant. The Ninth's veterinarian lived in similar quarters.[14]

Statistics on the number of families in detached residences are deceptive, because they include some who lived in shanties, such as the one

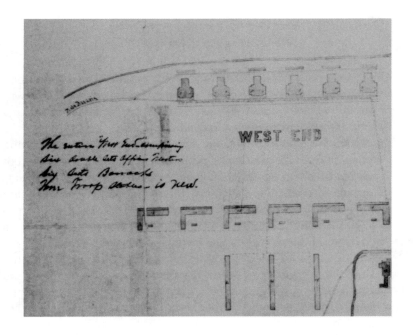

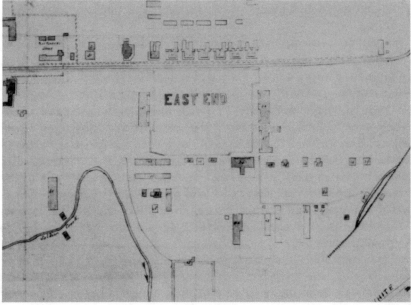

This **1888** map shows the recently constructed buildings of the new post as the "West End." Six sets of officers' duplexes faced six L-shaped barracks, with three stables behind those. The old post was called the "East End." Laundresses row was the long building just west of the bend in Soldiers Creek. The original post bordered the parade ground. Officers' quarters lined the northern side, and barracks faced each other on the western and eastern side. The westernmost of the three small buildings on the southern edge of the parade ground was the guardhouse where Crazy Horse was mortally wounded. Directly east of these three structures, at the southeast corner of the parade, was the "Bee Hive," the original cavalry barrack that was the site of the Cheyenne outbreak and the 1898 fire that took the lives of two Ninth Cavalry children.

Misc. Fortifications File, Ft. Robinson, #27, RG 77, NA

Surgeon Kean graphically described. The 1891 total for those living apart was twenty families. These included fifteen black families and four white ones. The twentieth was the Indian family of scout and interpreter "Little Bat" Garnier. The four white families were the dependents of members of the post non-commissioned staff. Although they resided in separate one-story cottages, "that many a second lieutenant might envy," they had no sewer connections.[15]

Around the turn of the century, probably when the Ninth left and the number of officers declined precipitously, the families of the non-commissioned staff moved into the sewerless old adobe officers' quarters. However, when the Tenth arrived, lieutenants again occupied the adobes. At that time, there were eleven non-commissioned officers who were authorized quarters with only one available set. That one, dilapidated and unsanitary, was shared by two families, while the others lived in even less sanitary places. After the Tenth left, the senior sergeants returned to the still sewerless adobes.[16]

There was little need for even these inadequate and unsanitary homes during the early years at Fort Robinson. Most men who enlisted for duty with units which served there were probably single, perhaps because of the still hazardous nature of duty in the White River area. Those who were married may have sought escape from wives and children. However these factors interacted, in 1883 only a half dozen "isolated log houses [were] occupied by the married sergeants and privates."[17]

During the late 1880s, several changes caused a rapid increase in the number of dependents on post. The railroad came through the region and towns grew where the Sioux once hunted. At the same time, the Ninth Cavalry came to the fort. Contrary to the assertion of Colonel James Biddle, the black trooper did not have "a greater affection and desire for women than his white brother." However, black soldiers did remain in the service longer. Colonel Biddle noticed this too and pointed out that his troops naturally tended to have larger families than white soldiers.[18] By the same token, more of them were married, and the post soon became crowded with dependents.

Statistics were not kept on what officers called "the civil population" until some years after the Ninth arrived. However, some families accompanied their men or followed immediately after the units that arrived in 1885. Private Rufus Slaughter of K Troop, for example, brought his wife Ella and two children, nine-year-old Gertrude and seven-year-old Sam. Other men also brought relatives, and by 1889 there were nearly two hundred dependents on post.[19]

The only census of women and children was taken in the summer of 1893. That compilation reveals both the number and size of the families of enlisted men. Fourteen white soldiers and twenty-five black troopers had families on post. Twelve families lived on Laundresses Row and five resided in the Bee Hive. Seven other families lived in officers' households, where they worked as servants, and fifteen lived in detached shacks or the small cottages set aside for the non-commissioned staff. In addition, there was a camp of Indian scouts, in which ten women and nineteen children resided.

The average number of children in these households was three. Only a few were larger. Ordnance Sergeant Christopher O'Brien, a white member of the post non-commissioned staff, had ten children in his bungalow. Two other white soldiers, Chief Musician Carl Gung'l and Sergeant Stone of the Eighth Infantry, had five children, while the largest black family was the four of Sergeant Edward McKenzie, I Troop, Ninth Cavalry. The census also shows one adopted child in a soldier's family, the white son of black Sergeant John C. Proctor of I Troop, Ninth Cavalry.[20]

More important perhaps than the size of each family is the overall structure of each group. The striking fact about the black families on post is that several extended beyond the customary unit of parents and minor children. Seven of the twenty-five black families on post had adult relatives living with them. Moreover, a sense of community extended beyond these enlarged family units to the other families and even to the years after military service. The cohesion within and among the families of black soldiers stands in contrast to the nuclear structure of nearly all the white families on post.

As time passed, the bonds between the men and families who served together surpassed those of mere co-workers. The close relationships which were forged were reflected in the resolution Sergeants Holloman and Dowd of the Ninth wrote for their fellows to mark the death of a comrade:

> Whereas the Almighty has, in his wise providence, removed from our midst our associate comrade, Sergt. Israel Valentine, Troop A, at Fort Robinson, Neb., June 21; therefore, be it Resolved, That as the last tribute we can pay to his memory, as one of our comrades, we record our appreciation of him, and extend to his family our sympathy in their bereavement . . . .[21]

Mrs. Valentine, who remained at Fort Robinson until she was forced off post, obviously valued the community in which she lived very highly.

There were several reasons for the families of enlisted men to form a closely knit social group. They lived in very close proximity and had mutual interests and social status. Race also drew the families of black soldiers closer. With the exception of a small black community in Crawford, largely made up of retired and discharged soldiers, the town was not a particularly warm place. Also, military tradition and class consciousness among the officers isolated the families of enlisted men from those of the commissioned personnel.

Ties impelled by a common condition and long association were sometimes reinforced by marriage. The wives of two Ninth Cavalry sergeants, Edward McKenzie of I Troop and George Mason of C Troop, were sisters. Another Ninth Cavalry wife had been born to a black cavalryman's spouse at Fort Ringgold, Texas, in 1875. Both she and her mother lived with their husbands at Robinson. The younger woman had literally spent her entire life in the Ninth Cavalry. Later, three Tenth Cavalry soldiers at Robinson married women with common backgrounds: they were all born in the West Indies, one in Cuba, and the other two—who were sisters—in Kingston, Jamaica. Another Tenth trooper, Cook Beverly Thornton, married Sallie Conley, sister of Quartermaster Sergeant Paschall Conley of the same regiment.[22]

The size of the garrison declined fairly steadily from the time of the census of 1893 to the war with Spain. However, after an initial drop, the number of women and children on post remained fairly stable. In 1894, there were only 117 women and 126 children. The number of women remained constant through the spring of 1897, while their offspring increased by eleven. By early 1899, most of these people had departed to follow their men, and only eighty-five dependents resided at the fort. This population increased after the Tenth arrived in 1902, but never grew to the size it had reached in the mid-nineties. In early 1904, for instance, only sixty-nine women and thirty-six children lived at Robinson.[23]

Although there is no complete tabulation of the number and size of families after the 1893 census, the record of births gives some clue to the size of Tenth Cavalry families.[24] In 1904-1907, nine children were born to the wives of eight different cavalrymen. The two born to newly married Regimental Sergeant Major Presley Holliday and his wife Estelle were their first. Of the other seven, only the children born to the wives of Private Carey McLaine and Sergeant Joseph Williams were their first-born. Two others were second and another was a third child. Mrs. Josie Jones, wife of Sergeant Edward Jones of A Troop, gave birth to her fifth, a son William, in May 1905.[25] Six of the nine were boys, and two proud fathers, Sergeant Major Holliday and Sergeant Dolby of the band, gave their own names to their sons. Only four more births were recorded through 1910. Three daughters and one son were born to wives of Eighth Cavalry soldiers in 1908-1909.

A few soldiers met their future wives while stationed at the fort. The women William Connelly and Martin J. Weber of the Fifth Cavalry married in 1883 and 1885, respectively, were probably daughters of other

The evening gun being fired by two Tenth Cavalry troopers. During the period of the Tenth's service at Robinson, the Army restricted enlistment in the artillery to whites, contending that black soldiers could not master the mathematics needed for service in that branch.

NSHS

soldiers. Private Simpson Mann of the Ninth met his future bride while she was employed by "another lady," probably an officer's wife. Three white soldiers in the small garrison which occupied Robinson during the wars in Cuba and the Philippines married local women, one of whom was the daughter of the Crawford *Tribune*'s publisher. After the Eighth Cavalry arrived in 1907, weddings became more frequent affairs.[26]

Only one black soldier's wedding was performed in a Crawford Church. Sergeant Major Holliday, the Tenth's senior enlisted man, and Estelle Hill married in the Congregational Church. At least one black soldier, Sergeant Ebbert Maden of the Ninth, had his wedding in Chadron. Occasionally a ceremony was held in the home of a black resident of Crawford, where either the post chaplain or a local judge presided. Most weddings took place in the post chapel. Here too, civil officers occasionally performed a ceremony.[27]

Throughout the entire period, post commanders exerted tremendous power over the families of enlisted people. This power did not have any statutory base. Rather, it seems to have developed naturally out of the military caste system. Assignment of quarters followed the same procedure it did with officers: rank and seniority determined the right to occupancy. However, other factors also came into play. Post commanders carefully scrutinized the wives of their men and refused to permit women whom they considered of questionable virtue to reside on post. Of course, this kind of examination was unnecessary for officers' wives. But when it came to enlisted men, the commanding officer assumed the role of moral guardian.

At times, subordinate commanders pleaded the causes of their men when a commander sought to cast out a wife. Captain Charles Parker of K Troop asked Lieutenant Colonel James Brisbin to at least stay the banishment of Trumpeter Frank Lewis's wife until after payday so that he could find a place for her and their children. Brisbin was inclined to agree that this would be just. Then he noted that a woman of Mrs. Lewis's character could not be allowed to remain and ordered her banished immediately.[28] That this kind of treatment did not drive Lewis out of the regiment—he was still on post ten years later—suggests the paucity of options available to him.

Only a month after the Lewis episode, Private George Fredericks of the same troop came under the scrutiny of Colonel Brisbin. Captain Parker recommended quarters be assigned Mrs. Fredericks. Brisbin directed the captain to investigate charges that she was still married to another man. Mrs. Fredericks acknowledged a previous marriage but claimed to have been divorced. Her husband corroborated her story. The Frederickses had a marriage certificate, but Captain Parker was unsure of its legality: "Whether she is a bigamist or not I cannot say." Brisbin pondered the evidence and initially recommended the discharge of Fredericks. In the interim, he confined the hapless soldier in the guardhouse. Department headquarters settled the matter by dismissing it. Since Fredericks had enlisted with the understanding that he would not receive quarters, the question of his wife's previous marriage was irrelevant. She could not live on post in any case.[29]

In the following year, Colonel Edward Hatch summarily expelled Fannie Fletcher and Annie Cox, the wives of two Ninth Cavalry soldiers, with instructions that they never return. Five years later, Colonel James Biddle dismissed the request of Private Drayton Moffett, a teacher in the post school, for quarters. There was, Biddle said, as if speaking of an item supplied by the government, "no authority for Private Moffett to have a wife." A year later, Biddle handled a similar request from Private Wheat of A Troop in the same abrupt manner: "It is understood that his wife is not a desirable woman."[30]

In the summer of 1890, Colonel Joseph Tilford banished Suzie Barton, wife of an I Troop soldier. Then he found that his decision inconvenienced Lieutenant Edgar Hubert of the Eighth Infantry, who had hired her as a servant. Tilford rescinded the order but reversed himself again when Captain Guilfoyle of I Troop confirmed his assessment of her character. Within a week, he informed Lieutenant Hubert that Mrs. Barton's conduct had been "scandalous and unjustifiable." She would be allowed to stay only until Mrs. Hubert recovered from her illness. As soon as her services were no longer needed, Hubert was to report the fact to post headquarters.[31]

During the next summer, Corporal John Rogers of I Troop and his family were evicted from their quarters and the post at large. Even this failed to satisfy Captain Corliss. Because the family had been involved in a fracas, he recommended the discharge of Rogers from the service.[32] Four years later Colonel Biddle upheld the banishment of Mrs. Rogers as in the best interest of the service.[33] Fourteen years of service and heroism during the extremely arduous 1881 pursuit of the Apache Nana did not help Rogers in pleading his case.[34]

Biddle appeared at times to exercise his power with a complete lack of compassion. After Sergeant Israel Valentine died at Camp Bettens, Wyoming, during the summer of 1892, his widow remained at Robinson. In February of the next year, Colonel Biddle sent her away, explaining to Lieutenant Joseph Garrard that the quarters were for the families of enlisted men, not widows. He considered the sentimental attachment between her and A Troop to be irrelevant.[35] Biddle may have been right, but other commanders at other posts showed more sympathy with similar plights. After First Sergeant James Brown of I Troop, Tenth Cavalry, froze to death in a blizzard near Fort Assiniboine, Montana, his wife remained on post. Nearly a year after Brown died, a Tenth Cavalry sergeant said Mrs. Brown "ain't going to want for bread while the 10th Cav. has a ration left."[36] Nobody threw her out into the cold.

Biddle's apparent meanness was part of a calculated effort to keep the number of dependents at an absolute minimum. He admitted to being "very strict with the women" at Robinson, whom he "fined or sent away" for any indiscretions. In response to a plea for quarters on behalf of Private Wheat, he explained to Captain Garrard that he had given no authorization for any soldiers' wives to occupy quarters and that "none will be given." He justified his policy by stating that there were "too many wives of soldiers on the post." He maintained this policy in spite of his own belief that the black men under his command "were inclined to remain passive and to do [their] duty if allowed social and sexual intercourse."[37]

Regulation of the social lives of the enlisted men gave Biddle no joy. Captain Guilfoyle protested to him in late 1894 about Provost Sergeant Edward Fletcher's impromptu searches of the quarters of some men of I Troop, including Sergeant Proctor's. Biddle replied with a catalogue of misdemeanors, which ranged from harboring expelled women to dispensing illicit liquor. He dwelt at length on the unsavory character of members of Blacksmith Walker's family. One daughter, who had slashed a soldier with a razor, had been expelled but repeatedly returned. Walker's other daughter was pregnant by an unknown man. She would be banished when her baby became old enough to travel. Blacksmith Walker's problems were many, but Biddle dwelt on his own. He rebuked Captain Guilfoyle sharply regarding the conduct of the Proctors and Walkers, directing him to see that "no nuisance is inflicted upon the commanding officer or the Post by either of these families and see that under no circumstances is there any liquor sold at either of these houses."[38] This incident illustrates some of the more substantial problems of the post commander as overseer of morals. It also shows Biddle's attitude toward such problems. They were simply a nuisance. And the fewer families there were on post, the smaller the annoyance would become.

Colonel Biddle's explicit hostility toward the dependents of his men did not have much impact on the number of marriages. The War Department authorized the reenlistment of only nine married troopers in 1890-1894. In the next two years, while Biddle remained post commander, this figure jumped to twenty-three. Over the fifteen months between Biddle's retirement and the Ninth's departure, another fourteen married men were allowed to re-enlist. Of the forty-six men granted the privilege of having wives in this period, forty were black cavalrymen. The others were on the post non-commissioned staff.[39]

The re-enlistment of married soldiers was sometimes allowed with the explicit understanding that they would receive no quarters on post. This was the case with Private George Fredericks, whose difficulties have already been discussed. Another instance involved Lincoln Washington, who sought enlistment in the Tenth Cavalry. Captain Charles Grierson informed Washington in June 1902, that there were no quarters available for married men. He could enlist, but would have to find housing for his wife off post. Washington had been a sergeant-major in the Ninth and an officer during the Philippine Insurrection, and may have thought Grierson's conditions severe. However, in 1910 Washington was again a sergeant major.[40]

During the Tenth's tour of duty at Robinson, commanding officers continued to scrutinize the character of their soldiers' wives. Chaplain William Anderson approved the practice as "having a healthful effect." He drew a cause and effect relationship between being "blessed with good behavior" and keeping unsavory women away. He pointed out that it was difficult to keep evil women from coming on post. Some persistently returned, as did the wife of B Troop's quartermaster sergeant, William Bell.[41]

Sergeant Bell was a twenty-three year veteran, who had been recommended for a Medal of Honor for heroism in the assault on San Juan Hill. His wife Lulu had worked on post as a servant for one of the officers. After she was expelled, the Bells established a residence in Crawford. She returned to the fort several times to attend social functions, such as the dance of

July 25, 1904, given in honor of Sergeant Perry of L Troop. During the party she and her husband quarreled. Mrs. Bell settled the matter by pulling out a pistol and shooting him twice. He died of the wounds on the following day.[42] Chaplain Anderson bemoaned the loss of such a good soldier, who had been "much loved by all who knew him." He concluded that the presence of women like Lulu Bell had a "demoralizing effect on the good."[43]

This incident raises the same questions Colonel Biddle's complaints about Blacksmith Walker's family brought out. On occasion the social reality of life at Fort Robinson seemed to justify the arbitrary power of the post commander. Chaplain Anderson surely agreed that it did. However, Crawford was only three miles away, and expulsions merely put problems out of sight. Thus, while officers acted out of concern for the health and safety of their commands, they were ultimately powerless to prevent an occasional tragedy. Moreover, the exercise of their power restricted the functioning of the adult human beings who served under them. The questions were difficult and perhaps explained the contradictions in Colonel Biddle's thinking. While certain that his men performed better if their women were present, he strove to reduce the number of women on post to a minimum.

Not all officers were as ambivalent about soldiers' families. Surgeon Adair revealed his class bias as well as his favorable view of the women on post: he said they exhibited "an exemplary character as wives and mothers, comparing with women of the laboring class in civil life." Surgeon Kean observed that the presence of married men benefitted the entire community. While the wives of the men served as cooks and washerwomen for officers, they also supplemented their husbands' meager incomes. They also exerted a wholesome influence on their men, who spent much less time on the sick list than their single counterparts. Adair added that soldiers with families were less likely to desert. In sum, the married soldier was committed to his trade, and was "not constantly studying how to better his condition." Kean also took the eminently equitable position that officers were permitted to have their families accompany them and enlisted men should be entitled to the same consideration.[44]

Doctor Adair later wrote that banishment to Crawford, which was the only reasonable alternative to residence on post, was a distinct disservice to the families involved. The village sanitation system was defective and travellers were likely to pass venereal infections to the women. Both of these factors promised only to increase the sick lists. At the same time, Adair believed that residence in the hovels on post at least offered pure water, ice for food preservation, and military supervision to compensate for the sanitary evils.[45] He did not mention, and perhaps did not know, that residence on post also offered soldiers a community based on occupational cohesion, long friendships, and even intermarriage.

Chapter 6

IN THE BARRACKS

THE SOLDIERS who arrived with the Sioux Expedition in March 1874, made their first homes in tents near the Red Cloud Agency. They remained under canvas through the first summer but, following the practice of the time, completed three sets of barracks for themselves before the year ended. The buildings of native timber stood on the rim of a parade ground: the two infantry barracks faced each other from the eastern and western borders and the cavalry quarters stood on the southwest corner of the field, next to the adjutant's office. Each had a kitchen, mess hall, and storeroom as well as a dormitory.[1]

In 1883 the men of F Troop, Fifth Cavalry, built an additional log building, which they occupied in December. The structure stood between the infantry quarters on the eastern border of the parade ground and the original cavalry barrack, then occupied by a company of the Fourth Infantry. The new building, called the most substantial log dormitory in the Department of the Platte, had tightly mortared joints and a shingled roof. The main room, in which the troopers had their bunks, measured 118 feet long and had a ceiling over 13 feet high. This long bay was flanked by a library on the left and the company office, known as the orderly room, on the other side. The wing that extended back from the left front had a central hall leading to the mess room at the rear. On one side of the hall, a

An L-shaped log barrack at Fort Robinson.

NSHS

Black troops inside one of the 1887 barracks.

NSHS

series of rooms contained a barber shop, tailor, cook room, ration room, and closet. On the other side was a shop in which carpenter, saddler, and shoemaker worked together, a washroom, a bathroom, and a kitchen. The building cost the government $521.[2]

The 1883 building was the last barrack built by the men. The six adobe and two frame dormitories that went up in 1887-1891 and the two brick structures added in 1909 were built by contractors. All but one of the log barracks were vacated when the first adobe buildings were completed. Thereafter, some of the original buildings were converted to storage. At least one, the cavalry barrack of 1874 where the Cheyenne prisoners had been held briefly during the winter of 1878-1879, was taken over by enlisted families. The unfortunate infantry company which stayed in its log quarters until 1894 endured wretched ventilation in the generally dilapidated building. When these men departed for a new station, a recently arrived cavalry unit moved into the "very rotten" quarters and remained there until they left for Cuba.[3]

The adobe and frame quarters faced north across the new parade ground to the officers' homes which were built around the same time. Behind them to the south stood rows of cavalry stables, all luckily downwind. Each building was L-shaped and contained an orderly room or company head-quarters, first sergeant's room, store room, and squad room or dormitory in the main section. The wing included the dining room, kitchen, bathroom, and a second store room, as well as a shop for either a tailor or saddler, and the cook's room. The only significant difference between the infantry and cavalry billets was the size of the squad room: the former housed fifty men and the latter seventy.[4]

Private Simpson Mann of F Troop, Ninth Cavalry, arrived on post in early 1888 and joined his company in one of the new adobes. His dormitory's interior was covered with dove-colored plaster. A lone portrait of Abraham Lincoln adorned the wall, and curtains purchased by the men covered the windows. The beds consisted of iron frames strung with wire to support straw-filled mattress sacks which were folded over into rolls for inspections. A pot-bellied wood stove provided uneven heat.[5] By 1890 four "mammoth Rochester burners," fueled with kerosene, lit each squad room well enough to read newspapers—provided that the men contributed money to supple-ment the inadequate fuel ration.[6]

Mann recalled that there were spittoons in the room for tobacco chewers. The rest of his description was negative: no rugs, no day room or recreation area, no trash can, no pool table, and no drinking water. Some units made up for this last deficiency with a barrel of water outside the building. A chunk of ice from the post pond cooled the water but, after an epidemic of diarrhea was traced to the ice, most soldiers went to the hydrants in the bathrooms for refreshment. Private Mann dealt with the lack of potable water by hiding a gallon of whisky in his foot locker.[7]

Infantry troops in a nearby barrack also had their own solution to the lack of entertainment. Captain Charles M. Bailey's men purchased a pool table by subscription for use in their barracks.[8] From curtains and decent lighting to billiards, the men used their own initiative and meager financial resources to make their quarters habitable.

The adobes were built because the log buildings and the surrounding yards were a shambles. Four months before Company I, Eighth Infantry, moved to a new billet, Surgeon Walter Reed complained that waste water from the overflowing cesspool behind the dormitory saturated the soil under the building. Conditions in the cavalry barracks were no better. Defective drainage from C Troop's bath facility caused a similar problem. General George Crook said the log barracks had been thrown together in a "horrid manner," leaked, and were infested with bugs. Mann remembered that the new barracks, occupied soon after Reed and Crook complained of the old, were "clean as a ribbon," but full of bed bugs nonetheless.[9] Poor sanitation persistently troubled post doctors and menaced the health of troops, even in their new quarters.

The wash rooms of each barrack had two iron bath tubs. Hot water was piped in from an upright boiler, and soldiers bathed and shaved weekly. In summer the men enjoyed bathing in the White River and may have done so more often. The major obstacle to cleanliness under these arrangements was physical discomfort. While hot water was available, a warm room was not. The facilities were unheated and a winter bath must have required great determination. Surgeon George Adair noted that cold was not the only obstacle to cleanliness. The number of tubs was only a third of what he thought each company should have.[10]

The privies also caused sanitation problems. As late as 1892, the Army failed to provide sufficient lime or "dry earth" for these facilities. The area around the barracks of D Company, Eighth Infantry, was particularly repellent. The outhouse, close to the trader's store and post exchange, was used by many men on their way past. This traffic frequently overturned the nearby kitchen slop barrel. An appalled surgeon called the yard "the foulest three hundred square feet in the garrison," and a typical cholera center. Doctor Henry McElderry considered replacement of the privies by water closets the most critical requirement of the post. Five years later, however, the outhouses still stood, drawing "innumerable flies" in the summer. To add insult to injury, they were thoughtlessly located only a few feet from kitchen doors. Surgeons bemoaned the persistence of this problem particularly because the sewer line which removed waste from officers' homes ran directly behind the unhealthy outhouses.[11]

In 1900 and 1902, the Army built five lavatory buildings, complete with indoor plumbing and steam heat. The new facilities, which cost over $14,000, eliminated the long-standing problem of the outhouses but created the new difficulties of clogged and overflowing toilets. Moreover, the new buildings still required the "men to go out of doors for some distance to wash or attend to the calls of nature . . . ."[12]

There were problems with the barracks themselves as well. During the 1890s accommodations were simply inadequate for the size of the garrison. At times cavalry units had to live in the smaller, more crowded infantry barracks. Troops also lived in buildings not originally intended as quarters. In 1895 headquarters clerks were forced out of their quarters and shunted into a small annex of the post library to accommodate a troop of cavalry. Seven years later, the Tenth Cavalry band had to take up residence in the old amusement hall, because of the shortage of living space.[13] Even as late as 1909, the floor space per man was far below the Army's standard of one hundred square feet. Actual space ranged from sixty-nine to eighty-three square feet.[14] In that year, however, the problem was solved with the construction of two large red brick buildings.

One additional difficulty which plagued residents of the barracks was ventilation. Surgeon McElderry wrote in 1894 that none of the buildings permitted adequate circulating air. Only one allowed any flow of air from under the floor, and the men shut this opening during winter months for warmth. McElderry's statistical summation of air and floor space included a note that the fresh air that entered with doors and windows shut was just too small to estimate. He believed that the eighteen tonsillitis cases which occurred in the barracks during January 1895, reflected this problem. An influenza epidemic two years later, which incapacitated 112 men for an average of eight days each, was also blamed on the stuffy, stale barracks air. In 1909 Fort Robinson reported more tuberculosis cases than any other post in the country. This too was traced to the foul air which accumulated during winter months.[15]

Two of the most important rooms in the men's quarters were the kitchen and dining room. Each unit had its own facilities in the barracks, over which a cook chosen from among the men presided. This kind of amateur chef had prepared enlisted men's meals since the middle of the Civil War. The system, labeled "crude and traditional" by the Adjutant General in 1887, lasted until 1894. From that time, cooks were appointed permanently at a sergeant's rate. Ten years later, the Army established training schools for cooks.[16]

Saturday inspection for the men of I Troop, Tenth Cavalry, with an L-shaped dormitory behind them. The frame construction represented a considerable improvement over earlier log structures.

At Fort Robinson company kitchens in the log barracks were over-crowded and ill-fitted eight-by-ten shacks. In these and the larger rooms of later years, cooks and their kitchen police assistants prepared meals. Private Simpson Mann said the food in his troop's dining room was satisfactory. If so, cooks and helpers did more than creditable jobs with limited resources. The standard ration for Mann's F Troop consisted of eighteen components, two of which were candles and soap. The food elements were meat (pork, bacon, beef), bread (flour, cornmeal, yeast), vegetables (dried beans, peas, rice, hominy), coffee and tea, and condiments (sugar, vinegar, salt, pepper).[17]

This basic ration was supplemented by produce from post gardens. Commanders and troops all looked forward to the growing season, so much so that impatient soldiers occasionally conducted informal harvests. While the Ninth Cavalry spent the summer of 1892 in Wyoming, white infantry-men ransacked their garden repeatedly. The cavalry's gardeners, who were the only men important enough to be left behind at Robinson, could not stop the raids. Captain Corliss had to place the garden off limits before the depredations ceased.[18]

As early as 1878 Surgeon William H. Corbusier at nearby Camp Sheridan showed that a great variety of crops could be grown. In his family garden, he boasted of tomatoes, squash, and spinach as supplements to the dried issue vegetables. Robinson gardens yielded a similar variety, including an occasional asparagus crop. In 1893 the harvest yielded corn, beans, peas, lettuce, radishes, cucumbers, egg plant, squash, okra, parsnips, beets, tur-nips, rutabagas, peppers, cabbage, and potatoes.[19]

The complexity of the management of post and unit gardens illustrates their importance. Commanders ordered seeds from as far as Detroit, even before the railroad connected Robinson with the East. Troops erected fences to protect their plots from the domestic animals that roamed the post and used an array of agricultural implements more complex than their ordnance. In 1892 Lieutenant Colonel George Sanford instructed his quartermaster to requisition plows, harrows, rakes, cultivators, four kinds of forks, and other tools. A lieutenant served as officer in charge of the garden and super-vised the operation.[20]

When the agricultural operation was consolidated into one large post garden, as it was in the 1890 season, work parties frequently included black and white privates. They weeded and watered together under the super-vision of the corporal assigned as post gardener.[21] In spite of their appreciation of the result, troops did not always enjoy work in the garden. Private George Lanam of the Ninth Cavalry refused to obey Corporal Charles McTrammick's order to sort cabbage heads. McTrammick threatened to have him jailed, and Lanam replied, "I don't give a damn, put me in the guardhouse." A garrison court honored his preference and gave him twenty days.[22]

Commanders of newly arrived units had to purchase the garden plot of a departing outfit with troop funds. Captain Gustavus Valois and the men of C Troop, Ninth Cavalry, bought a Fifth Cavalry garden in August 1885 for $70. Valois made a down payment of $35 and sent the balance to the Fifth at Fort Supply, Indian Territory. He thanked the commander for the sale: "The garden is a very fine one and we are glad to have had the opportunity of purchasing it."[23] This transaction was facilitated by revenues received from C Troop's old garden at Fort Sill, also in Indian Territory. Lieutenant Charles J. Crane of the Twenty-fourth Infantry sold C Troop's produce and sent Valois the proceeds of over $91.[24] The Sill garden not only paid for the purchase of the new one but left a substantial profit.

The post hospital financed a separate garden for patients from its own fund. Soldiers from the regular garrison were occasionally detailed to care for it. Hospital produce sometimes included more exotic plants than the general harvest. In 1891 the surgeon reported that he planted fruit trees and strawberries as well as vegetables. The hospital also kept its own dairy cows, identified by leather neck bands inscribed "H. C. Cow."[25]

Local contractors supplied milk for the regular mess halls at least as early as 1893. W. H. Pullen, who furnished milk from 1896 to 1900, probably gave at least one surgeon ample justification for the maintenance of a hospital herd. Doctor Louis LaGarde complained in 1897 that Pullen's dairy was dirty and that the milk was probably unsafe. Two years later Surgeon Albert Simonton renewed complaints about Pullen's yards and sheds: manure covered the ground and fouled the air. Pullen also skimmed the milk so that it contained less than half the specified cream. Moreover, he refused Simonton's request that he examine the Army's dairy regulations. The doctor then recommended that the post get its milk elsewhere.[26]

The complaints continued into the next year. Simonton found sediment of cow manure in samples taken from the bottom of Pullen's milk cans, and concluded that the milk was "a constant menace to the troops stationed here, of bowel troubles and typhoid." The milkman's practices so enraged the surgeon that he called Pullen "devoid of moral principle," and finally had his license revoked. Peter Cooper, a Crawford dairyman, received the contract and apparently performed satisfactorily thereafter. The scattered cases of typhoid which had plagued the post disappeared, the cream content of the milk trebled, and the post finally received a safe and reliable supply of the beverage.[27]

Milk and fresh produce added considerable variety to the foods issued by the commissary. However, D Troop's menu for a week of February 1893, which Adair called "a just representation of the ordinary fare of the soldier," still contained far more bread and meat than anything else. Breakfast consisted primarily of roast beef or hash, with potatoes, bread, and coffee. The mid-day meal also featured beef and bread, and sometimes bacon. Beans, rice, sauerkraut, turnips, and cabbage were each served once. Supper was the lightest meal, usually bread and gravy and either coffee or tea. The troops had milk at five of their twenty-one meals. Summer menus probably offered a wider variety, but the fare was still drab though reasonably well-balanced and nutritious.[28]

As the menu suggests, the men consumed large quantities of meat. The official ration allowed nearly nine pounds of beef and over two pounds of pork for each man every ten days. A Crawford rancher furnished the meat in 1894 and 1895 for about six cents a pound. Herman Rincker, who had the contract for those two years, received nearly $15,000 for the period.[29]

Although the Army converted to the purchase of chilled beef from large packers to supply most posts in the mid-1890s, local ranchers furnished Robinson meat for many years thereafter. The contract went to Chadron after the turn of the century, and post medical officers had to rely on Department of Agriculture agents to inspect the meat. They frequently claimed they were too busy to do so. This distressed Surgeon James Church, but the Secretary of Agriculture denied requests for more systematic checks.[30]

Civilians also provided other items for the soldiers' tables. For many vendors, particularly the early ones, sales on post were probably extremely important sources of cash. This boost to local agriculture was less important than the protection the fort offered but substantial nonetheless. Several of the first families who settled in the area regularly visited Robinson with butter or vegetables, either to trade at Benjamin Paddock's store or to sell to mess halls. One farmer and his family arrived frequently with wagon loads of ice-packed buttermilk cans. They sold glasses of the chilled, farm-fresh beverage to parched cavalrymen at a nickel a serving, much like later ice cream vendors.[31]

Units on post further supplemented their diet by raising small herds of cattle and swine. These animals yielded milk as well as meat, albeit sometimes at the expense of other meal components. Porcine raids on the post garden brought angry threats from post headquarters of deductions from the vegetable allowance for owners of miscreants. Troop herders were also warned about grazing their animals too close to the ice pond. Companies managed to hold on to their animals in spite of these problems. Several troops of the Eighth Cavalry offered livestock for sale when the regiment left in 1910. One unit had two milk cows, three sows and three shoats. Another departing troop advertised six poland-china sows and forty piglets.[32]

The availability of supplements like milk and fresh vegetables, therefore, often depended on the men themselves. Similarly, any improvement over the drab issue tableware also came from the troops. Until the late 1880s the Army distributed large tin mugs and plates with iron utensils. These were dropped in favor of white ironstone chinaware. Some units on post purchased barrels of more attractive dishes from commercial suppliers, adding some color and patterns of their own choice to the dining room monotony. In 1898 the Army also tried to provide more attractive gold aluminum utensils. One Ninth Cavalry troop at Robinson used the experimental items but reported that they spotted and corroded easily.[33]

Meals and living conditions generally remained simple and drab. Alleviation of the monotony depended in large measure on the actions of unit commanders and the privates themselves. Their initiatives frequently resulted in better meals and more pleasant quarters. The soldiers, both black and white, were not oblivious to their own welfare, and used their small pools of funds to enhance their daily lives.

While soldiers on post worked together to ameliorate conditions, they also quarreled and brawled. Most incidents involved only two men, but some became more general. Private Thomas Herbert of B Troop, Ninth Cavalry, a career soldier who later won a Certificate of Merit for distinguished service during the Cuban war of 1898, started one such fracas. Not satisfied by hurling epithets at Privates Charles Daniels and William Davis, Herbert threw a rock at Davis. The intended victim dodged the missile, which struck Private James Cook. When Corporal Gus Bailey tried to arrest Herbert, he became the object of Herbert's blows. Several men finally subdued the soldier, who spent thirty days in the guardhouse for the multiple assault.[34]

Barracks scrapes never involved black and white privates against each other, even though there was ample opportunity for such conflict. While housing by company meant racial segregation, there were occasions when whites resided with black cavalrymen. This occurred when the garrison was entirely black and whites either enlisted on post and waited for assignment or were left behind by units as gardeners. In 1897 five privates of the Sixth Cavalry and one Eighteenth Infantry soldier slept and ate with the Ninth Cavalry for varying periods.[35] Similar situations took place in other years, and the temporary desegregation never resulted in violence. Perhaps the few whites with whom the African-Americans shared their barracks behaved with caution in such circumstances. Perhaps fear of their officers' reactions restrained the blacks. Whatever the reason, black and white soldiers were able to share life in the Spartan and uncomfortable barracks.

The austerity and discomfort of barracks life paled quickly into insignificance for soldiers incarcerated in the guardhouse, which was among the first buildings erected in 1874. It faced the parade ground from the southern rim, where it stood between a warehouse and the adjutant's office. This log jail remained in use for ten years. In 1884 a new one was built alongside the original. Only three years later, the Army advertised for bids to erect still another lock-up, perhaps out of concern for the miserable conditions inside.[36]

Surgeon Adair complained at least twice about the filthy interior of the building. He noted that the only remedy for the overcrowding, which went beyond the limits of health and decency, would be a larger, better ventilated structure. Two months later, Doctors Adair and Jefferson Kean made a thorough study of conditions at Colonel Joseph Tilford's request. They found the prisoners "like beeves in a cattle car, with the advantage of pure air on the side of the latter." An average of twenty-two men slept in a single thirteen-foot square room. Three more serious violators occupied isolation cells, where they had nearly three times the floor space of the others. Air entered the larger room from the outside through two cracks around the windows. The lack of fresh circulating air made malaise, nausea, and bronchitis common problems. Generally, Kean and Adair concluded that men were kept there in "reckless disregard for the laws of health."[37]

Crowding became so incredibly bad that prisoners at times had to stand all night. Three convicts were released to lessen the crowding, and the guard detail vacated the building so the prison room could be enlarged. Colonel Edward Hatch had already ordered that every effort be made to keep soldiers out of the lock-up by use of disciplinary measures short of courts-martial. He feared corruption of minor violators through association with "the most worthless and vicious men . . . ." The surgeon added that confinement of petty offenders who still had their self-respect and decency would only disgust them with the Army.[38]

In 1891 the Army authorized $8,470 for a new, more commodious jail. George Jewett of Sidney received the contract and completed the building the following year with only $1,300 in cost overruns, modest by twentieth century standards. An indoor water closet, steam heat, and large rooms gave the building some comforts even the barracks lacked. Both the surgeon and the post commander now hinted that prisoners were being coddled.[39]

Convicts in the guardhouse wore obsolete military clothing without the buttons. For a time their garments were dyed a dark blue, then butternut. In 1911 a "P" was added to further set them apart. Their food was the same as that served in unit dining rooms, and the cooks of the outfits

The new guardhouse around 1898.

in which they last served were responsible for feeding them. Several problems arose out of this practice. Soldiers on kitchen police sometimes rebelled against delivering the meals. In addition, cooks resented the extra work involved in preparing prisoner meals. A directive that the officer of the guard inspect all meals to insure that they contained properly cooked portions of adequate size could have reflected deliberate negligence in the kitchens. Even these instructions did not bring much of an improvement. On at least one occasion prisoners refused to eat the supper brought them. Since the westernmost barrack was over a quarter mile from the guardhouse some complaints were inevitable. Food served on winter days never stayed warm, and neither did the men who delivered it.[40]

The unpaid labor of convicts was fairly important in the daily routine of the post. Colonel Hatch even asked that convicts be sent to him from elsewhere in the busy construction year of 1887. Private Mann, who escorted parties of chained prisoners to work as an armed guard, said they dug ditches and scrubbed buildings. Prisoners also worked with a small "police cart," picking up litter around the fort. In May 1902, Colonel Jacob Augur directed the daily release of a Tenth Cavalry prisoner to work as a lineman for the Signal Officer. A month later Augur had to rescind the order. Finally, in 1908, the Army allowed post commanders to employ those serving three months or less as mechanics and teamsters in the quartermaster department.[41]

Work outside the guardhouse benefitted the prisoners as well as augmented the post labor force. Men who misbehaved were taken off work parties, which was no small punishment in the odorous old jails. Other incorrigibles were locked in small cages, fed bread and water, or placed in irons. Myles Smith, a nineteen-year veteran of the Ninth Cavalry who deserted to take a job as a waiter in Douglas, Wyoming, spent two months in irons. An officer of the guard shackled Sergeant Barney McKay and deprived him of reading material, a severe penalty for a man who worked as a newspaper reporter as a civilian.[42]

Although there is little information on how soldiers of the guard treated their charges, two incidents suggest both the range of permissible behavior and the pressures of guard duty. Sergeant Alfred Pride of the Ninth lost his stripes and $20 for allowing a prisoner to escape. On the other hand, Sergeant John Jackson of the same regiment fractured a white prisoner's skull because the convict threatened him. The victim, Artificer Cornelius Donovan, later died, but Jackson was exonerated. Colonel James Biddle expressed surprise that Jackson had acted with such restraint and did not shoot the infantryman outright.[43] Sergeants of the guard must have learned from these incidents that escapes would be costly but that any means could be employed to keep the prisoners submissive.

Sergeant Jackson's assault on Donovan was one of very few violent episodes involving white and black soldiers. Another more explicitly racial incident occurred when Private Jacob Schwartzentroup of the Eighth Infantry objected to a sergeant's efforts to escort him to the guardhouse. When two black troopers came to the non-com's aid, Schwartzentroup's anger mounted. He tried to strike the men and raged that he would not go with "a damned black nigger son of a bitch." He went, of course, and his outburst cost him an additional thirty days.[44]

The capture of escapees represented one of the few ways soldiers could gain official recognition during peace-time. Colonel Hatch offered three cavalrymen of the Ninth "any favor within my power" as well as five-day passes for an 1887 capture. Sergeants Ebbert Maden and William Vrooman of the Ninth also received the gratitude and praise of Colonels George Sanford and Biddle, respectively. Civilians received a monetary reward for the same service. As early as 1888 a Dawes County deputy sheriff claimed and received the customary $30 reward for apprehending and returning an escapee.[45]

Many more made good their escape, in spite of the vigilance of soldiers and civilians. From 1877 to 1909, at least twenty-one left successfully, perhaps to be apprehended months later at distant posts. Some broke loose from work parties while others crept out of hospital wards. Two men bored a hole through the guardhouse floor and crawled through the coal cellar to freedom. Some of these escapees had special incentives: they disappeared just before being taken to the disciplinary barracks at Fort Leavenworth to serve long sentences.[46]

Post officials showed little interest in the prisoners except as potential escapees and as laborers. Before the completion of the 1892 facility, officers worried a bit about the influence of confinement on men they considered minor miscreants, rather than hardened criminals. But this was an effort to keep some men out rather than to help those inside. Chaplains visited the prisoners from time to time, but only Chaplain Alexander Landry, who served on post from 1911 to 1915, showed any consistent concern. One of his first acts was creation of a weekly bible class in the lock-up. As long as Landry remained, the program continued. When he left, the Sunday school closed.[47]

Chapter 7

RACE AND RANK
IN THE NINTH CAVALRY:
THE STANCE AND McKAY AFFAIRS

RACIAL SOLIDARITY was an important motivational force among black soldiers, at Fort Robinson as well as elsewhere. From the so-called San Pedro mutiny of 1867 to the Houston riot fifty years later, black enlisted men frequently acted in concert against hostile whites.[1] For the men of the Ninth Cavalry at Fort Robinson this cohesion took a variety of forms, ranging from establishment of their own fraternal organizations to threats of violence against the entire community of Crawford.

The violent protests of black troops against white racism have been fairly well documented, but the limits of the cohesion on which these actions were based have not received the same attention. The experience of the Ninth Cavalry at Fort Robinson provides some insights into the factors which divided blacks against each other and in some cases thwarted efforts to establish unity. Two incidents in particular, the murder of First Sergeant Emanuel Stance and the court-martial of Sergeant Barney McKay, illustrate some of the divisive elements at work.

Emanuel Stance was a tough old campaigner of nearly twenty years experience when he rode into Robinson with F Troop in 1885. He had served well on the southern plains and the Medal of Honor he won for heroism against the Kickapoos in 1870 was the first awarded to a black soldier after the Civil War. Stance was wiry, battle-hardened, and mean. He had already lost his stripes once in 1873 for a fracas in which he had bitten off a chunk of another sergeant's lip. After he came to Robinson he became the center of a series of disputes and brawls which hit F Troop during the last half of 1887.[2]

The first confrontation, which took place in the odorous and fly-infested stables, did not involve Sergeant Stance. On a June morning Private Frank Bowser decided he had had enough of these conditions and strolled out of the corral to his barracks. Quartermaster Sergeant Robert Harris ordered him back to work. Bowser refused angrily: "Why the devil don't you make some of these other men do something?" Harris escorted the private to the guardhouse, ignoring Bowser's threat to "fix" him. The sergeant brushed the warning aside and demanded silence. Bowser, defiant to the end, replied "You can't stop me from talking."[3]

On the same day that Bowser received a twenty-day sentence, two other men, Private Norbin Harris and Corporal Robert McKeen, confronted each other at the stables. Harris scorned an order to adjust a horse's tether. Like Bowser he felt persecuted and snapped at McKeen that he was "tired of you God damn niggers bulldozing me and I will not stand it!" When Lieutenant William McAnany asked why he spoke so disrespectfully, the surly Harris answered that, "They have been cursing me ever since I have been in the troop and I am tired of it." A garrison court-martial gave him thirty days.[4]

One of the incidents at the post stable involved First Sergeant Stance, who reprimanded Private Henry Royster for carelessly watering the horses and threatened to jail Royster if he persisted. Royster was as defiant as Privates Bowser and Harris had been: "You can take me . . . none too soon, that is fine, I am ready to go." And he went—for ten days.[5] This incident was the third in six days in which privates had disobeyed and defied non-commissioned officers.

Relations among the sergeants themselves were not entirely harmonious. On the morning of November 13, a quarrel erupted at the stables between Sergeant Ebbert Maden, then in charge of the stable guard, and Quartermaster Sergeant Harris. Maden called Harris a liar, and Harris knocked Maden to the floor. Private Lewis Glenn rushed in from his sentry post and tried to stop the fight. Harris demanded that Glenn "dry up or he would break his damn head," but others broke up the scuffle. Later a garrison court-martial fined Harris a month's pay and reduced Maden to the ranks.[6]

Private Glenn may have already had his share of conflict. He had clashed twice with First Sergeant Stance, for which he had paid five dollars and spent ten days in the lock-up. One confrontation occurred in the barracks, when Glenn ignored an order to wash his trousers. The other took place in the corral. Stance ordered Glenn to stop jerking a horse he was watering. The private denied any misdemeanor and demanded to see his commander. He warned that he was "tired of your bulldozing me, Sergeant Stance."[7]

The dining room was hardly calmer than the stable. On June 23, Private David Kendrick smashed a bowl over Private William Smith's head. Smith had to have surgery before he could return to duty.[8] Private George Jones, obviously displeased at kitchen police duty, started another mess hall fracas. At first light on November 20, Cook William Perrin assigned Jones to carry breakfast to the prisoners in the guardhouse. Jones called Perrin "a son of a bitch," told him to go to the devil, and refused to serve the convicts. The outburst disturbed his comrades who still slept in the adjacent squad room and cost Jones $3.[9]

Only two days later, Private Jacob Blair also disrupted the early morning quiet of the barracks. He came in at three o'clock, drunk and extremely disorderly. Blair laughingly flung his boots about the place but amused none of his comrades. He paid $2.50 for the commotion. At breakfast that morning, Blacksmith George Waterford, perhaps unsettled by Blair's display, created a disturbance. Sergeant Stance ordered him to be quiet. Waterford growled back that "anyone who approaches me this morning is tired of living."[10]

These ten petty difficulties involved eight different privates and four non-coms, in a company of only about forty-five and ten, respectively. Discipline was significantly less than perfect. Captain Clarence Stedman, a veteran of seventeen years with the Ninth, surely bore ultimate responsibility for this condition. As one of his privates complained, Stedman did not know as much about his troopers as he should have and depended too much on his sergeants for information.[11]

First Sergeant Stance, the senior non-commissioned officer, not only failed to maintain harmony but was himself the focus of much discontent. Six of the ten altercations involved privates and their non-coms; four involved Sergeant Stance. The military caste system was more than a simple dichotomy of white officer and black soldier. Black privates responded to what they considered to be harassment by their black non-coms with belligerence and threats. Moreover, when Emanuel Stance was found dead in December, the soldiers of F Troop became prime suspects.

Lieutenant Joseph Garrard discovered Stance's bullet-riddled body on the road to Crawford at about eight o'clock on Christmas morning.[12] A few days after the funeral, Major Andrew Burt, post commander during the absence of Colonel Edward Hatch, sought legal advice from a Federal jurist in Omaha, in a remarkably humble and deferential letter. Burt "very respectfully" apologized to the judge for the "trespass on your valuable time," and asked a series of questions concerning the judicial process. Major Burt confessed his ignorance of jurisdiction over the crime or the proper legal authority to whom to report the matter. He emphasized the importance of the case, which he thought involved "the whole interests of the service."[13]

On the same day Burt complained to Governor John Thayer that the Dawes County Sheriff had not apprehended any suspects. Thayer offered a $200 reward for the killer. Colonel Hatch later protested that the sum was insufficient and urged an increase to $1,000. He shared Burt's anxiety and sense of gravity of the matter because the Stance murder "was the third cold blooded murder" of soldiers at Fort Robinson in eighteen months. Privates Thomas Menlow of C Troop and Henry Roberts of F Troop had been killed in late 1886, and their cases were unresolved. Moreover, "no one has as yet been punished for the crimes."[14] Hatch and Burt feared that they were losing control of the garrison.

The sheriff finally arrested a suspect, Private Miller Milds of F Troop. Burt remained apprehensive and wrote that it was of "importance, vital importance," that no effort should be spared to "prevent Milds' escape if guilty."[15] Yet, by this time Hatch and Burt had already made a costly and foolish error. In 1887, the state legislature had explicitly ceded judicial and legislative jurisdiction over the military reservation to the United States. Both officers should have known this, but they wasted precious time by taking the case to a Chadron state court, which decided in late February that the crime was committed on the military reservation and declined jurisdiction. Hatch then jailed two cavalrymen for complicity while continuing to hold Milds. The colonel then turned to the federal court system, but he did not know which circuit court had jurisdiction or how to bring the matter to trial. He feared for the safety of the garrison because "the men who are engaged in these murders are impressed with the belief that the law cannot reach them."[16]

Within a few days of Hatch's plea for help, three Federal officers—a district attorney, United States commissioner, and marshal—arrived to examine the evidence. The commissioner decided Milds was the principal assailant and sent him to Omaha for trial. Nearly a year passed before proceedings continued. Incredibly, the delay was attributed to a lack of funds for the prosecution. By that time some witnesses had died, while others had been discharged and could not be located.[17]

Colonel Hatch approved Captain Stedman's recommendation of a dishonorable discharge for Milds and forwarded the request to Omaha. Hatch called Milds "a worthless scamp," and reported that the soldier had contracted syphilis. Hatch thought the condition was chronic. Milds was in the hospital "and in all probability will spend most of his enlistment there." He was dismissed from the service in January 1889, at Fort Robinson.[18]

Milds was never convicted for the death of Sergeant Stance, and post correspondence contains no proof of his guilt. However, the evidence still points strongly toward the men of F Troop. Captain A. W. Corliss believed "men of his own troop" probably killed Stance. Private Simpson Mann, who joined F Troop shortly after the murder, heard that two or three soldiers had killed one of their sergeants. When he recalled the incident years later, Mann called the victim "dirty mean," and said he had beaten soldiers and lied to officers about them.[19]

Mann commented that the murdered man's replacement, Sergeant Nathan Fletcher, represented an improvement. This is no surprise: the shooting may have temporarily subdued many a belligerent non-com. More significantly, Mann concluded that the sergeants "all were about [the] same."[20] An earlier court-martial of a private in C Troop supports the aged veteran's recollection and evaluation. The court convicted the soldier of striking First Sergeant Thomas Bannister. General George Crook, commander of the Department of the Platte, overturned the decision. Crook noted that the sergeant provoked the assault when he struck the accused on the head with a carbine and then chased the soldier through the barracks. The calm that overtook F Troop did not endure indefinitely either. In 1891, Private Edward Ross became insubordinate to First Sergeant John Turner. When Sergeant Edward Fletcher ordered him to the guardhouse, Ross called Fletcher a "damned son of a bitch" and struck him.[21]

Officers like Hatch, Burt, and Stedman either failed to appreciate the fact that sergeants browbeat and even terrorized private soldiers, or they condoned this behavior in the name of discipline. One officer wrote that Stance was "a very strict disciplinarian," and that he "stood high in the esteem of his superiors." Probably the same officer observed that Stance's troop "needed a strong hand, and it took a pretty nervy man to be 1st sergeant."[22]

Stance was more than a strict disciplinarian. He hounded his troops and apparently condoned similar behavior by his subordinate non-coms. If he was killed by one of his own men, as the evidence suggests, the shooting may well have been the ultimate protest against this kind of leadership and the command structure that condoned it. Awareness of this possibility may

John Guilfoyle as a West Point cadet.
USMA

have been what prompted Hatch and Burt to such vigorous pursuit of Stance's killer. Post officers had not been nearly as energetic after the earlier murder of Menlow and Roberts. While their actions after Stance's death were surely prompted in part by their respect for the victim's previous service, their near panic suggests that more basic factors were also involved.

Rank did not always divide the black cavalrymen among themselves. In 1891 the privates and non-commissioned officers of I Troop united in a protest against their commander, Captain John Guilfoyle. Colonel Biddle described Guilfoyle as "a most excellent officer," and "one of the best captains" in the regiment. However, even Biddle, who was no egalitarian in racial matters, acknowledged that the captain was a "man of extreme prejudices." The men of I Troop agreed. Following the example set by black infantrymen at Fort Bayard, New Mexico, a few weeks previously, nearly forty privates and noncoms composed and signed a complaint against Guilfoyle and left the document on Major Guy Henry's desk. They petitioned to have Captain Matthias Day replace Guilfoyle, who they charged had called them a "damned mob."[23]

Major Henry met with the complainants, whose names he tactfully forgot. He advised them to present their grievances through military channels, which meant to Guilfoyle himself. Henry recognized that "nearly the whole troop" had signed the petition but claimed they had "acted in ignorance." The unflappable major then tore up the complaint, hoping to close the matter at that juncture.[24]

Guilfoyle was apparently still ignorant of the petition when Henry decided to squelch it. The post commander probably had not considered that the men could work secretly or that their captain would not know of the conspiracy. When Henry told Guilfoyle about the complaint, the captain responded with court-martial charges. Major Henry reluctantly forwarded the charges and recommended a general court-martial, even though he did not believe the matter could be proved.[25]

The Department Commander was as unwilling as Major Henry to try the case. Henry informed Guilfoyle of the decision and added that his office would not forward any more correspondence on the issue. He told Brigadier General John Brooke that a public hearing would only injure discipline in the regiment.[26] Henry probably believed the matter was finally settled, but it still troubled him. When he relinquished command at Robinson in late May, he praised the officers and men "for their attention to duty and zealous cooperation in all requirements of the service." But he also suggested "less public criticism of comrades and a willingness to sacrifice personal desire for the good of the regiment . . . ."[27]

John Guilfoyle was a stubborn man. A month after Major Henry's departure, he pressed charges again. Lieutenant Colonel Alfred Smith surveyed the evidence and reported that he could only prove that three men, a private, a corporal, and a sergeant, had asked others to sign the petition. Nevertheless, the difficulties probably did not cease until Guilfoyle went to the University of Nebraska in the fall of 1895 to replace Lieutenant John Pershing as professor of military science and tactics.[28]

Post officers did not always treat the protests of enlisted men as cavalierly as Major Henry had done. Not long after the complaint against Captain Guilfoyle had been quieted if not settled, an incident in town brought a markedly different reaction. The trouble erupted when James Diggs, an ex-cavalryman of the Ninth who had been dishonorably discharged in 1887, was nearly lynched in Crawford. In mid-April 1893, Diggs had been cleared of misdemeanor charges by the police court in town. Apparently, some citizens believed justice had not been done and decided to override the judicial process. A soldier-pamphleteer, obviously enraged by the episode, wrote that, "human ghouls and blood-fiends filled the night air with the cry of 'Nigger!' 'Nigger! Let us lynch him,' and they would have doubtlessly duplicated the brutal horrors of Paris and Texarkana, Texas, and Fort Gaines, Ga., if they had caught Diggs." The mob's prey managed to escape his pursuers, among them three saloon-keepers and town marshal A. Morrison, with the help of some of his friends in the Ninth Cavalry. The fiery broadside repeated verbatim a number of passages used a few days earlier by the columnist "Yellow Cape" in black Chaplain Henry V. Plummer's regular "Fort Robinson Dept." in an Omaha race paper, as blacks called their own journals. It closed with an unambiguous warning to the townspeople: "You shall not outrage us and our people right here under the shadow of 'Old Glory,' while we have shot and shell, and if you persist we will repeat the horrors of San Domingo—we will reduce your homes and firesides to ashes and send your guilty souls to hell." The author signed the warning "500 Men With the Bullet or the Torch."[29] Other circulars, found after the episode, were signed just as menacingly by "Skull and Crossbones."[30]

Lieutenant Colonel Reuben Bernard wasted no time seeking legal advice. With a nearby newspaper predicting "a merry time between the nigger soldiers and saloonmen and gamblers at Crawford almost any time," he threw Sergeant Barney McKay of G Troop into the guardhouse and placed Crawford off limits.[31] Within two months Sergeant McKay was convicted of bringing the incendiary broadside cited above into his barracks, dishonorably discharged, and sent to the military prison at Fort Leavenworth for two years.[32]

While he awaited his trial in the guardhouse, McKay had his first brush with Captain John Guilfoyle. As officer of the guard, Guilfoyle refused to allow McKay any books or newspapers. Colonel Bernard had to order that McKay be permitted reading matter, provided that "nothing of any improper nature" was smuggled in to the prisoner.[33]

Captain Guilfoyle sat on the military court which tried McKay for conduct to the prejudice of good order and discipline. To no one's surprise, the defendant challenged Guilfoyle as prejudiced. Guilfoyle had not only tried to prevent McKay from reading in the guardhouse, but had also stated that he would convict McKay "on general principles." Besides, his attitude toward the black enlisted men was widely known. Guilfoyle's temper flared at the challenge, and he told McKay he could not use his legal privilege to attack a member of the court. He considered the challenge a personal insult and promised to resent it as such.[34]

The court rejected the challenge to Guilfoyle. Among those voting on the matter was Captain Matthias Day, who was himself later challenged and excused. When Day left, the resentful Guilfoyle became the senior officer on the tribunal and therefore its president. McKay was convicted, of course, but of very little. The charges had included bringing the circular into the barracks of G Troop and distributing it among the men. The court found him guilty only of bringing it into the dormitory.[35]

The three soldiers who testified against McKay during the trial experienced considerable pressure from their G Troop comrades. Private Matthew Wyatt, one of the three, complained that he was "treated pretty rough lots of times" and virtually ostracized from the time he agreed to give evidence against McKay. Private Drayton Moffett cursed Wyatt for his treachery, calling him "a cock sucking son-of-a-bitch," and accusing him of "pimping around the troop and among the white folks." Both Wyatt and Sergeant Arthur Ransom, another prosecution witness, had reasons for breaking the unit's silence. Wyatt had been convicted by a summary court of a minor violation based on McKay's testimony, and told several men he relished the opportunity for revenge. Ransom had killed a dog and had a heated argument with McKay over the matter. First Sergeant Thomas Goodloe had stopped that dispute by warning Ransom he would "mash his mouth." The third witness against McKay, Private Thomas Byron, had no apparent motive for his testimony. However, he was not the most reliable of men. Three months later, he was convicted of four specifications of lying to his commanding officer and sentenced to a month's confinement.[36]

The McKay court martial sheds as much light on the limits of cohesiveness in G Troop as it does on the fears of post officers. Some men apparently saw an opportunity for revenge on McKay. Others grew alarmed and tried to enforce unity with threats. Old soldier Goodloe sadly summed up the situation: "The niggers won't hang together; they are always ready to hang one another."[37]

Others were also in a hanging mood. Lieutenant Montgomery Parker, McKay's counsel and the son of abolitionist Theodore Parker, saw the court's decision as based solely on race prejudice. Parker committed a daring act for a junior officer, and referred the case to black Congressman John Langston of Virginia. Lieutenant Parker viewed the matter as "one in which the color line was drawn." He identified all the judges as southerners, and said the proceedings spoke for themselves.[38]

The prosecutor cited a related matter which may also have influenced the court. Lieutenant Alfred Jackson told the panel of judges that McKay had been involved in the shooting at Suggs, Wyoming, during the previous summer. Jackson's evidence did not match his rhetoric: McKay had been convicted by a summary court of absence without leave during the night of the affray, no more and no less.[39]

With the memory of Suggs, racial bigotry, and G Troop's internal divisions all against McKay, his conviction and two-year sentence were not surprising developments. The judgment was approved at headquarters in Omaha and McKay was shipped to Leavenworth, even before the Judge Advocate General reviewed the case. As McKay later noted, this was a clear violation of military due process.[40] This blunder caused his release from prison in November, after five months.

McKay's conviction probably did not satisfy Colonel Bernard. He believed Chaplain Plummer was responsible for the entire affair. In a confidential letter to department headquarters, he claimed to have "some very suspicious evidence against him but not enough to warrant me in taking action." Bernard wove a complex web of circumstantial evidence against Plummer. Central to his case was the resemblance between Plummer's "Fort Robinson News" column and the "500 Men with the Bullet or Torch" circular. Others, among them the editor of the Crawford *Tribune*, had also noticed the similarities and suggested a connection. Bernard said the other officers on post, including black Lieutenant John Alexander, considered Plummer "a very disturbing element."[41]

Colonel Bernard's suspicions of Plummer remained unproved. No connection between the chaplain and Sergeant McKay was established. All Bernard could say with confidence was that the affair had been "consummated by a few of the best educated men in the command . . ." Presumably, he meant McKay, who later published a newspaper in Newark, New Jersey, and wrote Republican campaign literature, and the seminary-educated Chaplain Plummer.[42]

After Congressman Langston obtained McKay's release, the ex-soldier barraged Washington officials with requests for reinstatement. He continued to write various congressmen and executive officers up to World War I, and even succeeded in getting two bills for his relief introduced in Congress, one in 1894 and another in 1899.[43] Throughout this long period he maintained his faith in the Army and in the ability and willingness of the government to give him redress.

The case of McKay and the broadside contrasts strikingly with I Troop's protest against Captain Guilfoyle. In the earlier episode, officers did not take seriously the charges made by the black troopers. But in McKay's case they acted hastily and harshly, sending a man to prison for possession of a leaflet. Clearly Colonel Bernard and his officers viewed the threat of armed insurrection, which was implicit in the broadside's reference to San Domingo, as a real possibility. The memory of Suggs might have convinced post officers and particularly Guilfoyle, who had played a prominent part in restoring order at Suggs, that this possibility was imminent.[44]

In their reactions to the petition against Guilfoyle and to the McKay case, post officers seemed unable to accept the complaints of their men at face value. Both protests were directed at racists, an officer in one case and a community in the other. Major Henry had thought the first one was a result of ignorance, a strange interpretation of a petition stating a specific grievance and remedy and signed by forty men. Colonel Bernard saw the second as a call to insurrection. In neither case did post commanders make any effort to remove the source of the problem. Rather, they tried to make the complaints themselves disappear.

The trial of Barney McKay and the events surrounding the earlier murder of Emanuel Stance also show some of the limits to racial solidarity. In the Stance case, the men of F Troop split along lines of the enlisted rank structure. The division of G Troop during the McKay court-martial was based on personal animosities. Problems like these did not always block cooperation in black units. But these difficulties could still be potent forces at critical times.

Chapter 8

ENTERTAINMENT

AS CHAPLAIN George Prioleau once told readers of the Cleveland *Gazette*, the enlisted men at Robinson enjoyed every kind of amusement available to officers. Troopers and their families rode horses, picnicked, hunted, and wined and dined one another. For many years, white residents of Crawford did not share the social life of enlisted soldiers. African-American cavalrymen on post had no white guests—except an occasional officer—at their dances. They organized numerous social clubs, such as the Tenth Cavalry's "Young Men's Social Club," "Dog Robbers," and "Syndicate," to arrange off-duty entertainment.[1]

Ninth Cavalry soldiers also organized to meet their social needs. As early as 1896, troopers of the regiment established "Crispus Attucks Lodge" of the Knights of Pythias. Corporal George Goff, a Tennessean who later won a Certificate of Merit for heroism in Cuba, led the group as "Sir Knight Captain" in 1897. Goff was also secretary of K Troop's social organization, the "Diamond Club," over which First Sergeant George Jordan presided as president. Ninth Cavalry troops had at least two other clubs in 1893-1894. Men of the band created the "Oak and Ivy" dancing club, and G Troop's soldiers had an organization known as "12 Brothers."[2]

White units also arranged many of their own off-duty activities, but their gatherings frequently involved townspeople as well as the military community. Sixth Cavalry units on post in 1897-1898 had a dancing club which held periodic entertainments at the Syndicate Opera House in town. Apparently large numbers of civilians attended these affairs, as they did Eighth Cavalry parties a decade later. One 1912 dance and supper, arranged by Twelfth Cavalry troopers, lured two hundred guests from as far away as Alliance and Valentine. The Twelfth's "Social Club" also gave at least one dinner at a Crawford restaurant.[3]

On post, troopers celebrated the promotions of their fellows with banquets and receptions. Ninth Cavalry sergeants organized such a dinner in honor of Sergeant Major Benjamin F. Davis to commemorate his advancement to Post Quartermaster Sergeant. Some years later, the Eighth Cavalry's Chief Musician, William Brinsmead, and Sergeant Andrew Donnan of the Hospital Corps arranged a smoker to honor Quartermaster Sergeant Benjamin Anderson, before his departure for Fort Terry, New York. Anderson, a twenty-year veteran and crack shot, was black and his hosts white.[4] This party suggests the same conclusion indicated by the irregular desegregation of living quarters and duty assignments: black and white enlisted men found it fairly easy to deal civilly and even cordially with each other.

From the earliest days of Fort Robinson, the post trader's store was a social center for off-duty soldiers. When the Army first established Camp Robinson in the early spring of 1874, J. W. Dear already awaited the business of the garrison at his Red Cloud Agency store. Dr. J. J. Saville, the resident Indian agent, had appointed Dear to the post in the previous year, removing the original trader, Jules Ecoffey, to accommodate Dear. Clay Dear, a relative of this trader, soon followed and established another store in the vicinity. Between them, the Dears sold provisions to the Indian agent, illegal whisky to the Indians, and tinned oysters to officers' wives. They also provided stage transportation from Sidney south of the Platte River to adventurous and illegal miners, whom they deposited at Red Cloud to find their perilous way into the Black Hills. Their partially legitimate business enterprise received early competition when the Army began to issue traders' licenses for Camp Robinson.[5]

John Collins, who operated the Fort Laramie store, opened a branch at Robinson within two weeks of the arrival of the Sioux Expedition. He held his temporary franchise until the autumn, when R. O. Adams gained the license on the recommendation of Nebraska's Senator R. W. Hitchcock. His 1875 successor, W. F. Kimmel, had the support of Army officers at Fort D. A. Russell and—more helpfully—W. R. Steele, Wyoming Territory's congressional delegate.[6]

In 1876 Frank Yates opened another store at Red Cloud. He and his father-in-law filled the demand for stage transportation into the Black Hills

The post sutler's store.

NSHS

with a line to Custer City that they opened in January of that year. In this way Yates helped bring on the Indian war in which his brother, Captain George Yates of Custer's regiment, died.[7]

These early storekeepers all came and went fairly rapidly. In January 1877, Benjamin S. Paddock, who later was very important in the development of Crawford, received a license as trader. The post council at Robinson urged his appointment, but his father, Senator Joseph Paddock of Nebraska, probably provided more material aid. Paddock operated his store with partner W. E. Annin until the Army abolished post trading establishments in the early 1890s. Annin also worked as Senator Paddock's secretary in Washington and was married to the younger Paddock's sister. Benjamin Paddock maintained his store and residence at the northwest corner of the post, about 400 feet from the near end of the original line of officers' adobes. This location placed him in the center of his market and gave much needed protection in the early years. When the Cheyennes fled Fort Robinson in January 1879, they chose to raid Clay Dear's store near the agency rather than Paddock's on post.[8]

For several years Paddock's store and saloon were the main entertainment center for soldiers of the garrison. The whisky he dispensed also caused the major disciplinary problems. Drinking sprees led to most of the court-martial offenses. Commanders eventually required that Paddock keep lists of the men who bought liquor and that he limit enlisted men to two drinks a day—and those three hours apart.[9]

After the imposition of these restrictions, neither the trader's store nor the post canteens of later years created much of a discipline problem. In 1887, a year in which the many garrison court martials indicated a near collapse of discipline, only two trials involved the trader's establishment. White Private William Jones chose to play a little cards at Paddock's store rather than obey his commander's order to stay in his quarters. Two months later black Private Clayton Woody engaged in a minor brawl with one of Paddock's employees. When First Sergeant George Jordan tried to stop the altercation, Woody turned on the Medal of Honor holder and contemptuously brushed him off: "You need not think because you wear the stripes that I give a damn for you." Both Jones and Woody spent ten days in the guardhouse.[10]

Paddock's log store provided more conveniences than whisky by the drink, including a post office, money orders, and general merchandise. In exchange for his services, Paddock received the privilege of cutting wood for his own use from the post timber reserve as well as his profits. In turn, he paid a tax of three cents per man per month to the post fund for his franchise.[11]

Trader Paddock enjoyed full access to the social life of officers and their families. He joined the party of officers who went to Fort Niobrara for an 1889 ball given by Colonel August Kautz and dined at the home of Captain Corliss. He also attended the intimate wedding of Colonel James Brisbin's daughter and the twenty-fifth wedding anniversary celebration of Captain and Mrs. John Loud. The only officer with whom he had a disagreement was apparently bad-tempered Captain James Hutton, who hit Paddock in the face several times after an argument in the officers' club.[12]

In May 1888, Colonel Edward Hatch established a post canteen in competition with Paddock's store and the bars of recently established Crawford. The new tavern provided beer at low prices and a profit to units on post. The War Department closed the canteen in October as an infringement on the vested rights of the post trader. One officer complained that the garrison reverted back to times when pay day brought a crowded guardhouse and alleged that desertions were on the rise again.[13]

Despite the decision to close Hatch's canteen, the days of the post trader were numbered. Only four months passed before Secretary of War William Endicott decided to abolish trading establishments where canteens were feasible. In preparation for the change, a board of officers assessed the value of Paddock's buildings for reimbursement. The canteen itself went into operation in the autumn of 1889, supplying the troops with sundries and comfortable entertainment at modest prices. Colonel Biddle allowed the canteen to open on Sunday as long as it closed for church services.[14]

Paddock's buildings were appraised at $600 and the quartermaster general authorized their purchase by the post commander. The trader's friends among the officers tried to come to his aid, and Colonel Tilford asked reconsideration of the revocation of Paddock's license. Tilford argued that the store had been a great convenience to military personnel and neighboring civilians. Colonel Biddle later renewed pleas on Paddock's behalf. He did not think Paddock's store threatened the canteen and claimed the trader should at least be allowed to reopen for six months to dispose of his stock. In addition, Biddle stated that most of the officers desired Paddock's continued presence at Fort Robinson.[15]

Paddock remained on post through 1893, probably hopeful that the pleas of his friends would enable him to regain his franchise. At the end of the year and again six months later, Biddle ordered him to dismantle his buildings, save the one in which he operated the post office.[16] After a long transition period, the days of the post sutler finally ended.

By that time the deposed trader had made an indelible mark on the development of Dawes County. Several early settlers, among whom L. N. Freeman who later served six terms on the Crawford City Council was most prominent, found steady employment in Paddock's store. Moreover, the trader, probably with the help of his father, brought the Burlington to the site of Crawford. The town was then surveyed on the tree claim of his partner, who sold the land to the Pioneer Townsite Company of the Fremont, Elkhorn, and Missouri Valley Railroad.[17]

By the time that he lost his trading license, Paddock was a rich man. His store, Army forage contracts, the postmastership, and his land deals proved a potent combination in an area which knew few wealthy men. As an Omaha reporter noted in 1888, the two railroad lines and Benjamin Paddock owned the town of Crawford.[18] However, his business practices as trader obstructed the efforts of settlers substantially. At least four residents who came before the railroad drove horse-drawn wagons as far as Sidney or Valentine to obtain their supplies. Only one of them explicitly stated that Paddock's prices forced them to such lengths, but no other reason for the long treks can be adduced.[19] In light of this evidence, it is hard to see what Colonel Tilford had in mind when he argued Paddock's importance to civilians around Fort Robinson.

The canteen provided most of the items trader Paddock had stocked. Soldiers could obtain Schlitz beer over the bar, first by the bottle but later, as breakage mounted, by the glass. Officers could purchase food items unavailable through the commissary. Pool and billiard tables also made the store something of a social center for the men, who were allowed to purchase items on credit. The limitation of credit purchases to one fifth of a man's monthly pay meant a leeway of $2.60 to privates in their first year of service.[20]

The canteen shortly came to be called the post exchange. The adjutant general explained that the change was designed to eliminate the connotation of a "place of conviviality and dissipation." An exchange council, made up of commissioned officers, administered the combination recreation hall, tavern, and store. An exchange committee of non-commissioned officers, a biracial group in which the Ninth Cavalry's Sergeant Major Jeremiah Jones was the senior man, served as an advisory group. The only recommendation of this body which survives showed the importance of class divisions among the enlisted men, albeit on a less volatile and explicit plane than the difficulties in First Sergeant Stance's F Troop. The committee of five blacks and four whites asked Lieutenant Colonel George Sanford for permission to purchase beer for consumption in their homes. They said the "better class" of non-coms did not care to drink at the bar with privates and frequented saloons in town rather than rub elbows with their inferiors. By the end of 1893 the non-coms at least had their own room in the exchange. The rest of the building was divided into five other rooms: bar, lunch, sales, billiards, and an office.[21]

For the first four years of its existence, the Robinson canteen employed soldiers as stewards and bartenders. This duty probably provided some men with valuable commercial training and experience. These benefits were distributed among the racially mixed garrison in a patently unfair way. In 1889-1892, when black soldiers comprised between fifty-six and seventy-four per cent of the garrison, twice as many white troops served in the exchange: seventeen whites worked twenty-one tours of duty and eight blacks served on eleven. The difference was even sharper than these figures suggest. Private Ebbert Maden of F Troop, Ninth Cavalry, worked four of the eleven periods allowed black soldiers.[22] Maden was undoubtedly a bright and competent man. He rose to high non-commissioned rank three times in spite of two reductions to the ranks for various indiscretions and served as a lieutenant with the Forty-Ninth Infantry in the Philippine Insurrection. However, he was not the only intelligent man in the Ninth Cavalry. The choice of the minority whites for canteen duty on post simply reflects the oft-revealed racism of post and regimental officers.

In January 1893, the adjutant general halted employment of soldiers at the exchange. Retired soldiers and other civilians were then hired to operate the store and bar, although occasionally soldiers were used when other competent employees could not be found. The civilians pleased Colonel Biddle, who believed that they were less inclined to pilfer exchange stock. Several black retirees found work in the exchange, including Corporal John Denny, a New Yorker who had won a Medal of Honor for heroism against Victorio in 1880. Retired sergeants Alfred Bradden, Simon Franklin, and William Howard also labored there.[23]

The canteen did a high volume of business at a low margin of profit. In the year 1891-1892 the establishment grossed $15,174 and reported a profit of only $415. Beer sales, which totalled $7,757 in 1893-1894, must have accounted for a large part of total business every year. In the first six months of 1899, when a battalion of the First Infantry garrisoned the post, over ten thousand pints were sold although nearly a third of the men claimed that they did not drink beer.[24]

A junior officer, usually a lieutenant, served as exchange officer and supervised day to day operations. One exchange officer, Lieutenant James A. Swift of the Ninth Cavalry, became caught in a scandal that involved embezzlement of exchange funds and a possible relationship with a local woman. Swift killed himself in January 1896. Most officers disliked the duty, partly because they did not have any commercial training and partly because they thought shopkeeping beneath their station. An occasional blunder reflected this lack of education and inclination. On the day after the departure of the Ninth and Sixth cavalry troops for Chickamauga depleted the garrison in April 1898, Lieutenant George Hamilton accepted a freight car full of beer from the railroad. Then to compound his overestimation of the appetites of the fifty men left on post, he refused to sell the cargo to an interested Crawford saloon keeper.[25]

Units which served on post owned shares of the exchange in proportion to the number of men in each company. So each transfer to and from Robinson required an inventory and appraisal of exchange stock. Companies coming in had to buy a share; those which departed received their portion for the unit fund. Boards of officers made the necessary assessments for the transactions, which resembled the purchase and sale of company gardens.[26]

Four senior non-commissioned officers at Robinson were polled by the War Department in 1899 concerning the exchange. They agreed with their superiors that the exchange served them well. The sergeants stated that the sale of beer on post kept alcoholism and court-martials to a minimum. Commissary Sergeant Karl Thompson also said that abolition of the beer bar would bring the men into greater contact with "the lowest town element," much to their moral detriment.[27]

The only officer to dissent fully from this opinion was Chaplain Henry Plummer of the Ninth cavalry. Others who did not completely approve the canteen did so because they believed the system did not extend far enough. Colonel Jacob Augur said even whisky should be sold in the exchange. At least the men who wanted it could then get good quality liquor. Captain Corliss converted from his earlier opposition to the canteen as a "damned nuisance," suggested that beer should be served in the dining halls and even permitted in the barracks. Practically all the officers whose opinions were recorded agreed with Colonel Biddle that the sale of beer in the exchange benefitted discipline.[28]

While nearly all military personnel concurred that the exchange provided useful services, the institution met considerable hostility in town. In 1896-1897, the post exchange became the center of controversy as Crawford and Dawes County tried to extract revenue from Fort Robinson. On the first day of April 1896, Dawes County authorities arrested the post exchange officer, Lieutenant Eugene F. Ladd, and retired Sergeant Bradden. They were charged with selling whisky on post without a state license. Major Charles Ilsley and Captain Philip Powell posted their bond. The pair were convicted in a Chadron court, but freed on a writ of habeus corpus obtained from Judge Shiras of the United States Circuit Court, District of Nebraska, who cited the 1887 session of jurisdiction over the military reservation by the Nebraska legislature and ruled that the arrest had been made without "due warrant of law."[29]

The black cavalrymen on post exerted great pressure on local entrepreneurs to drop proceedings. The soldiers agreed on a boycott of Crawford businesses and threatened any violators with "a sound thrashing." The *Army and Navy Journal* observed that the men knew "their rights and are going to maintain them, even if the merchants of Crawford have to be starved out . . . ." The boycott was apparently effective. Local politicians surrendered to get the troops back into town, even before the Federal Court decision. However, Crawford had never united behind the threat to the post exchange. About a week before the suit was filed, fifty-five businessmen wrote the post adjutant, disclaiming responsibility for the legal action. Their resolution claimed the suit was "uncalled for" and tended "to mar the hitherto very pleasant relations" with the troops. They acknowledged that "the unexcelled prosperity of Crawford is largely due to her very cordial relations with the people of Fort Robinson, "which they hoped to restore."[30]

A year after the renewal of quiet and local commerce, Dawes County officials tried anew to obtain tax revenue from Fort Robinson. This time, the county attempted to impose its property tax on the exchange and the personal property of officers and civilian employees who resided on post. An assessor who came to Robinson to inventory the stock of the post exchange was denied permission to make the appraisal by Colonel David Perry, who sent the functionary away and asked his superiors in Omaha for legal advice. Perry apparently obtained the needed guidance in short order. Within a week he stated his case to the County Board of Commissioners: the fort was not within the county's jurisdiction. In case local officialdom had forgotten, he quoted in full the Federal Court decision in the Ladd case.[31] This letter was the final word in the controversy. Tax records showed no assessments on military personnel who resided on post. The Crawford *Tribune*, once confident that the fort would be taxed, now had no comment.[32]

After these efforts to tax the canteen failed, the post store still faced opposition from two groups. According to Lieutenant Milton F. Davis, local saloon keepers and their allies resented the exchange "for very good reasons." The hostility of the other group, "meddling W.C.T.U. women . . . and itinerant preachers," arose from "ignorance and fanaticism." Captain Jacob G. Galbraith added all Crawford merchants as the enemy. He said local businesses would have "unlimited extortion on sales of many articles now procured through the exchange . . . ," if it closed.[33]

The opposition won its victory in early 1901, when Congress prohibited the sale of alcoholic beverages on military posts. The secretary of war glumly reported that soldiers took to going off post, drinking bad whisky, and associating with "abandoned men and even more abandoned women." Colonel Augur also noted a decline in morality and discipline, and officers and men at all posts in the region agreed that "the abolishment of the sale of beer in the canteen was a mistake."[34]

In spite of the end of beer sales, the exchange survived as a permanent institution on post. In 1901 the store moved into the old concrete post hospital. Four years later, the Army built a new exchange for over $27,000.[35] Local merchants probably remained dissatisfied, but after beer sales ended soldiers spent more time in town and probably spent money on other items as well as drink. A soldier at nearby Fort Meade, South Dakota, commented that "Since the canteen has been abolished the road to Sturgis is kept well beaten and soldiers under the influence of drink are frequently met with."[36] The road to Crawford was also well travelled.

Soldiers did not spend all their off-duty hours tippling. Organized sports of many kinds were popular on post. Athletic contests provided release for pent-up energies as well as an important framework for relatively relaxed meetings between black troopers and white townsmen.

During the Ninth Cavalry's long tour of duty on the White River, baseball was a favorite sport. Black cavalrymen and white foot soldiers played together on the post teams, occasionally against visitors from Niobrara, Laramie, and other forts. According to Private Simpson Mann of F Troop, Ninth Cavalry, the men played well. They also played intensely: an umpire's decision in a game with Fort Laramie nearly precipitated a riot. Post officers encouraged the men to play for a variety of reasons. Major Andrew Burt simply loved the game. Others probably agreed with Surgeon George Adair that the sport helped the troopers keep physically fit while it lured customers from local brothels and taverns.[37]

Only a year after the Ninth arrived, Chadron's "Magic City nine" came to play Sergeant John Jackson's "Robinsonians." Civilians and soldiers lined the post athletic field and watched the cavalrymen come from behind to tie Chadron and almost win before the train schedule rescued the "Magic City" team. Before departure, however, the Chadron captain promised a rematch for Independence Day. He and Sergeant Jackson agreed to a $100 wager for the second contest.[38]

An additional $500 was bet by the time the Ninth's team rode the Elkhorn line to Chadron. When the players arrived, they found that the opposition had disappeared. The Chadron captain claimed he could not find his men and wanted to cancel both the game and the wager. Sergeant Jackson and his team refused, took the field at the appointed time, and claimed the victory by forfeit. The soldier who claimed Chadron backed down because of "either ignorance or prejudice" was wrong.[39] There was probably $100 worth of wisdom at the core of the decision.

Other towns also played the cavalry troops. A touring squad from Alliance received two thrashings on post, 24-4 and 35-9. Alliance retained an interest in the post's team, and an Alliance *Grip* reporter gained some measure of revenge for his community. Later in the month he watched the "big" match with Fort Niobrara and reported that Robinson lost in a "rather poor game."[40] Before that weekend was over, the post team lost two more games to Niobrara, as well as a substantial amount of money. Before the visitors could leave, however, the home team produced a footracer and asked for challengers. The Robinson man won and "corralled all the boodle the Niobrara team won on the ball game."[41]

After the black cavalry left for Cuba, Crawford nines began to play fort teams. From that point until Mexican border duty depleted the garrison in 1913, they competed frequently. Other towns like Gordon, Harrison, and Chadron also challenged the soldiers. Post squads travelled as far as Sheridan, Wyoming, and into neighboring South Dakota, where they played in Ardmore, Hot Springs, and Deadwood. As many as fourteen games a year were played against outside opponents, as baseball became a significant meeting point for military and civilian communities, even when the garrison was black. In neighboring Wyoming, baseball provided practically the only consistently friendly or at least civil meeting ground for black soldiers

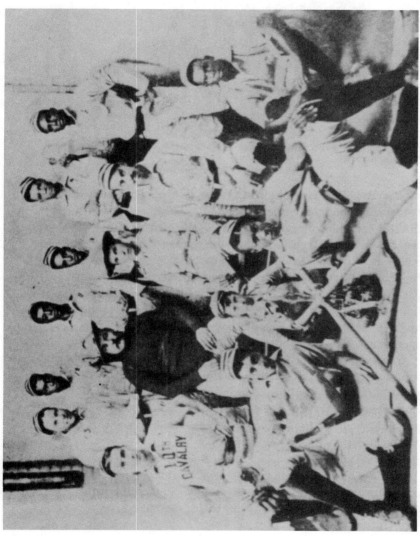

The Tenth Cavalry baseball team. The manager, Sergeant John Buck, is seated, wearing a sweater. Buck was a fine marksman and was recommended for a Medal of Honor for heroism in Cuba. The boy with the dog is Richard Hay, whose brother William later recalled learning to play baseball and shoot dice from the Tenth Cavalry. Copied from *The Colored American Magazine*, vol. 7, January 1905.

104

K Troop's football team. Copied from *The Colored American Magazine*, vol. 7, January 1905.

The Moorland-Spingarn Research Center, Howard Univ.

and white civilians. At Fort Robinson too the baseball diamond was an important setting for biracial gatherings.[42]

Gambling remained a regular feature of the contests. In 1899 a local newspaper observed that a considerable sum of money changed hands after a Chadron team, accompanied by a special train full of supporters, lost 34-16 to the soldiers. In a game between Crawford and the Tenth Cavalry, a $10 stake was the winner's prize.[43] Perhaps the nine members of the winning team each took a dollar and awarded the extra greenback to the umpire.

Usually Tenth Cavalry teams did not need the aid of umpires against town opponents. The regimental squad's members were "of excellent calibre," as Private Thomas Clement boasted, and won most of their games. The team was made up of the best players from all troop nines, and managed by Sergeant John Buck, a former volunteer officer and veteran of frontier, Cuban, and Philippine service. The players ranged from young, agile privates like violinist Howard Roan to relative oldsters like Beverly Thornton, the forty-three-year-old cook of K Troop.[44]

Unit teams, which were also quite capable, played a round-robin schedule each summer. Commissioned officers of the regimental athletic committee scheduled the intramural contests. At the end of the season, the leader received a pennant. Even teams that could not win on post evoked admiration in town. In May 1905, B Troop came from behind to beat Crawford, 13-11. The *Tribune* said "it was like the charge the 10th made at El Caney."[45]

The officers also played. Those few that were good enough played on their unit teams. They also had their own team and ventured off post twice for games with a team of Crawford businessmen. Their privates and sergeants were apparently more adept at the game. The officers lost both of their contests in town.[46]

Football was a popular pastime at Fort Robinson as early as 1893. The parade ground provided a convenient if sometimes overly fertilized gridiron. The growth of interest in football delighted Surgeon Adair, who preferred to deal with sprained ankles rather than venereal infections. Other officers also enjoyed the game, and some coached teams or officiated at matches.

After white troops came to the fort, civilian teams arranged matches with the soldiers. Crawford and Fort Robinson began a series of contests in 1907. Before the season ended, Chadron Academy and Alliance teams also clashed with Robinson squads. All the civilians held their own against the garrison, and the Chadron team regularly won its matches.[47]

Basketball did not gain popularity at the post until the Tenth Cavalry departed in 1907. The post gymnasium was already three years old, but local citizens were apparently reluctant to engage in contact sports with the black athletes of the Tenth. A local opera house was modified for basketball in 1912, and a Crawford team known as "The Sewer Rats" divided two games with the fort squad. Post teams also entertained opponents, such as a group of railroad employees, at home.[48]

Track and field meets known as Field Day were important in the sports program as early as 1897. These contests, held regularly during the warm months, included individual and team events. In 1897, several unusual and difficult matches included mounted fencing, gymnastics, and wrestling. Colonel Perry ordered the whole command to attend, and Sergeant Major Jones, then preparing to depart for Fort Whipple, Arizona, as ordnance sergeant, marched the conscripted spectators to the baseball ground.[49]

Colonel Augur of the Tenth Cavalry continued the meets and supported departmental competitions as fostering participation and interest. However, the men of the Tenth were already enthusiastic about field days. Private Clement, who later left the Army to work as a miner, railroad man, and musician, before becoming minister of the largest African Methodist Episcopal Church in Texas, Houston's Wesley Chapel, observed that contestants received "the hearty applause of comrades," as well as banners and cash prizes. While Clement was at Robinson, the competition included races, broad jumps, and military contests such as tent-pitching by eight-man teams. There were also exotic events such as bare-back mounted wrestling by four-man teams. The day's competition also usually included a horse race and a concluding baseball game between the two squadrons. Each troop's points were tallied and the unit with the highest score at the end of the season won the athletic banner.[50]

Occasional horse races at post or in Crawford drew crowds of black soldiers as well as civilians at first. On July 4, 1903, a soldier and civilian started a fight. Several troopers drew guns, and only the quick action of Captain Eugene Jervey and Lieutenant Bruce Palmer saved the situation. Later, soldiers still attended the races but were not allowed to disperse among the crowds.[51]

The first boxing match at Robinson was a sparring exhibition arranged by a touring promoter in 1892. In later years, matches were also held in Crawford. The first recorded contest at Fireman's Hall pitted Dan Donovan of Los Angeles against a black infantryman named Hamp Ireland, who came from Niobrara to knock Donovan out. Two Tenth Cavalrymen fought in a preliminary match.[52] In the next few months, boxing grew quite popular on post. Troopers like "Rabbi" Henderson, "Lightning" Murray, "Shin" Brown, and "Everytime" Mack slugged it out with each other and the occasional professional who strayed into northwestern Nebraska.

W. H. Gaston was the *Tribune's* favorite soldier-pugilist. Gaston put Lightning Murray in the post hospital with a broken jaw after only forty-five seconds in the ring. Most Crawford bettors had placed their money on "Lightning," but the *Tribune* man must have bet on the winner: "Here's to Gaston, the champion of the 10th U. S. Cav., and the coming champion of the northwest." Three months later, when a healed Lightning Murray fought for the post lightweight title in "a grand boxing carnival," heavyweight champion Gaston lured spectators with a bag-punching display. In 1906 one Tom Schumacher came to Crawford to fight the great Gaston. The match had to be moved from Fireman's Hall to "a canvas enclosure just outside the city limits, near the Northwestern stockyards," presumably to accommodate a large crowd. Amidst the combined stench of manure, sweat, and cigar smoke, Schumacher easily beat Gaston and returned to Denver. "The coming champion of the northwest" never fought again at Robinson.[53]

Hunting and fishing gave the men of the garrison as much pleasure as spectator sports, as well as meat for their tables. General Philip Sheridan, while commander of the Military Division of the Missouri, emphasized the practical aspect of the sport. In 1880, he ordered that hunting leave for officers not be charged against their annual leave.[54] Parties frequently went out to supply unit messes or holiday tables with game. Lieutenant Colonel Joshua Fletcher approved a ten-day hunt before Christmas, 1886, and provided the infantrymen with an escort and forage.[55] One year later, a soldier who called himself "Africus," reported that hunting parties scoured the countryside to provide meat for Christmas feasts. A thirty-day hunt during the fall of 1890 by Sergeant Curtis Rouse and five men of I Troop, Ninth Cavalry, served a similar purpose.[56]

But there was more to the practical side of hunting than bringing in meat. There was also learning the terrain. When Lieutenant Frank Armstrong, fresh out of the Military Academy, joined the Ninth Cavalry at Robinson in 1891, he found it very easy to get away on hunting trips. Colonel Biddle encouraged all of his officers to get out and become familiar with the country. So while Armstrong learned to rough it and to fill a corncob pipe with Lone Jack tobacco, he also got acquainted with the hills and gullies over which he might someday have to chase and fight Indians.[57]

Sometimes black and white soldiers went on the same expedition. Lieutenant William A. Mercer of the Eighth Infantry took three black cavalrymen as well as three of his own men on one such trip. The party camped on Sage Creek for thirty days in the fall of 1887 and enjoyed a pleasant vacation while laying in meat.[58]

At times officers went hunting purely for recreation. Captain Corliss and his son Bob frequently pursued ducks and prairie chickens. On a much grander scale, Colonel Hatch and Lieutenant Matthias Day went on a twelve-day safari in Wyoming, just after Hatch took command. They camped near Douglas, in Converse County, where scout Baptiste Garnier joined them. At the time, Garnier received $60 a month as an Army scout.[59] He and other employees frequently served as guides for vacationing officers and their civilian companions. In 1888 J. S. Collins, an Omaha friend of General George Crook, informed President Rutherford B. Hayes's son Webb of a planned excursion. Collins expected that Hatch would provide "a good outfit . . . 'Bat' and an Indian," and added that Hatch was "a tip top fellow." In later years, Collins continued to advise Webb Hayes to seek equipment and transportation from Hatch. Colonel David Perry later accommodated eastern industrialists like railroad magnate Seward Webb with excursions into Wyoming. The department commander, Brigadier General John Coppinger, joined Seward Webb for the 1896 and 1897 outings. Private George Byers of the Ninth Cavalry served them well on the first trip, so Coppinger asked for Byers again the second time. Byers, an extremely fair-skinned man who had originally enlisted in the white Sixth Cavalry but had been reassigned to the black Ninth, recalled these excursions with delight forty years later.[60]

Hunting was occasionally as dangerous to the men as it was for the birds and animals. Private William Miller, the post telegraph operator, was killed by a fellow sportsman in August 1886 on the military reservation. Miller was whiling away some off-duty hours at the time. After his death, the post went without a competent operator for some time.[61]

While outdoor activities continued year-round as the weather permitted, much of the indoor social life of the men centered on important holidays. Troops on post regularly celebrated four holidays, Decoration and Independence days, Thanksgiving, and Christmas. Most of the men had these days to themselves, with all duty but essential guard mounts and work parties suspended. Frequently the men even had the entire week between Christmas and New Year as leisure time. Festivities varied in scope but the two winter celebrations usually received the most attention.

Prior to the arrival of the railroad, the acquisition of Christmas toys presented a major logistical problem. Corporal Martin Weber, who later settled in Crawford, recalled that in 1882 he and a driver took a six-mule team to Fort Sidney to pick up holiday goods. Weber was almost blinded on the return trip through a blizzard, but made it with his cargo. As he drove in, the children spotted the rig and began to chant "The Christmas wagon has come." Later in the decade, holidays apparently passed without such frantic and perilous episodes.[62]

Thanksgiving in 1886 was marked only by a dance at the Amusement Hall. At Christmas, two years later, each unit had a "nice dinner," and a dance with music by the Ninth's string band.[63] In later years elaborate day-long festivities engaged the entire garrison. The men and their families enjoyed worship, athletic contests, and elegant banquets.

Thanksgiving, 1904, began for the Tenth Cavalry with an early morning serenade. Principal Musician Thomas Hammond, a Pittsburgh native who played violin and cornet, led a volunteer band through the post. The musicians played selections at each barrack and the hospital. Later in the morning, Chaplain Anderson conducted the service at the Crawford Congregational Church, and preached a "fine Thanksgiving sermon" to the soldiers and civilians in attendance. After church the troopers returned to post for what Corporal Charlie Simmons of K Troop called "the most important feature of the day," the football match between B and K Troops. Regimental officers refereed the contest, in which B scored two second-half touchdowns for a tie.[64]

The footballers then cleaned up and joined their colleagues in the K Troop dining room. First Sergeant Robert Johnson, one of the finest marksmen in the Army, served as master of ceremonies. After he welcomed the men and their guests, Chaplain Anderson invoked the blessing. Then the company sat down to its feast. Guests included Chaplain Anderson and the third squadron's Sergeant Major L. L. Vaughn, who had served in K, with his wife. Five other guests also brought their spouses. Among them were Regimental Quartermaster Sergeant and Mrs. Paschall Conley, who celebrated their twentieth anniversary together four months later. Other married guests included Cook Beverly Thornton, who had just married Conley's sister Sallie, Commissary Sergeant and Mrs. William Hill, and Sergeant and Mrs. Eugene Frierson.[65] The company seems to have been as much an extended family as a military unit.

After dinner, the sated assemblage departed "feeling very jubilant." Members of other units probably felt as comfortably full: "All the troops had elaborate dinners . . . and the visitors as expected were many." The festivities ended with a grand ball, sponsored by the "Young Men's Social Club." L Troop's orchestra provided music for the affair, which was "a good time for all."[66]

Yuletide observances began on Christmas eve with Chaplain Anderson's annual service át the post chapel. Over 200 people attended in 1904, and many officers joined the gathering. In some other years, officers held separate Christmas tree parties for their children, but this time the entire community had a single celebration. One of the officers dressed as Santa Claus and appeared from behind the Christmas tree with a sack of presents, "much to the delight of the little people." Christmas day itself was beautiful: "the weather was fine . . . with a slight remnant of snow from the preceding week." After a breakfast that included egg nog, the regimental band serenaded the garrison. Troopers visited with each other, wished their fellows a merry Christmas, and examined gifts.[67]

Early in the afternoon, dinner, "the climax of the Christmas day festivities," was served. Corporal Stephen Barrow, a waiter in civilian life who stayed in the Army to become one of the first black warrant officers after World War I, supervised the decoration of K Troop's dining room with cedar boughs. Many of the same people who dined with the men at Thanksgiving came to the reception which preceded dinner. The troop orchestra played while the men and visitors, including the troop's three white officers, chatted. First Sergeant Johnson again welcomed the guests, and Chaplain Anderson said grace. Then Captain Harry Cavannaugh responded to the requests of his men with a short speech, which showed he was "well pleased with the troop of which he has been commander for a number of years." Oyster soup was followed by four entrees and eleven desserts, plum pudding to pumpkin pie. The repast was capped with cigars and coffee. Nostalgia accompanied the meal, as the men reminisced about Christmases past.[68]

The men visited with friends in the garrison during the afternoon. In the evening, "quite a number of church going soldiers" went to chapel, where Anderson spoke on the origin of Christmas. The festive spirit lasted until New Year's Day, when more banquets marked the end of the holiday season.[69]

Musical entertainment was not reserved for a few special holidays. Since Fort Robinson housed a regimental headquarters almost uninterruptedly from 1887 to World War I, a regimental band served on post near-ly all the time. These bands proved a valuable source of entertainment, not only for the garrison but for Crawford and other neighboring towns as well. The musical organizations' primary function, of course, involved regimen-tal drills and parades. They also gave weekly concerts on post to civilian and military audiences as early as 1889. During Colonel Biddle's tenure, these musicales became daily affairs, held every morning at the Biddle home. After the post gymnasium opened in 1904, the Tenth's band and a smaller string orchestra gave regular presentations, which many civilians eagerly attended.[70]

George Tyrell, the leader of the Tenth Cavalry's band, was an able and creative musician. Among the pieces played in concerts at Crawford by "Tyrell's famous Tenth U.S. Cavalry Band" were several of his marches. Some of their titles, such as "Colonel Augur" and "Colonel Whiteside," showed his understanding of the source of his sustenance. He and his band did rise above such celebrations of their superiors, and played their share of selections by Verdi and Rossini.[71]

Bandmaster Tyrell also had an imaginative side. A local paper reported his plans for "a grand military spectacular production presenting Sitting Bull's capture," called "Tyrell's Pine Ridge Campaign." His plans in-cluded his skilled band, a 100-voice chorus, fifteen soloists, a company of soldiers, and an entire Sioux tribe, not to mention a "battery of electrical artillery," and a "corps of pyrotechnists," as well as nurses and corpsmen, presumably to treat damaged eardrums and other injuries.[72] There is no record of a presentation of Tyrell's extravaganza. Had it been performed, it could not have escaped notice.

Tyrell's signal contribution to the community was the training of a local civilian band. He gave several evenings over to the encouragement of local musicians. Whether any of his black bandsmen aided him is unknown. However, they certainly had the skills to do so. Several of them played more than one instrument. J. F. Hendricks played clarinet, sax-ophone, organ, and cello, and Atlantan Albert Lowe played violin, trom-bone, and trap drums. At least three other members of the fourteen-piece ensemble were proficient on at least two instruments.[73]

Tyrell and his band also brightened social activity for other Pine Ridge towns. The Tenth's orchestra furnished music "par excellence" at the Chadron opera house for a New Year's gala and played for an Eagles' dance at Edgemont, South Dakota. Even minuscule Unit in Sioux County occa-sionally paid musicians from the fort to entertain the town. In Crawford the band played for stock growers' meetings, fire department benefits, frater-nal orders, and Decoration and Independence Day celebrations.[74] Other

Mitchell Harris of the Tenth Cavalry band. Copied from *The Colored American Magazine,* **vol. 7, January 1905.**

The Moorland-Spingarn Research Center, Howard Univ.

The Eighth Cavalry band on post in 1910.

The Tenth Cavalry band marches in Crawford's 1905 Fourth of July parade.

military units also participated in parades or athletic contests. Many of the men went to town just to watch the festivities and spend their money.

During some of the early years, post commanders forbade their men from attending town celebrations. In at least 1888, 1889, and 1893, the black cavalrymen stayed on post. In the last of these three years and perhaps in others, racial problems led to the boycott. Independence Day in 1893 came less than three months after the near lynching of James Diggs. Colonel Biddle kept the ban on travel to town which had been imposed after the episode by Lieutenant Colonel Reuben Bernard. Biddle politely refused an invitation for the garrison to attend the town's celebration and did not mention the prohibition or the tensions which had convinced Bernard to impose it. However, it is still likely that concern over a reoccurrence or retaliatory violence by his men prompted his decision.[75] Such withholding of patronage in early years stimulated local citizens and particularly merchants to more judicious treatment of the soldiers. After 1893 Robinson garrisons regularly joined with the town to commemorate national holidays.

Independence Day brought the most spectacular celebrations. Indian dances, horse races, parades, baseball matches, and even an appearance by "Blue Belle, the diving horse," all contributed to the carnival atmosphere. In some years troopers added bareback wrestling and steeplechases to the programs. Giant tugs of war—"Tenth Cavalry Against the World"—also drew crowds of as many as four to five thousand into Crawford. During the 1897 celebration, the Twenty-fifth Infantry's experimental bicycle corps pedalled through town on their way from Montana to St. Louis. Thousands of curious spectators lined the street and the Ninth Cavalry band played "Annie Laurie" as the black infantrymen rode by.[76]

Although the Crawford *Tribune* may have exaggerated a bit in calling one July 4th carnival "four days of ecstacy," the Crawford festivities delighted most visitors, as well as local merchants. For only a minimal outlay for the regimental band, a few special policemen, and purses for races and ball games, Crawford businessmen purchased military attractions and drew military spectators as well as civilians to town.[77] Commercial leaders appreciated the lure of their military features, as indicated by advertisements for a "grand civic military celebration" one year and a "Grand Celebration and Military Display!" in another.[78]

Town leaders were careful to express publicly their gratitude for the post commander's assistance. Annual expressions of thanks, published in local papers, were never more effusive than that of 1902:

> The officers and enlisted men comprising the garrison at Fort Robinson—the fighting Tenth— have endeared themselves not only to the committee but to every citizen of Crawford for their invaluable aid, without which

the celebration would have been short of many of its most attractive features. The *Tribune* on behalf of this community desires to return thanks to the commanding officer and the entire garrison not only for their active participation but for their uniform gentlemanly deportment throughout the day . . . .[79]

Usually fairs and holidays enhanced relations between town and post as well as the profits of local merchants, but this was not the case during the "four days of ecstacy" in 1907. Holiday spirits were dampened when soldiers confronted a "uniforms prohibited" sign at a Syndicate Opera House dance. The City Council quickly apologized in a unanimously approved resolution which they delivered to Colonel Henry Kingsbury on post. On the same day, the newspapers extended its customary "most profound and heartfelt thanks" for the garrison's participation.[80]

Other towns appreciated and envied the advantage Fort Robinson gave to Crawford. Occasionally compliance with the many requests for troops meant that contingents lent a martial tone to more than one fair. In 1902, for example, most of the Tenth celebrated independence in Crawford, but a baseball team also played in Chadron. In other years, Robinson troops played county fair cavalry at Chadron, at the Box Butte County fair in Alliance, and the Sioux County fair at Harrison. Cavalry troops also participated in the festivities at Frontier Days, the annual rodeo extravaganza at Cheyenne, Wyoming, and the Wyoming State Fair at Douglas.[81]

Chapter 9

SCHOOLS AND LIBRARIES

THE ARMY operated several facilities for the benefit of members of the military community. Post schools, a reading room, chapel, and a hospital all offered necessary social services, particularly in years when comparable civilian institutions were not available. The services offered at Fort Robinson did not always satisfy the soldiers. When this was the case, the men provided their own remedies through clubs and schools of their own creation. Of the several officially sponsored facilities, only the post hospital seems to have been satisfactory at all times. The services provided by the others were at one time or another adjudged deficient by those who used them.

A complex school system served Fort Robinson. Sergeants and officers as well as illiterate privates attended regular sessions. Dependent children also received an elementary education at a school set aside for them. The superintendent, usually the post chaplain when there was one, ran the schools for children and privates. The military education of non-coms and officers was administered separately. School terms extended through the normal September-June year and included two daily sessions. All enlisted men were required to send their children who were at least six years old. This order was rigorously enforced to prevent youngsters from loitering about the barracks. Exceptions were allowed for children who attended classes in Crawford or elsewhere.[1]

Sessions took place in the versatile but inadequate amusement hall where conditions became so bad that at times students had to wear hats as a defense against rain and sand. Classes covered a variety of subjects. Children confronted arithmetic, reading, spelling, geography, and United States history. Soldiers learned the same subjects and received instruction in the Constitution, grammar, and military correspondence. The Army provided dictionaries, copy books, slates, and globes.[2]

The school still operated as late as 1912, when it was the only active children's school in the Department of the Missouri. Brigadier General Frederick A. Smith explained that the availability of good civilian schools near all other installations made post schools superfluous. Only at Fort Robinson did he consider the post school necessary.[3] Many post officers would have agreed with General Smith. In spite of the fact that Crawford schools opened in 1887, they sought other ways to educate their children. Captain Corliss' son Bob learned for a time from a tutor, First Sergeant John McMahon of his father's company. Then Corliss sent the boy to the post school but withdrew him after only two weeks. Finally, Corliss and other officers hired teachers from neighboring towns. The young women boarded at officers' homes and rotated every few months. This private school continued, perhaps with some interruptions, until at least 1905.[4]

Some officers and senior sergeants did send their children to Crawford, at least as early as the mid-1890s. Adaline Gung'l, daughter of the Ninth Cavalry's white chief musician, graduated from the high school with honors in 1897. In the next decade, first one and later two horse drawn wagons regularly transported pupils to town schools. After the Tenth Cavalry departed, white children from post and town began to share social gatherings. Periodically "Fort Robinson scholars" entertained their classmates on post.[5]

The children of black soldiers also attended Crawford schools, at least in the higher grades. Fort Robinson had no intermediate or middle school. Chaplain Anderson's wife created one, but it lasted only a short while before the town established its own. All post children then attended the one in Crawford. Black and white, they travelled together from post to town in the same wagon.[6]

The post school, private tutors, and the Crawford system did not exhaust the possibilities. Around 1901 a few enlisted men and officers began to send their daughters to private St. Agnes Academy in Alliance. At least one officer, Lieutenant Colonel George Sanford, who served at Robinson in 1891-1892, chose a boarding school for his children.[7] Officers who did not want to mingle with their men, whites who wished to avoid blacks, and those who sought a better education than that available on post had ample options. But no matter how hard parents tried to protect their off-spring from the less positive influences on post, the children had their own ideas about what they should learn. Captain W. W. Hay's son William, who was 12 years old when he came to Robinson with his father in 1902, not only learned to play baseball from the soldiers in his father's troop of the Tenth Cavalry. He also learned how to shoot dice.[8]

At Robinson and most other posts private soldiers taught children as an extra duty. They received thirty-five cents a day compensation, which substantially increased their thirteen-dollar-a-month base pay. Throughout the late 1870s secretaries of war repeatedly urged that this extra duty pay be increased or that teachers be recruited at the rate of senior non-commissioned officers to obtain capable men.[9] None of these suggestions were adopted and the schools muddled on with available manpower.

At times the situation at Fort Robinson reflected that general problem. Colonel Joseph Tilford complained in 1890 that a white sergeant, Harry Ogilvie, was "the only thoroughly competent man in the garrison . . . ." However, this does not generally appear to have been the case.[10] During 1892-1898, the number of men listed as competent teachers on the post's monthly returns often exceeded the number employed, even during the busy months of November to April, when enlisted men as well as children attended classes.

A commander's mistake occasionally exacerbated the problem of scarcity. Private William M. Jackson of F Troop, Ninth Cavalry, enlisted as a laborer but found himself teaching school at Robinson. Only after Jackson asked to return to duty with his troop did Lieutenant Colonel James Brisbin rectify the error. Another part of the difficulty with instructors was simply that the teachers were also soldiers and had to attend to other duties and training as well as teach children. Colonel Biddle acknowledged this difficulty in an 1892 plea for an additional instructor. One teacher who had also to be a soldier could not properly teach thirty children.[11]

During 1886-1894, when the garrison was made up largely of the black Ninth Cavalry and some units of the white Eighth Infantry, eleven men from each regiment taught sessions at Fort Robinson. Private Walter Pulpress and Sergeant Joseph Moore of the Ninth each instructed four sessions. Sergeant Moore, who organized the Ninth Cavalry's Sunday School in 1886, must have taken his consciousness of his community and past into the classroom. During his years at Robinson he proposed that the black regulars raise money to purchase the site of John Brown's Fort at Harper's Ferry for a monument. He also helped collect $150 on post for black Nebraskans impoverished by a flood in the Broken Bow area. Regardless of Colonel Tilford's partiality toward white Sergeant Ogilvie, the black children and privates must have benefitted from contact with Moore. Private Drayton Moffett of G Troop, who taught during 1891-1893, took a deep interest in Sergeant Barney McKay's case and strove to rally the unit to McKay's defense.[12] Black students at the post school did not lack race-conscious teachers.

After the Spanish-American War there were other role models for black children. Sergeant Major James W. Peniston, who taught in the post school during 1902, had been cited for bravery at Las Guasimas during the Cuban campaign and promoted directly from private to the senior non-commissioned rank. A perennial sharpshooter, Peniston even gave up his Sundays so he could teach at the post school.[13]

During peak months as many as six men were employed as instructors. Colonel Biddle explained that this unusually high number of men was necessary to serve his black regiment: "illiteracy among colored men is far greater than among white, they not having the same educational advantage in their early youth as their more fortunate white brother." He added that black recruits were especially eager to achieve literacy and that he desired to give them every chance. Chaplain Henry Plummer agreed with his commander. He called his pupils "studious, obedient, and earnest," while teachers were "competent, obedient, and zealous." Plummer summed up the attitudes of the men who attended his school by saying he had "never seen a class of men, who as a whole have shown a greater desire to improve their condition mentally, morally, and socially."[14]

Men who did attend had to be dedicated or coerced. The illiterates were indeed compelled to go, and post commanders had little patience with absentees. Chaplain George Prioleau, who superintended the post school for three years, complained that many of the men attempted to evade attendance to earn extra money. He claimed they "would rather go on the ice pond and cut ice than attend school." However, other men voluntarily gave up their leisure hours to sit in classes either at noon or in the evening after a full day's work.[15]

In 1894 the Army discontinued the enlistment of men who could not read or write English. After that, the number of conscripted students gradually declined to zero. The school was still maintained for those who wished to attend. The course of study available to the men did not cover the entire range of subjects required by the Army curriculum but extended beyond the "three R's" to physiology, elementary algebra, and grammar.[16] When Chaplain William Anderson took over the schools during the final phase of the war in the Philippines, he added Spanish to the curriculum. The demand for this course must have been substantial to justify Colonel Augur's request for fifty Spanish grammars. In general, the school provided the soldier an opportunity to "improve mentally if he wishes . . . ."[17] For many black soldiers the school may have offered a better chance than they ever had as civilians.

Examination of the post school, its curriculum, and attendance provides only an introduction to the possibilities for education and the desire of the black troops to grasp it. Men of Chaplain Anderson's Tenth Cavalry created their own institution, in which they could educate each other on matters of particular interest. When the Tenth came to Fort Robinson it brought a regimental branch of the Young Men's Christian Association. Chaplain Anderson and some of the enlisted men had established the organization in 1900, when the regiment garrisoned several Cuban towns. Members met on Wednesday evenings, both in Cuba and at Robinson. According to S. J. Willoughby of A Troop, programs were "nearly always along literary lines," and included recitations, musical presentations, essays, and debates. Many of the soldiers attended meetings, and Willoughby believed that the intellectual efforts of the men compared "favorably with those in many college literary societies."[18]

The quality of the programs may have been a reason for the association's great popularity. Chaplain Anderson noted in late 1902 that 450 men of the garrison were members, and as many as 342 soldiers attended a single meeting. Troops of the regiment planned and conducted the weekly exercises in rotation. This practice inspired rivalry among the units as they competed to provide the best programs.[19] The policy also assured that an evening's recitation or debate would be of interest to the spectators.

Some of the programs focused explicitly on the problems of black Americans. Essays such as the one presented by Beverly F. Thornton, K Troop's cook, show that physical and occupational distance from the black civilian community did not isolate the soldiers emotionally or intellectually. Thornton exhorted forty-six of his colleagues at the January 4, 1905, meeting to the assiduous practice of thrift. He argued that in order for African-Americans to become "a respected people," each man diligently had to place a portion of his income aside. Regular saving, he said, formed a buffer against servitude in times of want. Those who failed to save would be able to "neither command their time nor choose how or where they should live."[20]

Corporal Joseph Wheelock of K Troop also read a paper which emphasized race consciousness. His essay, entitled "Our Own Editors and Publishers," urged his fellows to patronize race magazines and newspapers. After listing the available periodicals, he bluntly asserted the alternative to loyal support in a pair of rhetorical questions: "Do we buy our papers and magazines from other people whose greatest aim is to show us in the worst possible form to the world? Do we patronize the man who at all times is ready to minimize our true manliness?"[21]

The YMCA occasionally obtained speakers from off post. These included Reverend John B. Carnes of Grand Island, Nebraska, a Methodist minister and state superintendent of the Anti-Saloon League. Carnes presented temperance lectures to 142 men in January 1905, and to ninety-six in October 1906. Mrs. Henry Highland Garnett, widow of the famed abolitionist clergyman, also addressed 118 men in August 1904. Neither she nor the temperance advocate elicited as much interest as a "Jubilee Concert," attended by over three hundred soldiers in January 1903. The Reverend Jesse Moorland, International Secretary of the YMCA, also visited the chapter at Fort Robinson. The visit pleased Chaplain Anderson, who said Moorland's encouragement and advice would enhance his association's work.[22]

Officers of the association also assisted the chaplain with church services. In one instance Reverend O. K. Hobson, a Crawford minister, accepted YMCA president James Buchanan's invitation to preach a sermon at a Sunday chapel service. A year later, while Chaplain Anderson took a brief vacation, members conducted religious observances on post.[23]

Through their own efforts the men of the Tenth provided what appears to have been a far more satisfying educational experience through the association than the Army offered in the post school. Certainly the organization offered a welcome supplement to the school and a forum through which men could express their views and exert their own leadership. The meetings also served to maintain ties with the black community at large. The black cavalrymen do not seem to have been "psychologically as well as physically" isolated from their civilian brothers.[24]

Non-commissioned officers also went to school to study military subjects, such as the articles of war, care of weapons, tactics, and map reading. For a time, the sergeants met in company barracks under the supervision of unit commanders. Later they moved to one of the old adobe officers' quarters and met in larger groups. Officers took this training seriously, and at least one non-com, Corporal John Parke of the Ninth Cavalry, paid a fine for his failure to master his lessons in tactics.[25]

Commissioned officers on post attended a formally organized lyceum to further their professional training. Emerging in a period of increasing professionalism along with professional associations, service schools, and journals, the lyceum began at Department of the Platte posts in 1888. Three years later, General Schofield extended the program to officers at all posts garrisoned by line units. Originally the assembly was intended to prepare the officers for promotion examinations, but it later stressed general improvement in knowledge of military affairs. The post commander served as president; majors and senior captains acted as instructors. Meetings were conducted in a less austere atmosphere than enlisted men's schools, either at the post library or the officers' club. A board of officers determined the subjects that officers discussed as well as the course of study for non-coms.[26]

At the end of each lyceum season every officer was required to read at least one "carefully prepared paper" on a professional subject to his fellows and the non-commissioned officers in the post chapel. Research materials for these papers were severely limited by the books at the post library or in personal collections. The lyceum owned some books of its own, such as a map-reading manual and a Spanish-English dictionary, but this collection was also extremely small. The papers nevertheless illustrate some of the issues with which the officers concerned themselves. With many volumes of the *Official Records of the Rebellion* on the post library shelves to augment the interest many had in the Civil War, it is no surprise that several of the papers assessed specific battles of the rebellion. Others dealt with European campaigns, like Hannibal's or the Crimean War battle at Balaclava. Some of the essays, such as Major Charles Ilsley's 1896 paper on "Our Coming War with England," were more speculative.[27]

Several lyceum papers dealt with the Army's role in civil disorders. Captain Corliss read essays on "Street Fighting" in 1888 and 1893. In the latter year Captain John Loud wrote on the same topic. Other officers studied "The Regular Army and the Labor Riots of 1877," and "Cavalry Against Mobs."[28] These papers reflected the transition from an Indian-fighting to a strike-breaking Army that took place in the mid-1890s. Officers in the lyceum, while still partially immersed in the Civil War, sought to comprehend and adapt to what they apparently perceived as a new role for themselves and the Army.

The post library, which provided some of the material for the lyceum essays, opened in 1883, in a first-floor room of the new administration building. At the time some of the companies on post already had their own reading rooms, so it is quite possible that organized efforts to make some literature available had long been underway.[29] An officer, usually the chaplain, and an enlisted assistant administered the collection of seven hundred volumes.

In eight years the collection grew by one hundred volumes. The additions came from several sources. The Quartermaster Department authorized funds from which post commanders could order reading material, and private religious groups such as the American Bible Society contributed to the collection.[30] Most of the books in the reading room dealt with military subjects. In July 1891, there were sixty volumes of the *Official Records of the War of the Rebellion*, as well as many military histories and reference books. Lieutenant Colonel Alfred Smith's request for additional material,

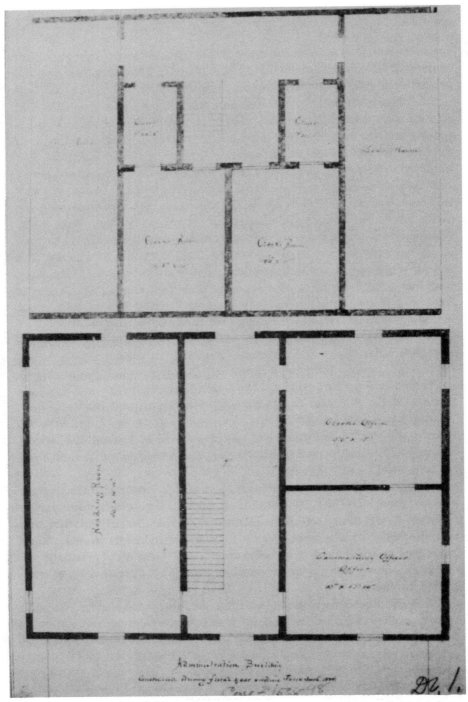

This plan of the 1883 administration building shows the commander's office and reading room on opposite sides of the hall in front. The rest of the building is taken up by store rooms and clerks' offices. Construction cost $1,508.98.

Misc. Fortifications File, Fort Robinson, #9, RG 77, NA

which was filled in the winter of 1892, included still more literature on warfare. He sought biographies of Washington and Napoleon, and American military fiction such as *Sailor Boys of 1861*. He also ordered novels by Alexander Dumas, Charles Reade, and Wilkie Collins.[31]

Two years later Colonel Biddle asked for still more military history and biography, as well as translations of some of the "higher class French novelists." He complained that few books had arrived since Smith's order, and inquired about the collection from abandoned Fort McKinney. The Department had sent the Fort Laramie library to Robinson in 1890 when Laramie had closed. Most of the books on post were old and worn, and Biddle would have welcomed the McKinney volumes.[32]

The post librarian and council of administration, all of whom were commissioned officers, determined which books to purchase. Their own tastes probably accounted for the emphasis on military literature. Captain Corliss, who noted some of his reading in his diary, claimed he tried to read about three hours a day "in some good military book." During one year on post he read Caesar's *Commentaries*, a history of the Union Army's Second Corps, and at least one work on tactics. A fourth book he read, *Ben Hur*, was by an American officer, General Lew Wallace. Corliss' other choices were Dickens' *Pickwick Papers* and Strutt's *Sports and Pastimes of the English People*.[33]

Fortunately the library also received newspapers and magazines. In 1886 Colonel Hatch's order included the *Army and Navy Register*, three daily newspapers, and four periodicals, including *Harper's*, *Puck*, and a black weekly paper, T. Thomas Fortune's New York *Freeman*. By 1892 the number of metropolitan dailies increased to six. In addition the library received six weeklies and four general magazines, *Harper's*, *Atlantic Monthly*, *Scribner's*, and *Century*. The selection included no race papers, and neither did the next year's list. Colonel Biddle did not correct this situation in his 1893 requisition for reading material for his 385 black troopers. Instead he asked for the *Journal of the Military Service Institution* and the *Congressional Record*. The post hospital, which ordered some periodicals of its own, also ignored the needs of the black soldiers. In 1902-1903 the surgeon subscribed to *Leslie's Weekly* and the New York *Times*.[34]

The available selections did not satisfy all observers. Mrs. Ellen Biddle and Chaplain George Prioleau both expressed satisfaction with the collection, but a private who signed himself "Africus" disagreed with the chaplain and the colonel's wife. He commented that a bulky package of books that arrived in late 1887 caused quite a stir in the garrison. The excited men speculated that the books might be by the French novelist Emile Zola or perhaps some of Captain Charles King's frontier romances. To everyone's chagrin the package contained only another large volume of the *Official Records of the War of the Rebellion*. Africus said he and his fellows were less than delighted with "the thrilling and intensely interesting narratives (?) in that literary treasure . . . ."[35]

Some units had their own reading rooms, so at least these could order literature more to the men's tastes. Members of C Troop, Ninth Cavalry, subscribed their money for book purchases, and the Quartermaster Department cooperatively shipped their choices to Robinson. Another outfit, C Company of the Eighth Infantry, had a handsome book fund from the will of retired Sergeant Thomas McKenzie. When he died in 1892 McKenzie left the unit reading club $600 and the company reading room another $500. This soldier, who worked in the post library for nine months in 1889, knew the deficiencies of the post collection very well.[36]

Chaplain Henry Plummer of the Ninth reported the presence of a "literary association" on post in 1892. Plummer said the association strove to encourage the study of useful literature among the enlisted men and that the organization had a comfortable reading room with space for forty users. "Some friends in the East" sent him books to distribute among the men, and once donated $200 for books, in addition to the papers, magazines, and books they sent "for mental and religious edification."[37]

The literature offered by the post library and the several collective efforts to provide more reading material did not exhaust the possibilities. Several major black weekly newspapers had subscribers among the black cavalrymen. The Cleveland *Gazette* published several articles from post correspondents between 1886 and 1898 and had an active agent at Robinson. This soldier, who signed his letters "Duranti," promised the editor in 1886 that his paper "shall be in the hands of every reading man in the Ninth Regiment of Cavalry . . . ." Later he wrote that he expected to present the *Gazette* with forty new subscribers as a New Year's gift. Some Ninth Cavalry soldiers read the Omaha *Progress*, which had a regular Fort Robinson department edited by Chaplain Plummer and written by an anonymous trooper called "Yellow Cape." The Ninth's cavalrymen also read the New York *Age* and the Richmond *Planet*.[38]

Troopers of the Tenth Cavalry also maintained contact with the black community through race journals. The Indianapolis *Freeman* had at least one Fort Robinson reader, C. J. Lewis of M Troop. The men of K Troop subscribed to the New York *Age*, which Corporal Joseph Wheelock called the "best colored newspaper in the Republic." In K Troop they also took the two leading black monthlies, *Colored American Magazine* and *The Voice of the Negro*. The latter journal even boasted that every man in K Troop had presented his wife or sweetheart with a year's subscription, an extraordinary act of support which may even have preceded Corporal Wheelock's exhortation to take race publications.[39]

First Sergeant Robert M. Johnson of K Troop was partially responsible for the strong support his men gave the black press. This veteran of the Apache wars paid the postage on subscription requests of his men. Corporal Wheelock said Johnson did so "simply . . . to advance a good cause."[40] His generosity helped assure that the men of his unit kept abreast of developments which concerned black Americans. It also corrected the Army's failure, either through negligence or design, to provide race literature for black troopers. On a much less lavish scale, Johnson performed a service similar to that of Sergeant McKenzie's bequest. Both contributed materially to their fellows' efforts to obtain a more rounded selection of reading material than the Army offered.

Chapter 10

RELIGION, THE CHAPLAINCY, AND THE COURT MARTIAL OF CHAPLAIN HENRY VINTON PLUMMER

FOR THE FIRST twenty years of its existence, Fort Robinson seldom had a clergyman. Chaplain George W. Simpson served briefly in 1880-1882, but eight years passed before John D. Parker replaced him. During the interim an occasional minister visited the fort to conduct services. For example, a Catholic priest from Cheyenne stopped on post for a few days in November 1883, celebrated mass, and christened three children before he returned to Wyoming. Infrequently, a pious Department commander like Brigadier General Oliver O. Howard expressed concern over the situation at Robinson and other Department of the Platte posts. Howard called the need for a chaplain at Robinson urgent. Men and their families were "cut off from ordinary religious and social privileges" at such an isolated post, and he believed the Army should assign a clergyman to meet their requirements.[1]

Some official efforts to fill the religious needs of the garrison were made in the 1880s. Though there was no chaplain, the post did have a chapel by 1887. A small building was erected for $1,500 and served both as chapel

Chaplain Henry Plummer, sometime between 1884 and 1888. Photograph copied from Nellie Arnold Plummer, *Out of the Depths or the Triumph of the Cross* (Hyattsville, Maryland: 1927).

The Moorland-Spingarn Research Center, Howard Univ.

and amusement hall for everything from dances to Grand Army of the Republic meetings and boxing exhibitions. During the day it was also used for the post school. A private soldier, sometimes a white infantryman and at other times a black cavalryman, reshuffled furniture after each of its various uses and kept the building clean.[2]

The combination church-school-arena was still in use when Henry Vinton Plummer, chaplain of the Ninth Cavalry, arrived in the spring of 1891 from Fort McKinney, Wyoming. The black chaplain's career already resembled a classic "up from slavery" story. He had fled from bondage in his native Maryland during the Civil War and enlisted in the Navy, where he served nearly two years. After teaching himself to read and write, he worked his way through a Baptist seminary in Washington, D.C. In 1884 his efforts were rewarded with a chaplaincy, the first appointment given a black clergyman in the post-Civil War Army.[3] Moreover, when he received his commission, he became the only black officer in the service.[4]

Chaplain Plummer attended vigorously to his duties, which included librarian and superintendent of post schools as well as the chaplaincy. He held worship services each Sunday evening, at which Mrs. Mary Garrard played the organ. As many as 187 people crowded into the small, uncomfortable chapel for his services, which he supplemented with Thursday evening song services and occasional revival meetings. One set of five meetings drew as many as 130 enlisted men as spectators. He also conducted a well-attended Sunday School for the children on post. In October 1893, for example, average attendance was twenty-one of the forty Sunday-School-age children.[5] Those kinds of services were more or less the stock in trade of any chaplain. Plummer went beyond them and organized an active temperance movement at Fort Robinson.

In March 1892, he held the first of fifteen temperance lectures, where he addressed 125 men on the evils of demon rum. Later the meetings became more complex and perhaps more interesting. In March 1893, he presided at what he called a "great mass meeting" of about 150 soldiers, as well as civilians from Crawford. A local minister shared the podium with Plummer, and a group of Crawford women entertained the audience with temperance songs. The "Loyal Temperance Legion" also gave a musical presentation. Plummer established the legion among the children at the post in the summer of 1892. Its members held regular meetings for a short time during the year, with as many as thirty attending a session. Later they aided the chaplain with songs at his meetings.[6]

Plummer's efforts generally pleased his superiors. Lieutenant Colonel George Sanford remarked that he had never seen such large church attendance at a military post. He attributed the popularity of religion to "the efficient manner in which the chaplain carries out his work," and concluded that Plummer was "entitled to high commendation." Other officers shared Sanford's view. Colonel James Biddle called Plummer "a good man . . . conscientious in the performance of his duty." Major Guy Henry agreed and added that he thought Plummer was "anxious . . . to do good."[7]

The harmonious relations between Plummer and his commanders did not last very long. Tensions and conflicts between the chaplain and his superiors ultimately destroyed Plummer's career. Less than three months after his arrival he said the great distance between the chapel and the barracks (about one tenth of a mile) reduced attendance at his services. In a later report he complained that "the very idea of divine services in a dance hall destroys much of the impressive solemnity which should characterize divine worship." Colonel Sanford agreed and recommended erection of an appropriate building. After all, no chaplain before Plummer had generated such widespread religious enthusiasm.[8]

Chaplain Plummer made other minor complaints. At one point he told Colonel Sanford his quarters were inadequate. Sanford replied that Plummer's residence was no worse than those of other officers. However, Surgeon George Adair disagreed and wanted Plummer's dank cellar filled with lime.[9] In another instance Plummer complained to Biddle about the support he received as superintendent of schools and drew a sharp rebuke for his indiscretion.[10]

The major dispute between the chaplain and post commanders grew out of Plummer's temperance activities. Almost as soon as he arrived he began to attack the post exchange system. This caused little difficulty with genial Major Henry, who disagreed with Plummer but observed that "water is the best beverage if men can be so persuaded." Colonels Sanford and Alfred Smith also disputed Plummer's arguments about the exchange, but they both knew the chaplain's quarrel was with the system, not with matters at Fort Robinson. Sanford believed Plummer was "one of the most efficient officers" among the Army chaplains and that his influence over the men on post was excellent.[11]

Plummer's report of March 1892 contained his most complete indictment of the post exchange. Sale of beer on posts made "legal one of the most pernicious and menacing evils that stands in the way of the physical, mental and moral development of the soldier," as well as undermined discipline. As a result many "of the most promising young men" became "confirmed drunkards, mendicants, and gluttons . . . entrapped and enticed" by the legality of the exchange. He claimed to have seen troops marched from the pay table to the canteen to pay their bills. In fact, while writing that very report, a soldier's wife had come to him and begged him to convince her husband to give her some of his pay. He was one of many who spent all their money on beer and gambling at the exchange. Still, Plummer made it clear that he objected to the system rather than the command at Robinson. He said—probably incorrectly—that troop commanders generally opposed the canteen and that post authorities did what they could to handle the matter satisfactorily.[12]

Colonel Sanford recognized that Plummer did not directly indict his command. He said Plummer agreed with him that the marching of troops to the canteen to pay bar bills occurred elsewhere and that discipline at Robinson was at least as good as at other posts. However, Plummer's charges had convinced the adjutant general to cut off beer sales at Robinson. Sanford wanted the order rescinded. He also passed to Plummer the department commander's instructions to document his case and state explicitly whether his statements applied to the Robinson exchange. A day later Sanford forwarded Plummer's reply, agreeing that prohibition would be the best policy. Sanford did not believe that was possible, however, and thought government control was the best available option.[13]

Continuing his campaign against tippling during Biddle's tenure as commander, Chaplain Plummer even succeeded in having the exchange closed on Sundays. At the same time he complained to Biddle that Lieutenant Colonel Reuben Bernard had both discriminated against and humiliated him while Bernard had commanded the post in the spring of 1893. Bernard replied that Plummer sought to discredit his tenure just as he had sought to slander Sanford with his attacks on the canteen. He called Plummer's charge "an effusion of falsehoods, with slight shades of truth intermingled in such a manner as to make the whole thing in spirit grossly false." Bernard even asserted that Plummer had acknowledged efforts to make Sanford's administration "as obnoxious at Washington as he could," though Plummer and Sanford seem to have been on fairly cordial terms.[14]

In the meantime Biddle's reports on Plummer's efficiency followed a curious trend. In 1891 Biddle had praised the chaplain as "a good . . . and conscientious" man, but two years later he said only that Plummer's "services comply with the law." By early 1894 Biddle denied his ability to judge clergymen, who he felt tended "as a class . . . to feel in conflict with the general code of military discipline." He said his views differed from Chaplain Plummer's, and he thought it would be unjust for him to even express his opinion of his subordinate.[15] Biddle's opinion of his own ability to evaluate his regimental chaplain changed considerably in three years. He may have been freeing himself for drastic action against Plummer.

Meanwhile, Plummer created even more trouble for himself. In the spring of 1894 he submitted an unusual and audacious proposal to the War

Department. Plummer sought authority to lead an exploratory and missionary expedition to central Africa, to introduce American civilization and Christianity. The enterprise would provide an excellent outlet for educated and trained black Americans and would help "remove the dread of Negro domination and be at least the entering wedge to the solving of the so-called Negro problem in the South." Furthermore, Plummer was eager for his people to "secure a slice of the African 'turkey,' " before other nations colonized all of the continent. He wanted to take fifty to one hundred black enlisted men with him. He explained that the troops were ideally suited to the mission, since they were disciplined to frontier life. Men of the Ninth Cavalry, he said, would voluntarily accompany him to Africa.[16]

The proposal drew support from diverse groups. Bishop Henry Turner of the African Methodist Episcopal Church, the leading colonizer of the day, backed Plummer, as did a convention of black churchmen in western Pennsylvania.[17] Bishop Turner believed the expedition would benefit the heathen of Africa, talented black Americans, and national commerce. Chaplain Plummer also drummed up substantial local support. In early May the Robinson Post of the Grand Army of the Republic forwarded a petition in favor of the plan. Twenty-five northwestern Nebraska veterans signed the letter, including black retirees like Sergeant Simon Franklin of the Ninth Cavalry band and the white marshal of Crawford, who had led a would-be lynch mob in 1893. The petition probably reflected the same conflicting motives which later made bedfellows of Marcus Garvey and the Ku Klux Klan. In spite of this and other endorsements, the War Department expressed no interest in the scheme. The adjutant general told Plummer no law authorized the detail of an officer "for such an expedition."[18]

Only a short time later, the aggressive and energetic chaplain faced court-martial charges. Lieutenant Colonel Bernard, who had suspected Plummer of responsibility for the incendiary leaflet which Sergeant McKay had taken into his barracks, initiated the action and placed Plummer under arrest on June 6. When Colonel Biddle returned from Omaha, Bernard reported that Saddler Sergeant Robert Benjamin complained of seeing Plummer "odorous with the fumes of liquor." Colonel Biddle immediately began an "unusually careful" investigation. He recommended a general court-martial as offering the only possibility of a "thorough vindication." He found no fault with Plummer's work with the schools and chapel but asserted that his usefulness "as an officer and chaplain"—which Biddle had earlier claimed he could not assess—had "virtually ceased." Three enlisted men, Sergeants Benjamin and David Dillon and Regimental Sergeant Major Jeremiah Jones, apparently witnessed Plummer's drunkenness.[19]

The trial did not take place until November. In the meantime, Chaplain Plummer worked to avoid the disgrace of dismissal from the service. First he applied for retirement, alleging an infirmity due to naval service in the Civil War and old age. Colonel Biddle eagerly recommended approval, in the "interest of the service." The adjutant general refused to act on the application until the post surgeon examined Plummer. Doctor Adair found no disability and Biddle changed his recommendation.[20]

When this failed, Chaplain Plummer prepared to defend himself. He collected affidavits from several prominent white civilians of Crawford, including two former city councilmen. These men agreed that the chaplain's conduct had been exemplary. T. G. Harris, the white post wheelwright, concurred. Not only had he attended Plummer's services but the chaplain had made pastoral visits to his home. He found Plummer to be "earnest in his ministerial work and gentlemanly in his deportment."[21]

The most unusual and most telling testimonial to Chaplain Plummer's sobriety came from Mrs. Garrard. Mrs. Garrard had played the church organ and worked in the chapel from the time of Plummer's arrival. She praised his "decidedly good" influence over the men, and noted that he worked "almost entirely without help or encouragement from the officers." Mrs. Garrard observed Chaplain Plummer closely "out of the pulpit as well as in it and even on numerous occasions at his own house on church affairs." During the several years of their acquaintance, she had *never once seen him, even to the smallest degree,* show any evidence of being under the influence of alcohol."[22]

Congressman John Langston commented that Mrs. Garrard's letter was "entitled to great weight." However, Plummer's own record spoke for itself as the "strongest reflections of these, the first reflections upon his character." The record of which Langston spoke certainly suggested little taste for strong drink. The chaplain's most strenuous efforts had been against alcohol. Still, neither the record nor letters from Langston and Bishop Turner could prevent Plummer's trial.[23]

As the court-martial grew closer, Chaplain Plummer showed great strain. Three days before the trial the post surgeon treated him for "nervous prostration." While Plummer grew anxious, Biddle became more confident of his ability to judge clergymen. He said Plummer did not show the "high character and purity of a Christian life," though he assured department headquarters he would treat the chaplain properly if he were retained in the service.[24]

Chaplain Plummer was not retained in the service. On November 2, 1894, a general court-martial convicted him of two specifications of "conduct unbecoming an officer and gentleman." The first count alleged drunkenness in the quarters of Sergeant Major Jones early in the evening on June 2. The second cited a drunken display at Sergeant Benjamin's home immediately thereafter. Only Sergeant Benjamin and his wife testified against Plummer. Jones and Dillon acknowledged that the chaplain had drunk with them, but did not corroborate Benjamin's tales of drunken disturbances. The affidavits of Private John Miller and his wife, who stated they had chatted with Plummer shortly afterward and found him completely sober, did not help. The sentence of dismissal from the service was carried out on November 10.[25]

Chaplain Plummer complained bitterly about the verdict. On the day before he left Fort Robinson and the Army, he protested his innocence and accused Colonel Biddle of concocting the charge "on account of racial prejudice toward me and my work as Chaplain." He said he was dismissed on false testimony, against which "patriotism and devotion to duty counts for naught."[26]

Biddle's behavior toward Chaplain Plummer was strange. And, as Mrs. Garrard complained, the officers did not support Plummer in his work. Two of his supporters suggested that this lack of encouragement was due to his "personal and friendly relations" with the troops, to which he was driven by the social ostracism of his fellow officers as well as the requirements of his position.[27] Chaplain Plummer lived in an untenable social position at Fort Robinson: as an officer he was expected not to fraternize with the men; as a black man he was denied the social life of an officer.

That ostracism was clearly not directed at Plummer alone. Two black line officers, Lieutenants John Alexander and Charles Young, also served on post and experienced the same aloofness. Other indications that racist policy extended down to the enlisted men are just as important for clarification of the context of Plummer's difficulties. A black weekly newspaper reported, probably on the basis of information provided by a Fort Robinson correspondent, that:

> There is considerable discrimination going on at Fort Robinson, Neb. There are three white clerks in the commissary department, two in the post exchange, two in the post bakery, two in the post adjutant's office, two in the officers' club and mess room, the post librarian is a white soldier, two white soldiers at the post pump house, a white non-commissioned officer in charge of the post saw mills, five white men in the post quartermaster's department. All these places are filled by enlisted men of the Eighth Infantry, of which there are only two companies at the post, while there are six cavalry companies, all colored. whew![28]

Plummer's aggressive and energetic behavior challenged the leadership structure in which blacks were clearly relegated to a secondary position.

He was well liked and respected by the enlisted men with whom he was forced to associate. Moreover, he had taken steps to institutionalize his popularity through the Loyal Temperance Legion. He had certainly probed the limits of "up from slavery." However, racism and jealousy of his warm relations with the men were not the only untoward aspects of the trial.

There are also hints of a personal vendetta against Plummer. Captain E. H. Crowder's pre-trial investigation disclosed that Sergeant Benjamin had borne a grudge against the chaplain for reporting his negligence while in charge of a bakery detail at Fort Riley before the Ninth moved to Nebraska. Benjamin also complained that Plummer refused to attend his social functions and to lend him money. To solidify his own case against Plummer, Benjamin apparently resorted to deception. Evidence presented at the trial suggests that Benjamin wrote himself a threatening letter, which was typed on the machine at post headquarters where he worked. The note warned him not to testify against the chaplain and was signed "We Thirteen."[29]

Sergeant Benjamin was promoted to ordnance sergeant only a week before the trial convened. Sergeant Dillon, who Biddle once described as a "reluctant witness" against Plummer, met a different fate. He was dishonorably discharged from the Army in September, about two weeks after the end of Plummer's trial, after only a shadow of a trial for conduct to the prejudice of good order and discipline. Dillon's crimes were violation of Biddle's order to stay away from the Benjamins and an attempt to quarrel with Benjamin.[30]

The Dillon trial proved two things. It established that Dillon was indeed furious at Benjamin for his role in Plummer's dismissal. It also showed Biddle's determination to protect Benjamin and the result of the Plummer court-martial. The instigator of the quarrel was never established. Sergeants John Jackson and Houston Lust and Trumpeter John Rogers all testified that a verbal clash had taken place between Dillon and Benjamin. Benjamin had called Dillon a "damn dirty Dutch Cur," and threatened to "blow your damn brains out." Enraged, Dillon called Benjamin "a God damn son of a bitch," and accused him of "running around here reporting Chaplain Plummer." "Now, God damn you," he added angrily, "you report me."[31]

The last comment referred to a rumor told Dillon by the wife of Sergeant Preston Brooks. Dillon testified that Benjamin's wife told Mrs. Brooks that Dillon intended to kill the Benjamins. Incredibly, Mrs. Brooks was never asked to testify at the trial. Moreover, Colonel Biddle, who affirmed to the court that he had ordered Dillon to stay away from the Benjamins, never explained why he had done so. The entire trial was rushed to completion in a single day in a procedure so shoddy it had to be deliberate.[32] David Dillon was railroaded out of the Army and the Plummer matter was closed.

Chaplain George W. Prioleau, who replaced Chaplain Plummer in
June 1895, had also been born into slavery. The new minister held two
university degrees and had taught in the theological department of Wilberforce University. In addition he had been a public school teacher in his
native South Carolina and a leader in the Ohio Conference of the African
Methodist Episcopal Church.[33] Chaplain Prioleau stayed at Robinson with
the Ninth until the Spanish-American War. That tour of duty on post was
his first in the Army and gave him a chance to develop a perspective on
the military environment. An article he wrote in 1897 also shows what
he thought of Fort Robinson. In spite of the Christian upbringing of most
of his charges, many men could not resist the "atmosphere pregnated with
evil and sin" which they found in the Army. The environment exerted great
force and the men were "tempted to fall in and content themselves with
the new situation."[34] In effect, he saw himself as straddling the road between the post and Crawford, keeping the men true to their upbringing and
away from the sin and corruption of brothel and tavern.

Whatever his figurative position, Chaplain Prioleau worked both ends
of the highway. He preached to Crawford audiences as well as the garrison.
Prioleau sermonized "most ably and eloquently" before the Congregational
Church of Crawford, from the Book of Judges. A year later Reverend H. V.
Rominger of the Congregational Church returned the favor and spoke at
Prioleau's Sunday evening service. Chaplain William T. Anderson, enroute
to Montana to join the Tenth Cavalry, also visited Fort Robinson. A
Crawford journalist reported that the urbane minister and physician "was
very much impressed with the appearance of our bustling city."[35] Ander-
son returned in 1902 and served the garrison for five years.

During his three years on post, Prioleau conducted Sunday School for
up to fifty children as well as weekly worship. Members of the command
and their dependents participated in his services as vocalists. One of his
last meetings, sponsored by the local chapter of the Regular Army and Navy
Union, memorialized the men killed on the battleship *Maine*. The chaplain
invited "all patriots, old sailors, and soldiers" to attend. Over 400 came
to hear Mrs. Garrard play the organ, Mrs. Annie Prioleau sing, and Prioleau
celebrate the patriotism of the *Maine* casualties.[36]

Between his departure and Anderson's arrival in 1902, no clergyman
served the fort. An occasional itinerant, such as Miss M. E. Brown of the
Omaha Methodist Hospital, solicited donations on post. However, the situation was not nearly as desperate as it had been before Plummer's arrival:
there were at least five churches in town and a white garrison on post. Officers now made small contributions to Crawford's religious life. Surgeon
Albert Simonton, for example, lectured on Cuban customs for the benefit
of the local Baptist congregation.[37]

Almost as soon as Anderson and the Tenth Cavalry arrived in 1902, they lost the combination chapel and amusement hall. The Tenth's band moved into the old building, after an expansion of the medical facilities drove them out of the old hospital. Anderson had to make do with the post schoolroom, which was too small for entertainments "that would prevent men from going to town and debauching their lives." Getting the men to church was no easy task with a comfortable chapel. But even the faithful probably attended reluctantly at a building whose dry earth closet had "enough feces on one seat to interfere with its proper use."[38]

The post gymnasium was completed in 1904, and the regimental YMCA moved into the new building. Perhaps Anderson also took his services into the gym, since the old chapel remained in use as barracks until 1908. In spite of the lack of proper facilities, some aspects of the situation pleased the minister. For example, the ladies of the post, probably officers' wives, donated the money for the purchase of a new organ and songbooks.[39]

The morality of the post troubled Anderson more than the facilities. He shared Prioleau's fear that debauchery and sin awaited troopers in town. Both had entered the Army from relatively prosperous middle-class Ohio churches. Anderson's ministry at St. John's African Methodist Episcopal Church, Cleveland's oldest and wealthiest black congregation, did not prepare him for druggists who dispensed opium or pistol-toting soldiers' wives. Anderson tried to improve this Sodom on the Pine Ridge in several ways. He believed the best way to keep soldiers out of trouble was to keep them out of town, and the YMCA helped provide sound entertainment on post. He also visited the barracks frequently and talked privately with the men, focusing his attention on "those who are inclined to give trouble to troop commanders and the garrison in general." He also urged the discharge of "bad characters."[40]

The chaplain's efforts pleased Colonel Jacob Augur. He wrote that Anderson did "good work among the men," and had "the interest of the men in all his efforts in their behalf." Contract Surgeon Samuel McPheeters agreed and added that Anderson "was very well thought of by the officers."[41] Episcopal ministers from Crawford and Chadron also held services on post during Anderson's tenure. Their evening meetings were for officers and their families. Thus, while Augur, McPheeters, and other officers thought highly of Anderson, they still desired to attend another church. That contrasted sharply with the situation faced by Anderson's replacement, Chaplain Neil Brennan, who served the Eighth Cavalry at Robinson. Brennan reported that many officers attended his masses and non-denominational regimental services. He praised them for setting such a good example for the men. The basic difference between the two situations, of course, was racial. One scholar has concluded that "eleven o'clock on Sunday morning was probably the segregated hour in America," and Fort Robinson was no exception."[42]

The Roman Catholic Brennan offered a more complex array of services than his Protestant predecessors. Weekday morning masses, catechisms, and confessionals became regular features along with Sunday services. The choir of the Crawford Roman Catholic Church helped Father Brennan celebrate at least one Easter high mass. This may have impressed his replacement, Chaplain Alexander Landry, who formed a glee club soon after he arrived in 1911. Brennan and Landry both taught Sunday schools, and Landry also instructed his guardhouse bible class.[43] In the twenty-five years which passed since the chapel was built, a wide variety of programs developed to meet the needs of practicing Christians.

Chapter 11

MEDICAL PROBLEMS AND SERVICES

IN THE YEARS before the Spanish-American War, the Army built its hospitals to last only ten years because longer use saturated them with hospital poisons and made them unfit for occupancy. This doctrine combined with imperfect planning of the size of Robinson medical facilities to produce a long sequence of construction activities on post. The first hospital was built of logs in 1875. An Omaha reporter called it "convenient, well lighted and well ventilated" in 1883, but the Army replaced it on schedule with a frame structure on 1885. From that year through 1909, two completely new ones and an annex were built, while the quartermasters also regularly remodeled older facilities. The Army spent close to $64,000 building and renovating Robinson hospitals. At least once plans were so poorly made that an annex had to be designed less than a year after a building was opened.[1]

An Army medical officer with the title of post surgeon administered the hospital. The surgeon actually worked at two jobs. As a general practitioner he had to treat everything from bullet wounds to gonorrhea. He also served as a public health officer, who regularly inspected post buildings and grounds for sanitation and brought deficiencies to his commander's attention in monthly sanitary reports. The men who filled these jobs showed dedication and ability. Surgeon Walter Reed, by far the best known of all Army doctors, served at Robinson in 1884-1887. Six years after he left,

138

The post hospital.

he joined the first faculty of the Army Medical School. Another Robinson surgeon, Jefferson R. Kean, became the first director of military relief for the Red Cross in 1916.[2]

Civilian doctors known as "contract surgeons" augmented the medical staffs at Army posts as early as 1866. Those men, who served six months on a contract, became important at Fort Robinson during the Cuban and Philippine wars. The Army expanded rapidly in those years, and experienced military doctors seldom remained at interior stations. At the turn of the century the contract paid $150 per month and quarters.[3]

The hospital steward was senior enlisted man at the hospital and a member of the post non-commissioned staff. Until the Army established a corps of contract dental surgeons in 1901, the steward's duties included tooth extraction as well as supervision of the detachment of the Hospital Corps, which was established in 1887 to provide trained enlisted assistants for doctors and stewards.[4] After the turn of the century an Army dentist visited Fort Robinson for two to four weeks each year.

Enlisted members of the Hospital Corps served as nurses and orderlies. Troopers received assignment to hospital duty from line outfits on post. Thus, when the garrison consisted of black cavalrymen and white infantry-

men, as it did in 1885-1894, the Hospital Corps was the only desegregated
unit on post, where the men lived and worked together daily. After the
Eighth Infantry left in 1894, the corps became all black. When the Ninth
went to Cuba in 1898, at least one black corpsman, former post school
teacher Walter Pulpress, remained behind, much to his dismay. He asked
for a transfer to Fort Grant, Arizona, or another Ninth Cavalry station. He
told the Post Surgeon that "he is a colored man and would prefer to serve
with colored men."[5]

Some cooperation with the town on medical matters was crucial for
the post's well-being. The military and civilian communities were physically
too close to each other for anything but close coordination of medical services. But before Crawford was founded, the only medical facility for many
miles was on post, and medical services were among the most significant
forms of aid to early settlers. The nearest civilian doctors lived in Sidney
or the Platte River towns. In addition, a midwife or two lived in what soon
became Dawes County. Mrs. Charles E. Ball, for example, served her
neighbors from a homestead halfway between the sites of Chadron and
Crawford as early as 1885.[6]

Civilians in need of medical attention gained admission to the hospital
only with the approval of the post commander. The best known patient
treated on post was Jules Sandoz in 1884. A mounted patrol found Sandoz,
who had smashed his ankle in a fall into a well, near the wagon road which
connected the fort to Valentine and the east. The troopers took him to the
hospital where surgeon Reed restored health to the man who later fathered
the writer Mari Sandoz.[7]

In the few months after Reed treated Sandoz, the railroad moved toward
the Pine Ridge, and a line of towns—Rushville, Gordon, Hay Springs,
Chadron, and Crawford—followed the laying of track. By the fall of 1886,
when Crawford was about three months old, George A. Meredith, an Ames,
Iowa, physician, had set up a practice in town.[8] Meredith's arrival took some
pressure off of Reed and his successors. But Robinson physicians still took
civilian cases, because their facilities were better than those in town or simply because rural patients came to the fort for help. Civilian employees of
the Army, who worked and sometimes lived on post, also received care.
In addition, the post surgeon had an obligation to treat retired soldiers. Last-
ly, some assistance was based on personal friendships.[9]

Doctor Louis LaGarde, who arrived in late 1896, went to considerable
lengths to maintain good relations with the physicians of Crawford. He invited them all to Fort Robinson to witness a modern hernia operation, which
he performed successfully. He also developed a series of culture tubes for
detection of dyptheria and displayed them at a Crawford drugstore for

the convenience of the local doctors. In early 1898 he entertained members of the regional Pine Ridge Medical Association, who came to Crawford for their annual meeting. The doctors dined at his quarters and returned to town in a military ambulance.[10]

The casual and informal cooperation suggested by these gatherings inevitably proved inadequate. The proximity of the two communities, and particularly the goods and services offered to soldiers in town, created problems that the troops brought back to post. These included a broad range of contagious diseases, from influenza to syphilis, as well as non-communicable but serious problems like narcotics.

Before Crawford was founded, the fort suffered few serious medical problems not directly related to unsanitary facilities. Whooping cough killed two children in 1876, and scarlet fever struck Lieutenant Colonel James Brisbin's family ten years later. Measles and flu broke out on post in 1888 and 1890, respectively.[11]

To that time none of the outbreaks were traced to Crawford. However, some infections apparently came on post from elsewhere. A Ninth Cavalry recruit arrived with measles in 1896, probably from the Cavalry Recruiting Depot near St. Louis, which frequently distributed disease as well as men to installations around the country. After the Cuban war, malaria contracted at Southern camps and in Cuba also came to Dawes County. But Crawford water, described as "notoriously bad" by Surgeon Edward Everts, also became troublesome. Everts thought soldiers who went to town caught malaria from water in Crawford wells. When typhoid broke out in town at the Stockmen's Hotel, Doctor Peter Field warned the garrison to avoid the well near the Crawford Post Office. Three months later, two more cases of typhoid brought a warning against all Crawford drinking water. The city boarded up one well in 1904, but typhoid continued to harass the two communities. After twenty cases were identified in Crawford in 1908, post children went to town schools only when armed with canteens full of water.[12]

When smallpox hit Crawford in late 1900, the city council declared an emergency and imposed a quarantine on affected residences. Doctor Albert Simonton, at the fort, thought the efforts were poorly enforced, and Captain Harry Wilkins closed the post to civilians for about six weeks. More cases were reported in town through the spring and scarlet fever also appeared later in the year. Both diseases continued to trouble Crawford until January 1902.[13]

At that time, military authorities finally established a formal procedure with the town for reporting communicable diseases. After the Dawes County surgeon suggested such an arrangement, Crawford's town council assented to Surgeon Field's proposal, and Doctor Anna M. Cross, the first town physician, alerted Field to all new contagions.[14] Field forwarded these notices to the post commander with his recommendations. Intelligent and rapid action was finally possible, provided local doctors diagnosed their cases promptly and effectively.

Doctor Cross and post physicians worked smoothly together, but other Crawford practitioners caused paroxysms of rage in the post surgeon's office. Doctor J. E. Hartwell examined a child who visited at a ranch near the fort. He diagnosed the problem as chicken pox but gave neither treatment nor instructions. When smallpox appeared on post, Surgeon Field looked at the same child and assessed the ailment as smallpox. George Meredith, the town physician, agreed with Field's diagnosis and the child was removed to the Crawford pesthouse. Field complained of Hartwell's incompetence to the city council. Because of his failure to take proper steps, "this whole post has been exposed in an outrageous manner."[15]

Meredith too was not held in the highest esteem on post. A post medical clerk, on entering a communication from Meredith in his ledger, wrote in the "Name of writer" column: "G. A. Meredith, Quack." Even before these incidents, however, post medical officers held the skills of local doctors in contempt. Surgeon R. C. Fauntleroy, who departed for Cuban service in the spring of 1898, discouraged Captain A. G. Hennissee from offering a contract to any of the local physicians. Hennissee finally offered the job to Doctor Ira Sanderson of Sturgis, South Dakota, who refused it. From Sanderson's rejections and the state of the profession in Dawes County, Hennissee concluded that he "had no hope of being able to make a contract with a competent surgeon here."[16] Relations with Crawford doctors continued to be civil so these opinions probably remained private.

A scarlet fever epidemic in January 1910, struck Crawford and later the fort. Surgeon James Church was among those hospitalized. Both town and post were quarantined and all local schools were closed. A ring of sentries enforced the post's isolation and thwarted at least one Eighth Cavalry trooper's efforts to escape the quarantine. Apparently doctors brought the disease under control before the end of the month.[17]

Epidemic infections visited the area only rarely compared to venereal diseases. At least one soldier was discharged with a chronic condition in sixteen of the thirty-one years from 1875 to 1905. A total of thirty-six sufferers, twenty-seven of whom were black cavalrymen, received medical discharges in the period. The largest numbers released in a single year were seven in 1904 and six in 1898. Statistics on discharges reveal only the worst cases, however. In 1903, for example, only one man had a case serious enough to warrant dismissal from the service, while forty-seven received treatment for fifty-six cases of gonorrhea, syphilis, and chancroids. In seven months of 1902 venereal infections at Robinson cost the Army 2,963 days of duty. In contrast, alcoholism, gunshot and knife wounds, and other injuries during the same period resulted in a loss of only 321 days.[18]

In early 1898 venereal disease became so serious that Lieutenant Colonel John Hamilton focused the garrison's attention on the problem in a general order. Army officers throughout the West normally turned a blind eye to prostitution, but the growing sick list finally made the situation intolerable and forced Hamilton to take notice. Hamilton stated that 160 days had been lost in January due to these infections: nearly sixty percent of all hospital cases stemmed from them. He directed his subordinate commanders to read the order to their men, and advised that "the vicious and faithless should be eliminated from the service."[19]

Colonel Hamilton and Surgeon LaGarde also went to town and complained to the city council. The council's clerk reported that the officers "suggested that some speedy and effective action be taken toward the prevention of the spread of venereal disease." In contrast, the councilmen discussed possibilities by which "the nuisance might be to some extent abated." The Army temporarily solved the problem by reducing the garrison to less than a company, and sending most troops south to prepare for war.[20]

In June 1902, when the garrison again grew to include several hundred men, venereal disease became a major problem once again. Captain Charles Grierson protested the town council's inattention and warned the city fathers that he might take drastic steps. Surgeon Field had recommended that Crawford be placed off limits in the event of a failure to reach an understanding. Grierson knew such a measure "would undoubtedly cause a loss to the merchants and others doing business with the private soldiers of this command." This warning had an effect. In July, the council appointed the first village physician, whose job was examination of prostitutes. Doctor Anna Cross, the wife of a horse dealer and graduate of the New York Eclectic Medical College, received the appointment and became the first woman to serve in any public office in Crawford.[21]

Medical inspections of prostitutes as a solution to the problem of venereal disease was not without precedent. Such practices had been tried in Europe as early as Napoleonic France. In the United States they went as far back as the early 1870s in St. Louis, Missouri, and were the subject of spirited debate at meetings of medical associations in the later decades of the century.[22] But questions of creativity aside, the city thus found a way to keep the whores and the business of the troops while satisfying Grierson's demands for action.

Following the St. Louis model, the council passed the cost of the examinations on to the proprietors of bawdy houses. The city fathers required "all the women who are paying a fine"—virtually a whore tax—to submit to inspection by City Physician Cross. In the first month two carriers of venereal infections were identified and expelled from town. The entire process was enforced by the city marshall through semi-monthly tours of the whore houses to check the certifications held by the residents.[23]

The town's policies, as carried out by Doctor Cross, pleased Surgeon Field. In January 1904, he announced the arrival of an era of safe sex: Robinson was free of incurable gonorrhea and all but one case of syphilis. To assure long-term success, Field proposed an exchange of names of prostitutes and infected men with the town physician, immediate inspection of any woman who was known to have infected a soldier, and her arrest or expulsion from town if she refused treatment by a respectable physician.[24]

Field's hard-headed, no-nonsense approach to the problem contrasted sharply with that of the city physician known to the post medical clerk as "G. A. Meredith, Quack." Meredith's report for March-April 1904, which was published in the *Tribune*, was no less than a paean to Crawford's system of quasi-legal prostitution. He said the physical examinations represented a reform of tremendous significance:

> We cannot possibly estimate the ultimate good our work may have accomplished. The influence of it must spread out far and beyond us. We can only deduce possibilities from results. We have added our mite to the cause of reform that is sweeping over the country for the benefit of all, morally and physically.

Meredith closed his tribute to the modus vivendi established between town, post, and whores by informing the city he would depart for the summer. Therefore, he would not be able to carry on the work of moral redemption.[25]

B. F. Richards became city physician and medical liaison with the fort when Meredith resigned. In early 1903 Richards had opened his Crawford practice in an office above the pharmacy of his brother, R. D. Richards. While physician Richards tried to keep venereal disease within limits tolerable on post, pharmacist Richards sold narcotics to soldiers across the counter of his drugstore. Chaplain William Anderson discovered that some of his men used opium and cocaine only a few months after he arrived. This should not have surprised Anderson. In the first place, the use of drugs, especially of opium, increased in the Army after exposure to them during the Philippine Insurrection of 1898-1902, in which the Tenth had just served before coming to Robinson. Moreover, alcoholism and narcotics were already intrinsic to the miserable lives of frontier prostitutes. Chaplain Anderson complained that Nebraska law did not prohibit trade in what

Colonel Augur called "pernicious drugs." He felt weaponless except for "moral suasion." The Crawford druggist and other citizens promised to prevent the sale of the drugs to troopers, but they did nothing, and given the likely prevalence of narcotics in whorehouses and gambling halls, probably could do nothing. All Anderson could do was lecture on the dangers of narcotics.[26]

Dr. George A. Meredith.

NSHS

As time went on, Chaplain Anderson, who was also a medical doctor himself, grew more fearful that the failure to eliminate the drug traffic would bring "terrible" results. One soldier had shot himself while under the influence of morphine and did not recall the event. Augur's frustration also mounted. He said use of drugs grew and he could not prevent their sale in town. Surgeon Field stated that narcotics presented a major obstacle to his efforts to control venereal disease. He cited a standard case history: "I went into the first saloon in town and don't remember anything after that," a soldier told him. "The fellows who were with me say that we went to most of the houses where women stay and I woke up in one of them." In his final monthly report, Field added "drugged liquors" to cocaine and opium as basic problems. Town officials "repeatedly promised to correct this evil" but failed to do so. Field identified the vendor of cocaine and laudanum over the counter as pharmacist Richards. Captain R. J. Fleming's servant Gertrude, who Field treated in January 1904, had obtained both drugs at Richards' store.[27]

Plainly the sale and use of drugs was not considered the scourge that they later became. In fact, in the United States a wide variety of medicines available over the counter or through the mail contained morphine, cocaine, laudanum, and heroin; and Coca-Cola did not replace the cocaine in its recipe with caffeine until 1903. Cocaine was a popular tonic, highly regarded for its amelioration of sinusitis and hay fever. In this situation, where the medical community was just beginning to recognize the harmful effects of these substances and legislators were starting to restrict and ban their use, the prevalence of drug use on post and in town cannot be determined. However, it is clear that drugs were a part of the problem that faced post doctors and commanders.[28]

Following the trend that was emerging nationwide in the decade before World War I, restrictions were finally imposed on the sale of narcotics, but the trade simply went underground. A man and a woman were arrested in August 1912, for selling cocaine. The latter was a long-time local prostitute who had apparently diversified her operation. Both were fined twenty dollars and costs by a Crawford court and released.[29]

Generally, in the years before World War I, Fort Robinson had both more competent medical personnel and more sophisticated facilities than Crawford. Post doctors found some of their civilian counterparts difficult to deal with and even incompetent. The town itself presented major public health and medical problems for the post. On the other hand, Fort Robinson rendered vital medical services to the civilian settlement in the early years.

Part III

THE
CIVILIAN COMMUNITY

Chapter 12

VETERANS
IN NORTHWESTERN NEBRASKA

WHEN A young man joined the Army he made a significant choice. For whatever reason he may have enlisted, military service usually meant he would be separated from his family for at least three years. For those who selected regiments that were actively engaged against hostile Indians, enlistment also frequently meant a substantial personal risk. But this was not the enlisted soldier's final critical choice. That came when his term expired and he confronted civilian life anew. A few reenlisted rather than face it, but the rest dispersed from posts like Robinson to either return home or try new places.

Some who chose not to go home from Fort Robinson made their homes on the Pine Ridge. Those veterans who stayed in northwestern Nebraska can be conveniently divided into three groups. There was an early group of whites, who served on post during the Indian wars and who appear to have done uniformly well in their adopted homes. The second group, black veterans who left the Army at Robinson between 1886 and 1907, also shared a common destiny, although considerably less prosperous and comfortable than that of the whites who preceded them. Whites who served at the fort after 1907 (and a few who were stationed there in 1898-1902) form a more complex group: some prospered and stayed; others failed and moved on.

Several early residents wore Army blue when they first came to the Pine Ridge. Some troopers homesteaded land near Fort Robinson. Daniel Kline and Henry Kreman, buddies while in the Fifth Cavalry at Robinson, claimed adjoining quarter sections in Sioux County. Kline rose to prominence in county politics but gave up his farm and went to West Virginia before the turn of the century. Kreman lived out his life on his Sioux County farm, as did another Army man, retired Sergeant John McMahon. Biographical information on other early veterans is very limited, but Kreman's daughter-in-law said "many of the soldiers stationed at the fort took homesteads along the river where there was plenty of fuel and water."[1]

At least two other Fifth Cavalry soldiers remained on White River. Martin J. Weber, a first sergeant and veteran of the Ute Campaign of 1879, established a ranch on the stream and later a feed store and elevator in Crawford. Weber served six years as a Sioux County commissioner before he moved to Crawford, where he won election to the city council in 1907. George Uhl, on the other hand, moved to town right away. The ex-sergeant, who had served ten years on the frontier, plied his barber's trade first in Harrison and then in Crawford. He held several minor offices, served two terms as city councilman, and was chief of the Crawford Fire Department for ten years.[2]

All of those men improved their status and accumulated some property. Even Daniel Kline, who went back east, was no exception. He left to perfect and market a milking machine he had invented on his Nebraska farm. Another inventor beat him to a patent, and he may have wished he had remained in Sioux County.[3]

The data regarding these first soldier-settlers has a bias built into it. Those who did not prosper or gave up early probably left no trace of their sojourn in northwestern Nebraska.[4] So caution must be used in generalizing about the opportunities for former soldiers. The careers of Uhl, Weber, and the others do at least show that in the early years some aggressive and able veterans could find respectable and comfortable places in the newly developing region. Northwestern Nebraska offered material comfort and political recognition for those early settlers, all of whom were white.

At least twenty-six African-American soldiers remained in northwestern Nebraska. The small community that they formed was by no means unusual. The Army played a significant role in redistributing the black population cityward and westward. Clusters of black veterans formed in small towns like Havre and Miles City near Montana posts as well as Crawford and Valentine in Nebraska. Other communities of former soldiers developed in larger cities. At the time of the war with Spain, at least six veterans of the Ninth Cavalry's G Troop lived in one Omaha neighborhood.[5]

In the Crawford group, retired Sergeant Simon Franklin of the Ninth's band, a Tennessean, stayed eight years before he moved to Arizona and opened a business near Fort Grant. Data on the remaining twenty-five is spotty but adequate for a general group portrait. Eleven qualified for retirement pay, and four others drew disability pensions. They at least had a basic income. In 1907, for example, a retired sergeant received $30.50 each month. Some, like Sergeant Allen Briggs who retired in 1897 with $168 in savings, also had small nest eggs.[6] A few found menial jobs in and around Crawford, but the two best employers were the Army itself and the Cook family's 0-4 Ranch near Agate Springs in Sioux County.

Veterans found several kinds of work at Fort Robinson. At least five men, including Sergeant Franklin, worked for a time at the post exchange, as cooks, bartenders, or other attendants. Pay was low, but a welcome supplement for those on pensions. In 1893 retired Sergeant Alfred Bradden, like Franklin a Civil War veteran, tended the billiard room for $10 a month, while Franklin received $25 each month as general attendant. Retired Sergeant William Howard earned a meager $5 a month as a laborer, while former soldier Lewis Toliver was paid $15 monthly as the lunch counter cook. Another retiree, Medal of Honor winner John Denny, also worked for a time at the canteen. Of these men, only Toliver did not draw a pension. Sergeant Bradden worked at the exchange for at least six years after his 1893 retirement, and his pay increased to $25 a month by 1899.[7] Most of the others probably lost their jobs in 1898, when troop strength and exchange operations declined precipitously.

Preston Brooks, who had served in the Ninth Cavalry at Forts Leavenworth and Robinson, was an oddity among the black civilian employees at Robinson. As post engineer he held a skilled and responsible position from 1893 to 1904, managing the waterworks and sawmill for $60 a month. He lost his job after severely thrashing a white employee, clerk J. A. Habeggar. Brooks claimed his son, who was being held on charges of theft of the Fort Robinson mail, had been framed by Habeggar and his wife. Perhaps Brooks was right, for his son was never convicted. However, the senior Brooks was fired when charged, though he was never found guilty of assault with intent to kill.[8]

Another black veteran of the Indian wars also worked on post. Caleb Benson, partially blind from an accident which occurred at Robinson, served Twelfth Cavalry officers as a domestic servant after homesteading for a short time. He and his wife Percilla, whom he married on his retirement

Preston Brooks, in the white shirt, shown on his job as post engineer in the pump house.

Tony Burroughs collection

in 1909, lived in Crawford for many years. Benson died there in 1937; his wife survived on his pension until 1966.[9]

At least three other black soldiers worked on the 0-4 Ranch for James Cook and his family. Two of the ex-cavalrymen used their talents as horsemen to get jobs as bronco-busters. Harold Cook called one, known only as Douglas, a competent and strong "big, husky Negro." The other, retired Sergeant John Butler, was "a very good hand with horses" as well as Harold Cook's "devoted friend." Ex-slave and retiree Butler apparently became a favorite of his employer. He earned their gratitude with a forty-mile ride through a blizzard to get a Crawford physician for Harold Cook's mother. His special position may have been partly responsible for the racial prejudice Harold Cook recalled other employees had shown toward Butler. Although the Cooks kept him on after he could no longer perform his work "for sentimental reasons," paternalism had limits and Butler was finally paid off and sent to Crawford to live. The senile old man died shortly after being robbed of his life savings on the way into town.[10]

Another former slave and ex-soldier who worked for the 0-4, Alex Stepney of Anne Arundel County, Maryland, began his military career as a servant for a Confederate officer. Stepney was hired as a bunk-house cook after his 1891 discharge. Later he moved to Crawford and worked as a mail carrier between the fort and railroad depot. He and his wife Fannie, the widow of another Ninth Cavalry soldier, lived in town until his death in 1918.[11]

The Cooks acted shrewdly in hiring both veterans and active duty men on furlough. James Cook and his family maintained excellent relations with post officers—Cook and Surgeon Louis LaGarde were particularly good friends—so they never had to take a chance on an employee without good recommendations from post.[12] Men like Butler, Douglas, and Stepney got good, steady jobs, and their employers obtained skilled, reliable workers.

The few remaining veterans for whom occupational data survives performed various tasks around Crawford. At least two of these former cavalrymen worked with horses, as did the men on the 0-4. George Wilson trained mounts for Dawes County sportsmen until he died at 67. Sandy Tournage drove for a local livery stable until he was gunned down in the spring of 1897, in a crime for which no one was convicted. Henry McClain and Rufus Slaughter tried their hands at farming, while William Howard and his wife hired out as farm laborers in Sioux County after he lost his post exchange job. James Williams opened a short-order restaurant in late 1905, but was unable to keep it open more than a year.[13] There is no job information available for the remaining old soldiers, four of whom did have their retirement stipends.

Preston Brooks was not the only former cavalryman to rise above this pattern of manual labor. Charles Price, a veteran of the Ninth Cavalry, can only be described as the local vice king and something of a legend. He served at Robinson before the Spanish-American war, but apparently came to Crawford from Fort Niobrara. Price operated a "honky tonk with gambling and bootlegging, where one could sin as he wished." After prohibition, he specialized in home-made whisky.[14]

These activities brought him considerable wealth and prominence in Dawes County. He and his wife owned real and personal property valued at $700 in 1912 and $1,000 in 1916. None of the other veterans accumulated estates that even approached that amount. In fact, only ten of the twenty or more veterans who resided in Crawford owned enough property to pay any taxes at all. In 1912, for example, when Charles and Rafella Price were assessed for $700, four others owned Crawford property valued at a combined total of $150.[15]

Only a small number of Afro-American families owned any real property. William Howard and his wife maintained possession of the same lot from 1902 to 1917 and perhaps longer. Alfred and Laura Bradden probably also had a residence on one of their five town lots. By 1917, only William Howard and Charles Price, who owned several parcels of land, and Alex Stepney, who bought a lot in that year, kept their property.[16]

In addition to sharing a similar status in town, most black veterans lived in physical proximity to each other. White Crawford did not formally impose residential segregation on black citizens, but shreds of evidence indicate significant public and private pressures against racial mingling. At least one restaurant advertised itself as "exclusively for white patrons," and blacks could not get haircuts from Crawford barbers. In addition, one prostitute paid her customary fine for what was apparently a double crime, prostitution and "being in company with a Negro on the streets."[17] So it is not surprising that blacks resided together in two clusters, one straddling the railroad track on the town's northwestern margin and the other a five block square east of the tracks in the southern part of Crawford. The lot on which the African Methodist Episcopal (A.M.E.) Church was finally built stood almost in the center of the second group of residences.[18]

The northwestern cluster included three parcels of land owned by Hannah Stephenson. One local source stated that she "became fairly well fixed" renting shacks to black families in the 1890s. She apparently paid less than $100 for each hovel and rented them for between $10 and $15 a month.[19] The pensions of veterans and the monthly pay of privates were both inadequate to pay such fees. Therefore, families or single men must have shared these dwellings. Rufus Slaughter and William Washington, "roommates" for a time in Crawford, could have pooled their incomes to rent a shack from Crawford's only civilian slumlord.[20]

The southern square contained a large number of lots owned by post officers and white members of the non-commissioned staff. These parcels of land included two directly adjacent to and across the street from the African Methodist Episcopal Church. Other officers' lots were next to those of black veterans. These officers had generally comfortable and spacious quarters for their families on post, and they probably purchased the land for use as rental property. Officers who bought town lots in the black sections of Crawford during the early years acted with substantial business acumen. Colonel James Biddle and other commanders to varying degrees imposed severe limits on the number of married enlisted men who could reside on post. Those who were denied quarters on post inevitably went to Crawford, where many probably rented quarters from Captain Corliss or Lieutenants Bettens, Hubert, McAnany, and Surgeon Reed. Although no evidence connects Biddle's harshness toward married men with these military landlords, the policies of one served the economic needs of the others nicely.

While black veterans in Crawford had little in the way of property, only a rigidly material evaluation could lead to the conclusion that they had nothing. They had each other, and lived in a closely knit, mutually supportive community. Those with small resources aided those with nothing; those in good health helped their fellows through sickness. Several examples illustrate this cohesion. Rufus Slaughter, one of the earlier veterans to put down roots in northwestern Nebraska came upon hard times as he aged. Rheumatism plagued him as early as 1889 but became acute after 1900. His wife had divorced him, and he lived in Crawford, first with ex-soldier William Washington and then alone. However, he was not alone when the pain rendered him immobile. For two months in 1904, former soldier Henry Wilson nursed Slaughter through a particularly bad period.[21]

Caleb Benson of the Tenth Cavalry also benefitted from the close ties which bound the men together. While serving at Robinson in 1903, he lost most of his vision. Benson had been cooking for a detachment camped on the timber reserve when the stove blew up in a storm and filled his face with ashes and cinders. After the dust cleared, he could see only dimly out of one eye and not at all from the other. He then received a medical discharge. Three years later, the Army granted the twenty-seven year veteran's plea to be allowed to finish his thirty years for retirement. In the interim, however, he tried unsuccessfully to find employment in Crawford. During this difficult period, men of his former troop provided Benson with financial aid.[22]

Another aged veteran lost his pension in 1918, when he left the government sanitarium in Hot Springs, South Dakota. Benjamin Hartwell, then seventy-five years old, survived on charity for twelve years before his pension was restored. An aged African-American washerwoman who lived near Crawford, probably cavalryman Henry McClain's widow Louisa, provided most of Hartwell's support during this long hiatus. If she was in fact Hartwell's benefactor, she continued a tradition she and her husband had established when they lived together. The McClains supported two adopted children and five of Henry McClain's brothers and sisters on their rented farm. On McClain's death in 1907, the *Tribune* praised "his manhood and integrity" with ample reason.[23]

As these few veterans' case histories show, the bonds forged while on active duty were not broken by discharges and retirements. Other incidents and episodes, which are discussed elsewhere, also underscored the endurance of these ties. The defense of former trooper James Diggs by Sergeant Barney McKay and others in 1893 and the deep desire of Sergeant Israel Valentine's widow to remain on post after her husband's 1892 death also showed that the bonds which held this community together crossed the lines of active service. Soldiers, veterans, wives, and children supported and sustained each other in time of need. The closely knit community probably convinced a good number of the men to stay in Crawford.

In addition to mutual aid and support, the community offered social opportunities beyond the few possibilities among the whites. No blacks ever held political office in Crawford, and very few even set foot inside a white church. Of all the fraternal organizations in town, only the Grand Army of the Republic chapter appears to have admitted African-Americans to membership.[24] So the only opportunities for leadership existed within the small, relatively poor, and informally segregated black community.

Ninth Cavalry soldiers and veterans organized a chapter of the Regular Army and Navy Union in 1895. The John H. Alexander Garrison of the mutual aid association was not the first all-black chapter. Twenty-fifth infantrymen had organized such a club at Fort Custer, Montana, in 1892. The Union probably filled a social void for veterans in two ways. It provided a regular, formal setting through which to sustain relationships with their friends who were still in the service, and served as a burial association. Veterans were assured space in the post cemetery even without the Union, but the organization provided the added assurance that friends would make funeral arrangements for them. Sandy Tournage, who drove for a Crawford stable, was a member, and his fellows laid him to rest after his untimely 1897 death.[25]

The black community had its own social life, which was infrequently covered in the local press. Masquerade balls at various town halls drew soldiers from post as well as civilians. The Tenth Cavalry orchestra furnished music for at least one such occasion. Crawford blacks also held barbecues at the fairgrounds and an annual formal celebration at Firemen's Hall. The only account of these galas indicates that some whites accepted invitations to attend the "Colored Folks Ball," and even danced with black women.[26] This is the only indication outside of Grand Army of the Republic meetings of biracial socializing.

The most significant and most difficult collective activity of the veterans' community was the establishment and organization of a church. A lot was acquired sometime between 1909 and 1912, and a cornerstone laid in June 1912. The building was completed in the autumn of the following year.[27] The time during which the church was established was significant. Up to 1907, when the Tenth Cavalry left, large numbers of black troops and families resided on post. The departing cavalrymen took their social clubs, YMCA, band, and other organizations with them, creating a void that made establishment of a church as a social center a community imperative.

Some whites apparently aided in the establishment of the church, which was called St. Paul's African Methodist Episcopal Church. The first pastor, Mrs. P. M. Maxfield, published a newspaper notice of gratitude. "I wish to thank my white friends," she wrote, "who have so kindly assisted me in building and establishing a church in this city, and also my own people who have worked so faithfully." She promised to "ever kindly remember them." Maxfield, who later served her denomination as a missionary based in Phoenix, Arizona, also ministered to a small congregation in Alliance, southwest of Crawford in Box Butte County. St. Paul's remained in operation at least until 1931.[28]

When the pastor first came to town, she stayed with Louisa McClain. From that time on, the surviving veterans and their wives played prominent roles in sustaining the church. Numerous dinners and socials were held to collect money until the church debt was liquidated in late 1916. The congregation used the home of Sergeant Bradden for a fund-raising social at least once. Sergeant and Mrs. Howard, who held the deed to the lot on which the church stood as trustees, operated a restaurant every Saturday during the autumn of 1916 for the benefit of St. Paul's. In addition, the officers of the "Willing Workers," a women's service club, included at least two veterans' wives. Annie Brooks, the widow of Preston Brooks, served as president, and Anna Beckett, the wife of a former Tenth Cavalry soldier, chaired the ways and means committee.[29] Veterans' families provided much of the leadership and material support needed to create the institution.

The various forms of segregation and discrimination which relegated black veterans to certain kinds of work and residences also ease the historian's burden. These veterans' families did form a more or less discrete and easily identifiable community. Assessment of the careers of white veterans poses different problems. They did not have to create institutions or community life, but merged into the civilian community, advanced through it, or left it for greener pastures. Those who stayed appear to have had little need for a cohesive community. They had fewer problems supporting themselves and hence less need for the mutual aid of other former soldiers. Don Rickey's conclusion that "many energetic, restless soldiers left the Army to pursue personal ambitions" in apparently booming areas of the West summarizes the motives of many white veterans.[30]

The physical mobility of whites who left the Army at Fort Robinson complicates assessment of their post-military careers. Those whites who served on post in 1898-1902 and after 1907 and stayed in northwestern Nebraska did not form communities like the blacks. Nor did they rely on such a limited number of employers. Norbert Frohnapfel, a tailor who left the Army at the end of 1898, first found employment in Cheyenne, Wyoming. Then he moved to Hemingford in Box Butte County. Lack of customers forced him to take work as a clerk in Alliance, where he finally opened his own general store in 1903. Another soldier, T. S. Jones of the Eighth Cavalry band, also went to Alliance, where he organized a band. Within a year, he resigned to lead a traveling show's eight-piece orchestra.[31] Men like Frohnapfel and Jones, who moved from place to place in pursuit of the main chance, make analysis difficult. They also verify Rickey's conclusion. They were indeed "energetic, restless" men with "personal ambitions."

Six of those white veterans at least passed through Crawford. One literally did just that. When last seen, cement-worker A. C. Hollander was running from the local police after forging his employer's name on some checks. Another, former First Cavalry Corporal Edward Bunnell, married the daughter of *Tribune* editor and publisher William Ketcham. Bunnell worked for the Burlington railroad, and also stayed only briefly in Crawford. Between 1901 and 1906 he and his wife lived in Chadron, Alliance, Sheridan, Wyoming, and Sterling, Colorado, as well as Crawford.[32]

The other four apparently found employment with little difficulty. Ralph Gardell left the Twelfth Cavalry in 1912 for a job as clerk with a Crawford clothier. However, it does not appear that he had any intention of staying. Eanes Phillips married a Dawes County woman and found work in William Sherrill's restaurant. A. W. Pifer opened a blacksmith shop in 1909, and stayed at least seven years. The fourth man, Levi Secrist, operated an apparently successful barbershop. He started as an employee in another shop in 1911. Within the year he had his own business and by 1916 he owned his own home. In addition, Secrist and his family occasionally vacationed in Cheyenne and even distant Chicago. He still owned his shop as late as 1930.[33]

Secrist's father-in-law, Benjamin Itskovetch, retired from the Army at Robinson in 1910. He had served as the Eighth Cavalry's quartermaster sergeant. Itskovetch stayed at Robinson until he died in 1946 and supplemented his retirement pay by measuring and reporting the level of the White River to the government each day.[34]

Ordnance Sergeant Christopher O'Brien, who first joined the post noncommissioned staff in 1891, also stayed on post after his 1896 retirement. O'Brien lived in government quarters and worked as postmaster at the fort until he died in 1901. His daughter, Elizabeth Hamilton, took over when he died. A son worked on post as a teamster until his death in 1903.[35]

Only one commissioned officer chose to live in northwestern Nebraska. Carter P. Johnson purchased a homestead in Sioux County soon after he arrived with the Tenth Cavalry. He bought his farm from the estate of John S. Tucker, one of the early White River settlers. Johnson stayed on post until he retired in 1910, and then served again in 1916. All the while he expanded his holdings, on which he began to raise cattle. Major Johnson may have used a standard cattleman's method to increase his acreage, paying others to file for land under the Kincaid Act. Other cattlemen employed soldiers and veterans in this way, for fees ranging from $5 to $150. Johnson is said to have used black families, so it is quite likely he paid soldiers of his own Tenth Cavalry to obtain land for him.[36]

Even while he served with the Tenth, Johnson prospered. In late 1905 he shipped at least three railroad cars of cattle to the Omaha market. He held ranch property in Wyoming as well as Nebraska, and "a beautiful southern type house with large white pillars on Buck Creek north of Glen." Apparently he even allowed his cattle enterprises to interfere with his military duties. In 1903 he drew a reprimand from Colonel Augur for an unauthorized absence from his squadron, which was then on detached service in Wyoming.[37]

There are no indications of any decline in Johnson's fortunes after retirement. In 1914 he sold at auction more farm machinery than most of his neighbors probably owned in a lifetime. In one sale he disposed of three McCormack mowers, a Deere binder, a corn binder, and two Deere gang plows. He also sold twenty-two head of cattle and twelve horses. Two years later he purchased a Ford car, one of the first automobiles on the Pine Ridge.[38]

Major Johnson accumulated much more property than the other veterans who stayed in the region. The earliest veterans who remained found comfort and security in the Crawford vicinity. McMahon's Crawford property reached a valuation of $1,375 before he died, and Weber's went as high as $872. He probably had additional holdings in Dawes and other counties. Uhl never reached this level but owned his home and held local office.[39]

These early settlers and Carter Johnson on one hand and the almost universally poor and isolated blacks on the other represent the limits of the available possibilities. In between, a small number of whites chased opportunity where they thought it existed. Some, like Frohnapfel and Secrist, may have found it on the Pine Ridge. Others were disappointed and tried elsewhere. Generally northwestern Nebraska did not offer abundant opportunity for former soldiers. Whites who came early prospered, but the blacks and most whites who came later did not do nearly as well.

All three groups, diverse as they were, shared an important characteristic. They represented an infinitesimal fraction of the 4,500 soldiers who were honorably discharged at Fort Robinson between 1882 and 1917. The overwhelming majority did not stay in northwestern Nebraska. When they left Fort Robinson they also left the Pine Ridge.

Chapter 13

THE MILITARY IMPACT
ON THE CIVILIAN COMMUNITY

OVER THE YEARS dependence on Fort Robinson influenced the nature of the community of Crawford in several ways. The level of public revenues, local attitudes toward vice, and the image of the community within the state were all determined at least partially by town decisions regarding exploitation of this extremely important source of income. Changes in economic activity in the town, as measured by fluctuations in postal receipts, frequently showed a direct relationship to the Army's expenditures for Robinson.[1] Military support for the local economy took a number of forms, including military and civilian payrolls and contracts for a variety of goods and services, such as forage, wood, and construction.

Crawford did have other sources of income. The small municipality served as a market place for neighboring farmers, though both Chadron and Alliance became more important at an early date. In addition, the Fremont, Elkhorn, & Missouri Valley and Burlington lines employed a few men in town. However, neither the railroads nor local agriculture were prominent sources of revenue. Crawford editors expressed no concern about either, while they frequently fretted over the slightest rumors of declining garrisons.[2] The attitude of the Burlington railroad demonstrated the insignificance of Crawford as both market and railroad center. Only one issue of *The Corn Belt*, the line's monthly magazine which advertised the railroad and the purportedly lush country it served, even mentioned Crawford. The region's sole noteworthy agricultural commodity was the Box Butte County potato crop.[3] Dawes County was a backwater region of little interest to the railroad that served it.

The post made large sums of money available. Some of the currency, such as the garrison payroll, indirectly flowed into the community. Other military money, such as locally let contracts for wood, coal, charcoal, forage, and construction services, entered the local economy directly. Still more funds became available through construction contracts and general purchases made by contractors whose home offices were elsewhere. Even firms located in distant Chicago and Minneapolis probably found it convenient to buy supplies in the vicinity rather than ship them into Dawes County. In all likelihood, these contractors also obtained much of their labor force near post. So the entire available pool of military expenditures had four components: military payroll, civilian payroll, local contracts, and construction contracts.[4]

The distribution of military expenditures in the years 1886-1911, shown in Table 3 at the end of this chapter, strongly favored Crawford. The rest of the northwest corner of Nebraska derived little immediate economic benefit from the military presence. Grain farmers located farther east, particularly in the more settled southeastern quarter of the state near Omaha and Lincoln, won some contracts. Through the entire period the town of Crawford received most of the money that flowed from the post. Comparison of military expenditures and the receipts of the Crawford post office during the years from 1891 to 1905, the only period for which data on both is available, showed the direct relationship between expenditures for the post and local economic activity.[5] Fluctuations in locally spent outlays for Fort Robinson, estimated in Table 2 at the end of the chapter and expressed graphically in Chart 1, were followed by changes in the local economy as measured by the shifts in postal receipts shown in Chart 2. In almost every instance, the town felt the impact of changes in military expenditures one or two years after they took place. For most of the period, the relationship between military expenditures and local economic activity was fairly explicit.

The distribution of local contracts had a significant social and political impact. Over $430,000 in government funds went to 102 bidders during 1887-1911. Eleven individuals received fifty-four percent ($291,000) of this money. Seven of these top eleven contractors served at least one term on the city council, and one held a seat for seven years. The contract outlays

Chart 1. LOCAL ARMY EXPENDITURES, 1889 - 1905

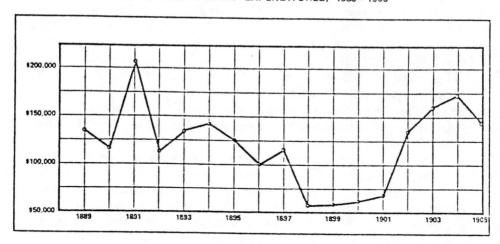

Chart 2. CRAWFORD POST OFFICE RECEIPTS, 1891 - 1905

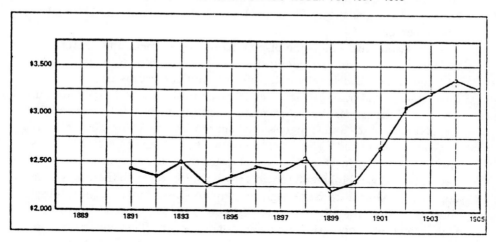

to the top local group both built and sustained political power. John Rowland, his brother-in-law Leroy Hall, and Hall's son Frank, were all in the top eleven, and received contracts totalling over $51,000—nearly ten percent of the total. Their eighteen contracts spanned 1887-1908, and their office-holding 1887-1912. Morgan J. Williams, the leading contractor, built his personal fortune on a series of nine construction contracts, which brought him $89,000, beginning in 1892. He later won election to the city council for five consecutive terms, 1898-1902.[6] Williams' daughter Cora Christina, who wed Lieutenant Herman S. Dilworth of the Tenth Cavalry in 1904, was the only Crawford woman to marry an officer.[7]

Any effort to correlate positions of city councilmen on issues with their economic connection to the post is exceedingly difficult, perhaps impossible. In the first place, city council minutes did not include records of debates. Moreover, the vast majority of councilmen depended on the post for their prosperity, a condition which mirrored that of the community at large. Sixty-four percent of the 159 full or partial yearly council seats held from 1886 to 1912 were occupied by retail merchants, tavernkeepers, and contractors who did over $3,000 in post business during their careers. Of the councilmen whose occupations are known, this group is an even higher eighty percent.[8]

The economic well-being of merchants, saloonmen, and contractors depended on two military conditions. The fort had to be fully garrisoned, and the troops had to have free and convenient access to the town's businesses. Local businessmen exerted no control over the first condition. The size of the garrison and construction activity on post depended on War Department policy and Congressional appropriations. On the other hand, Crawford leaders had a great deal to say about the terms on which soldiers spent their money in town. The lack of restrictions on prostitution, alcohol, narcotics, and gambling represented a town choice to which there was little opposition. Almost from the beginning the town systematically exploited those activities for public revenue. Taxes on saloon owners and prostitutes, which sometimes comprised over one half of the annual tax collection, supported local schools and paid for law enforcement. However, disputes over these activities eventually broke out when Crawford lost its bid to attract a state normal school to town. This failure may have destroyed local hopes of ever growing much beyond village status. It also marked the beginning of explosive political divisions and heightened voter interest, as the community wrestled with decisions regarding its social and economic structure.

The city council saw the liquor trade's potential for public revenue and levied the first occupational tax on saloonkeepers in the late summer of 1886.[9] Over the next three decades, until state-wide prohibition in 1916, the small municipality extracted a large portion of its revenue from taxes on saloons. This source of income depended on the continued success of the taverns, which in turn relied on the size and drinking habits of the garrison at Fort Robinson as well as Army policy regarding temperance and canteens.

The state of Nebraska permitted small cities and villages to establish their own license procedures and fees. The only restriction, obligatory annual re-issue of these permits, encouraged flexibility in rates. Crawford and other towns could regularly revise the levy to fit economic conditions and municipal needs. State law also permitted a tax on occupations and businesses as well as the saloon license fee. And Crawford extracted both the occupation tax on saloonkeeping and the license fee.[10] From the outset, the lucrative military market promised substantial public revenue through support of local taverns. The United States government had already rendered significant aid in 1881 by prohibiting the sale of spirits on Army posts.[11]

The thirty-dollar occupation tax of 1886, enacted in mid-year just after the town was founded, was supplemented by an additional $500 license levy in 1888. Moreover, the enactment explicitly designated the license fee to support "the common schools of the school district of the village of Crawford."[12] The village plainly intended to make the soldiers who frequented local taverns pay for the school system. This tax remained at $500 through 1912 and brought over $56,000 into the city treasury. The occupation tax, which rose to $1,000 in 1910, brought an additional $33,000 into the general fund. The annual collection, shown in Table 4 at the end of the chapter, varied considerably, and school officials may have experienced periodic droughts as well as surpluses, but in all likelihood the arrangement worked fairly well for Crawford. In fact, the annual sums collected for schools at times exceeded the need. City fathers then used the money for other purposes, such as the purchase of a hook and ladder truck for the fire department.[13]

The tie between the revenues extracted from saloons and the size of the garrison on post grew to be fairly explicit. Generally, the size of municipal receipts increased with troop strength. Thus, for example, during the period of the Spanish-American and Philippine wars the city took in $2,900 in 1897, the last full year of the Ninth's tour at Robinson, and $3,800 in 1902, the year the Tenth Cavalry arrived. In the four intervening years, revenue declined to $1,800. The saloonkeepers understood the fluctuations quite well. The spring of 1902 found them refurbishing and improving their places of business in expectation of the impending boom. One of them, Henry Armstrong, painted his saloon in "bright and dazzling colors," and installed a "handsome bar and fixtures."[14]

Crawford's volunteer firemen in 1892, before saloon revenues enabled the town to add a hook-and-ladder truck to its equipment. *NSHS*

The prize Crawford failed to win: the normal school at Chadron. *NSHS*

There were several exceptions to this rule over the years from 1887 to 1912, some of which can be tentatively explained. From 1888 to 1889, tax receipts almost doubled while the garrison remained nearly unchanged. The unusual increase in revenue may have been due to the closing of Colonel Edward Hatch's post canteen which operated for five months during 1888. Before the War Department ordered Hatch to close the facility, it provided a convenient alternative to town saloons and probably cut into their business. In other years deviations between the size of the garrison and saloon revenues occurred for different reasons. In 1905-1906, when the garrison declined but revenues increased, the significant factor may have been the approval of prohibition ordinances in Rushville and Hay Springs during the latter year.[15]

Changes in the racial composition of the garrison may have caused some of the more substantial deviations from the direct relationship between the size of the garrison and saloon revenues. Black soldiers, generally known to be more temperate than whites, may not have patronized the taverns as heavily as equal numbers of whites.[16] In 1897-1898 the decline in revenues was much smaller than the large reduction in troops might have warranted, perhaps because early in 1898 units of the white Sixth joined the Ninth Cavalry and the white First replaced both later in the year. Similarly, the replacement of the black Tenth Cavalry by a smaller number of Eighth Cavalrymen in 1907 was accompanied by an increase in saloon revenues.

Data for years in which nearly equal numbers of white and black troops resided on post yields similar results. In 1904, when Robinson was occupied by 563 black soldiers, saloon revenues were $3,400. In 1909 and 1912, a similar number of white cavalrymen resided at the fort and saloon revenues were $4,833 and $4,500 respectively. It is also possible that the pay increase of 1908 was responsible for the upsurge of spending in local taverns during the Eighth Cavalry's tour of duty.

While there are no ledgers available for the taverns, the evidence suggests that their proprietors accumulated substantial wealth and achieved considerable status in the community. John Bruer, a German immigrant's son who operated saloons in town for eleven years, sent his son on at least a second "annual tour of the United States and several other countries." Another saloonkeeper of German origin, James Hogle, ran a tavern for thirteen consecutive years, and rose to local prominence as president of the Crawford Eastern Star chapter. His daughter married a town dentist.[17] Some also achieved status in town politics. Bruer served three terms on the city council, George Barngrover was elected to four, and two others served one term each.

The profits of saloonmen and local tax revenues were probably enhanced by successful temperance drives in some nearby towns. Gordon, about sixty miles east of Crawford, voted for prohibition in 1889. When Rushville and Hay Springs followed in 1906, all of Sheridan County went dry. Alliance also prohibited intoxicants for some years but reversed itself in 1909. Chadron and Crawford, on the other hand, rejected prohibition in the same year. Nevertheless, the *Tribune* said in 1916 that state-wide prohibition was favored by an "overwhelming majority" except in Omaha, the largest and consequently most sinful community in Nebraska. John Barleycorn may have died "without much fuss or formality," but this probably depended on fortuitous circumstances. In 1913 troops on post went to Colorado to break a strike. Shortly afterward, practically the whole garrison was transferred to the Mexican border, where the men remained until American entry into World War I. Meanwhile, the city's property tax rate rose sharply from thirty-one to forty-eight mills in 1912-1916.[18] So the financial adjustments necessitated by the loss of saloon revenues were made when the troops pulled out, not when Nebraska went dry.

Crawford had a temperance movement of its own, but it was never strong enough to exert substantial political pressure. The only recorded Women's Christian Temperance Union activity before 1910 was establishment of a reading room. An Anti-Saloon League chapter also operated for at least a short time in the early twentieth century. Even some ministers of the local Methodist Church were soft on Demon Rum, although occasional acts of terrorism perpetrated by saloonmen and their allies may have influenced the clergy and other citizens.[19]

Temperance groups did rather carefully screen saloon licenses. Occasionally they protested issuance of permits to people they considered unsavory. In 1892 they successfully opposed the licensing of H. Newcomb, but he obtained his permit in eight other years. Seven years later a group of petitioners led by the minister of the Congregational Church, H. V. Rominger, forced the saloons to close for one day. The *Tribune* was furious, and called Rominger "a non-taxpaying itinerant, who has no interest here whatever except to stir up discord, which he does under the cloak of 'holiness.' " Under a new leader, Water Commissioner Samuel Stuart, the protestors soon withdrew their complaints on promise of stricter observance of laws requiring Sunday closure, the prohibition of minor patrons in the taverns, and full exposure of saloon interiors to public observation.[20] This challenge to saloons, perhaps made possible by the substantial decline in business during the Spanish War, might have served notice of the divisive possibilities of a protracted fight on the issue. The *Tribune*'s rhetoric painted a picture of a mad man and his cohorts seeking to sow disharmony rather than merely close four barrooms.

For nearly a decade after the Rominger affair, the community's moral guardians focused their energy on the Stuart petition reforms. Citizens also protested the presence of prostitutes in the bars.[21] With the exception of these few complaints, only an occasional violent incident indicated that saloons might be a nuisance.[22]

Marshal Joe Hand blamed the black troops for the violence, and most of Crawford probably agreed. Another old-time resident recalled that the community viewed the troops with hostility, but that local animosity was not racially motivated. Rather, local citizens identified the black soldiers with the town's saloons, gambling tables, and whorehouses.[23] Such conclusions were inevitable: from the founding of Crawford in 1886 to the departure of the Tenth Cavalry in 1907, the military garrison was overwhelmingly black.

Community decisions on attracting soldiers through institutionalized vice appear to have been based largely upon judgments concerning the exploitation of a black garrison. The evidence in support of this claim is tenuous and circumstantial but suggestive. In the first place, the Rominger protest of 1899 occurred not only in a period of declining troop strength but shortly after replacement of the black Ninth by white cavalrymen. This abortive effort to impose a new morality was not followed by another until 1907, the year another black regiment ended a five-year tour of duty on post. A month after the Tenth left and the white Eighth arrived, the *Tribune* discerned a "new order of things . . . both at Crawford and Fort Robinson." The "new order" on post referred to the arrival of the white cavalrymen. The "new order" in town began to manifest itself a month later when the town council approved a citizens' petition for the abolition of prostitution but did not crystallize until 1910, when the town lost its bid for a new state normal school. In addition, a series of prosecutions for gambling, the first since games of chance were banned in 1903, began in the fall of 1907. Even saloonkeeper and councilman Bruer paid a ten-dollar fine after pleading guilty to a gambling charge. Some of the penalties meted out in Chadron in 1910 reached $100 and costs. Prohibition of prostitution and punishment of gambling infractions may have only coincidentally taken place after departure of the black troops but no other reasons for taking these steps in 1907 can be adduced.[24]

Until 1907 town policy systematized, exploited, and encouraged harlotry. This pattern emerged mere months after establishment of the town. The town fathers used vagrancy, the "all-purpose violation [that] covered all sorts of minor offences," as Anne Butler characterized the misdemeanor in her book on frontier prostitutes, as the basis for this system.[25] In December 1886, prostitutes were classified as vagrants and so made liable to a fine. In March of the following year, city council instructed Marshal N. S. Jackson to collect five dollars from each vagrant. Two months later, council directed Jackson to compile a list of all "sporting women," collect five dollars every month from each, and pay the total into the city treasury. This policy of making the vagrancy ordinance the basis for regular collections from the prostitutes was not new. It had already been tried and found remunerative in many western towns, as early as 1868 in Cheyenne, Wyoming. The fines authorized by Ordinance Six amounted to a whore tax, rather than a penalty for criminality.[26]

Periodically the town marshal brought his collections of the tax to the city council. In keeping with the prevalent mode of discourse in discussions of prostitution, euphemism dominated the rhetoric of collection of the whore tax.[27] Monies were referred to as fines, and later as donations. When Marshal Messenger turned in $313 in donations for one-third of 1904, the Tribune approved the sum as "a pretty good showing."[28]

The allocation of funds accumulated in this manner is not clear. School superintendent Jeanette Meredith made a bid for the money in 1894, but there is no indication that the council approved her request. A December 1895, resolution directing the marshal to "pay himself by collecting donations from the prostitutes" died in council for lack of a second. A month later, however, such an arrangement was approved: the "donations" would go into a special fund out of which the city would pay the law officer.[29]

In some years the city treasury received substantial amounts from the whore tax. The available evidence on collections, tabulated in Table 1, indicates that the town tapped a source of revenue less lucrative than the saloons but still significant. If the tax was collected every month, the total would have been substantial indeed, particularly in relation to total receipts. In 1906 the large collection combined with $4,250 in tavern fees to yield nearly $6,000 in municipal revenues. Total city receipts for the year were only $9,515.41, so saloons and prostitutes accounted for over sixty percent of local revenue in that year.[30]

Efforts to control prostitution centered on keeping the women out of residential areas and saloons. The motive for the periodic harassment of prostitutes was clearly stated in a petition signed by "numerous citizens." They asked council to force all "lewd women" into residences in the same portion of town, where they would not be "an annoyance to respectable families."[31] Apparently efforts to create a discrete red light district were successful. By the last months of the Tenth Cavalry's tour on post, an area in the west end was identified as the home of prostitution and other vices.[32] This part of town was convenient to the post and occupied undesirable real estate near the railroad tracks.

Pressure from Fort Robinson in 1902 forced Crawford to alter its relationship with the prostitutes. Captain Charles Grierson, alarmed by the number of cases of venereal disease on post, threatened a military boycott of local businesses if corrective measures were not taken. The town responded with a program of physical examinations for the women, which was enforced by the marshal. This arrangement escalated the town's involvement in the enterprise and may have stimulated business significantly. Arrests surpassed previous records, perhaps indicating that more women engaged in prostitution than in earlier years. The city of Crawford may have created boom conditions by removing the fear of venereal disease from the minds of potential patrons.

The boom ended after the Tenth Cavalry departed. The city council passed Ordinance 114, banning prostitution, on July 16, 1907. In the autumn the mayor and county attorney jointly notified keepers and residents of bawdy houses of their intention to enforce the new morality. Thereafter, arrests decreased as prostitution either declined temporarily or went underground.[33]

By 1909 violation of the law became common knowledge. The *Tribune* reminded its readers that "houses of ill repute are . . . too plentiful in our city," and demanded a prompt end to the business. Almost a year later, Post Surgeon James Church counted six cases of venereal ailments in two months. More significantly, Church claimed that the city physician still examined and certified prostitutes. So three years after the passage of Ordinance 114, city officials maintained—perhaps surreptitiously—the old system of supervised prostitution.[34] The ban amounted merely to a final victory for those who wished to hide prostitution from the respectable citizenry.

Until 1910 vice did not generate visible tensions. The *Tribune* and occasional competitors for the town's small readership devoted their energy to boosting rather than muckraking. City council also systematically excluded evidence of bickering from its records. An informally established but effective policy kept records of debates on citizens' petitions for closure of saloons off of the books. There may in fact have been little strain for the papers and town council to hide. In most years municipal elections were tranquil affairs. Local political groups did not identify with national parties but called themselves "Independents," or "Citizens' Caucus." In 1894 the "Independents" and the "Peoples" ticket both ran saloonman George Barngrover for council. Three years later, the Citizens' Caucus celebrated their sweep of offices by dining with the very rascals they had displaced. In 1898, when the "good substantial citizens" of the Citizens' Caucus won without opposition, only fifty-nine voters went to the polls.

In the following year all council members kept their seats in an election described as "about the quietest ever held in the city." This "instance of the level-headedness of Crawford citizens," in which only forty-four bothered to vote, was followed by still another unopposed victory in 1900.[35]

While the local newspapers occasionally commented favorably on the reasonableness or respectability of a favorite candidate, town journalists made no effort to delineate issues. Taxes were low and, while no public resolutions of thanks were ever tendered to whores, saloonkeepers, and soldiers, everyone probably knew why. In addition only one dispute of any significance enlivened Crawford politics in the first two decades. A conflict over water rights between two powerful local political figures, Leroy Hall and Charles Grable, almost split the town into opposing camps. The *Tribune* identified Hall with "the has-beens of the village," and supported Grable and his irrigation scheme. Grable and his brother, an Omaha-based promoter, repaid their Crawford backers by going bankrupt and taking their State Bank of Crawford into oblivion with their personal fortunes.[36]

The only other dispute of any moment centered on the Rominger petition. No factions developed over prostitution or narcotics, although the availability of drugs troubled post officials greatly. Gambling also generated very little political interest. Prohibition of games of chance came almost effortlessly in 1903, to the delight of Chaplain William Anderson at Fort Robinson.[37] The ban on prostitution and gambling prosecutions also took place in a tranquil political atmosphere. The local consensus seemed almost impervious to issues related to vice.

In 1910 Crawford experienced a major political upheaval after it lost its bid to become the site of a state normal school. Crawford competed with Valentine and three panhandle towns, Alliance, Chadron, and Scottsbluff, in boasting of ideal locations and moral purity. While the State Normal Board inspected Chadron, Crawford, and Alliance, Crawford leaders supplemented newspaper advertisements by sending saloonman Bruer and Paris Cooper, shortly to be elected mayor, to lobby for the school in Lincoln. The *Tribune* recited Crawford's many advantages: railroad connections, White River fishing, scenery, and the town park all added to the fact that Crawford was "a town of churches, which would furnish moral tone to those so inclined." Troubled by a Lincoln paper's allegations that vice still flourished in Crawford, the editor said that public morality had improved considerably in recent years, and that Crawford was a "wide-awake, progressive town." In fact, rejection of Crawford because of the proximity of Fort Robinson would be foolish. Crawford's rivals were all railroad towns and therefore even wilder. Moreover, students at a Crawford normal would derive extra benefits through observation of military life and tactics at the post.

In addition to this newly discovered asset, Crawford boasted a Chautauqua and many churches.[38]

When Chadron won the school, the *Tribune* initially attributed the defeat to poor leadership in the campaign. Others believed that the proximity of the post was the vital factor in the State Normal Board's decision. However, Crawford's problem was more complex than that. An oldtime resident recalled that "Chadron had the railroad men and they were just as rough as the soldiers." To this citizen, the big difference was Crawford's substantial black population, which resulted from many years of black garrisons at Robinson. So the presence of the post combined with the resultant black civilian community and local vice discouraged the Normal Board.[39]

Loss of the Normal School ruined any hope the town might have had for growth beyond village status. Reflections on this bitter defeat and Crawford's persistent reputation as "the stink pot of Northwest Nebraska" brought on a crusade against vice which shattered the long-standing political consensus and generated deep divisions in the town. Soon after announcement of the school decision, the county sheriff arrested owners of twelve brothels, and Mayor Cooper himself was charged with ownership of one house as well as accepting blackmail to protect tavernkeepers from the law. Members of city council were also arrested for taking bribes to allow bawdy houses to operate. The habitual tranquility of local politics was shattered, and two parties began to develop. One, whose spokesman was the *Tribune*, embarked on a "crusade against vice." The other, whose views were articulated by the *Courier*, called the holy war a "black political plot."[40]

The sensational prosecutions were initiated by the newly created "Civic League." M. L. Birney, a prominent Methodist layman whose wife was vice president of the Dawes-Sioux County Women's Christian Temperance Union, led the group. The *Tribune*, which had attacked Reverend Rominger's efforts to close saloons in 1899 and had labeled the minister an outside agitator, supported the Birney crusade. The newspaper claimed to favor righteousness, justice, and equality in government. The editor believed the time was ripe for a clean-up.[41]

Two saloonmen, including Councilman Bruer, were singled out as violators of law and morality. City council initially refused to meet for consideration of demands to close their establishments, but was finally forced to act by a writ of mandamus. The city fathers, including Bruer, then unanimously revoked the two licenses.[42]

Meanwhile the case of the State of Nebraska versus P. G. Cooper opened in Chadron. Cooper was fined $100 and costs for ownership of one of the Crawford whorehouses. A week later, amid great community interest, he,

Bruer, and the other members of the city administration stood for re-election. While only forty-four had cast ballots ten years previously, over three hundred people turned out. The results reflected a deep split within the community. Two candidates from the Cooper slate, Bruer and Jones, retained their council seats. One member of the reform group, *Tribune* editor Conrad Lindeman, also won a seat. The fourth councilman, George L. Thorp, had won a two-year term in 1909. In spite of his failure to secure the normal school and conviction for owning a house of ill fame, Mayor Cooper won exactly half of the mayoral votes in his contest with pioneer resident Leroy Hall. A recount by a Rushville judge, to which both candidates agreed, gave Cooper another term. The reformers suffered a narrow defeat in their campaign for control of town government.[43]

Battle lines formed immediately in the new council. Thorp joined Lindeman in support of an ordinance doubling the $500 occupation tax on saloonkeepers. Bruer and Jones opposed the increase, and Mayor Cooper cast the tie-breaking vote to defeat it. Three days later public protests forced the councilmen to reverse their decision, which they did without dissent. They also limited saloon licenses to four. When applicants sought the permits, John Bruer was not among them.[44]

On May 20, 1910, a second wave of scandal broke. Raids disclosed five clubs that operated gaming tables and served liquor in violation of city law. Within a week, Cooper, Bruer, and Jones resigned, ending the short, tense confrontation with the reformers.[45]

In the election of 1911 reformers faced another contest for domination of the council. The Progressive caucus, chaired by Civic League President Birney, ran candidates for all four council seats. Lindeman and Thorp lost bids for re-election but the other two won. The Progressive candidate for mayor, Warren Acker, lost to lawyer Justin Porter. The total votes cast equalled those of 1910, but the margin was forty ballots.[46]

The men who defeated Lindeman and Thorp apparently favored a relaxation of laws against prostitution, so that Crawford might recover the post trade from Alliance and Chadron. Alliance had repealed prohibition in 1909, perhaps in an effort to lure the soldiers to town. Real estate promoter Arah Hungerford and hotelkeeper Charles Leithoff saw the restrictions on vice as restraints on business, and their victories suggest that many agreed. Before the election editor Lindeman railed against this view. He printed a letter from an angry resident, Charles B. Smith, which castigated the Porter ticket for efforts to lure the troopers with degrading activities while refusing to invite soldiers to parties, dances, and other social functions. A hint of recognition of the origins of the town's semi-public system of prostitution crept into Smith's letter, which closed with a plea that the soldiers be treated "more like white people." Editor Lindeman stated that vice was both a divisive issue and a restraint on economic growth. He acknowledged that reform might cost the town some business for a time but hoped that an improved moral climate would ultimately boost development. Lindeman accused mayoral candidate Porter of evading property taxes and of joint ownership of a bawdy house with John Bruer. The editor also claimed that the Canadian-born Porter was still a British subject, but this xenophobic appeal failed. Even reminders of the very recent normal school debacle and Crawford's reputation as "the stink pot of Northwest Nebraska" did not deter the electorate.[47]

Porter survived the *Tribune*'s allegations and served a full term as mayor. Bruer recovered his saloon license, and business went on as usual. Council treated no controversial issues during the year, but all incumbents, including Mayor Porter, were defeated in 1912. In future elections, the issues and tensions generated by soldier-supported vice became moot. Duty in the Colorado mine strike and on the Mexican border brought sharp reductions in the garrison, until it shrank to fourteen men and one officer at the end of 1916.

The elections of 1910 and 1911 focused the community's attention on problems which had developed out of the long dependence on Fort Robinson. Public and private decisions as to how the trade of largely African-American garrisons would be exploited tied municipal revenues to the size of the garrison and committed the town to semi-public prostitution. Efforts to alter this pattern came too late and were too half-hearted to have an impact when the normal school was established. Loss of the institution doomed Crawford to village status and marked the beginning of a period of explosive political divisions and heightened voter interest, as the community wrestled with decisions regarding its social and economic structure. Although the statewide ban on prostitution in 1911, the decline of the garrison on post, and prohibition in Nebraska all diminished the importance of the political struggles of 1910 and 1911, the debates of those years were very important when they took place. Unfortunately, the reticence of city council and the lack of one newspaper's files makes a full exposition of these disputes impossible. Nevertheless, it is clear that the arrangements developed over time to deal with Fort Robinson failed and that these same arrangements doomed Crawford's one opportunity to lure a stable and respectable institution to replace or supplement the post as a source of sustenance.

Despite the town's gross miscalculation of the best way to turn the post to municipal advantage, Fort Robinson's diverse overall impact on the development of the Pine Ridge was positive as well as significant. Before the first ranchers and town promoters came to the area, soldiers from Robinson participated in the subjugation of the Sioux and Cheyenne Indians. When whites began to trickle into the area, the number of services provided by the garrison multiplied. At least six men who arrived in 1887 or earlier worked on post, and many others probably laid adobe bricks in the construction years of 1887-1889.[48] Several early residents also found employment on post with trader Paddock. In addition, some families depended on Robinson troopers and mess halls as markets for buttermilk and garden vegetables. As the only stable source of income on the Pine Ridge, the fort played a crucial role in early settlement, particularly because the post construction boom of 1887-1889 coincided with the settlement of Dawes, Sioux, and Box Butte counties.

Fort Robinson also gave early settlers protection against the Indians. The threats perceived by these civilians were mostly illusory but nevertheless had to be taken seriously. Those who were troubled by rumors of war needed the military presence to allay their fears and stiffen their determination.

The influence of the post was not limited to the provision of protection, jobs, and a market for farmers. Fort Robinson's location also determined the routes and intersection of the railroads that passed through the Pine Ridge. In addition, the fort housed the only doctor in the vicinity during the years of settlement. With the exception of post trader Paddock, whose high prices forced some struggling pioneers to travel long distances for supplies, Fort Robinson aided and encouraged settlement of the Pine Ridge by its very presence.

This support of settlement and new communities represented a large public investment in northwestern Nebraska. This investment had significant characteristics which set it apart from privately financed activities. In the first place, fluctuations came primarily because of military exigencies, rather than business considerations. In addition, these outlays represented a large westward flow of money. Even if construction contracts are considered according to place of award rather than as local outlays, the bulk of the money spent on Robinson during the years from 1877 to 1911—over 87 percent—was disbursed in Nebraska. Thus, while private capital tended to generate profits for eastern owners, public investment—at least in this case— tended to create profits which moved in the opposite direction.[49]

Although the outlays for Fort Robinson had little immediate significance outside the Pine Ridge, such public investment acquired much larger importance when multiplied by the many instances in which it took place and when viewed over the great length of time over which it occurred.

Moreover, this phenomenon remains important today. As the twentieth century nears its end, construction and other projects financed by the national government still bring highly significant infusions of money to western communities that may have inadequate sources of other income.[50] As historian Gerald Nash has written, "to a considerable extent . . . the West was a creature of the federal government, and this dependence did not lessen during the course of the twentieth century."[51]

Clusters of settlement began near many western posts. Fort Concho, Texas, begot San Angelo, and Fort Assiniboine, Montana, spawned Havre. Numerous other examples of this pattern might easily be marshalled for virtually every state west of the Mississippi. While Crawford may not have been typical of the many towns near post in all its responses to the military presence, the conditions to which the community had to respond were probably common. Enlisted men sought entertainment, officers looked for investment opportunities, townspeople needed jobs, the Army wanted contractors, and the town as a whole required a basis of support and—for a time—protection. A parasitic relationship evolved quite naturally out of these diverse needs. The same general type of symbiosis probably developed wherever the Army was the only large enterprise in a community. Even in much larger and more complex cities, this kind of arrangement developed. Cheyenne, Wyoming, with state government and a large Union Pacific maintenance operation to supplement Fort D. A. Russell, still relied on the Army. As a city paper observed in 1909, "Fort Russell's relationship to the substantiality and prosperity of Cheyenne is so close that it may be accounted vital."[52]

For many years Fort Robinson was the sole support for Crawford. Other western towns experienced different degrees of a similar dependence, so the phenomenon of civilian community as military dependent was not unusual. The condition had far-reaching effects on the community. The source and level of public funds, local attitudes toward vice, the class structure, and even the availability of socially acceptable opportunities for mobility among women all depended in large measure on decisions made outside the community.

Perhaps no single phenomenon more dramatically illustrates the community's vulnerability to outside forces than the fluctuation in the number of marriages between local women and soldiers. For many years the racial composition of the garrison limited this obvious path to mobility for Crawford's young women. After the Eighth Cavalry arrived and a decent interval for courtship passed, marriages became frequent occurrences. While only four weddings took place before 1909, seventeen were celebrated between 1909 and 1914. Moreover, none of the couples remained in Crawford.

They either stayed in the Army or settled elsewhere.[53] It seems almost as if the long tenure of black cavalry on post had turned Crawford into a prison for young women in quest of a socially acceptable way out. The Eighth Cavalry quite literally came to their rescue.

Life on post, for the white troopers of the Eighth and the blacks who preceded them, closely resembled life in a company town. The four basic characteristics of the typical western company town, noted by James Allen in his book, *The Company Town in the American West*, were certainly present at Fort Robinson: a community hall, uniform and modest housing, a rectangular layout, and domination by a single company—in this case the Army.[54]

More important than the physical similarities was the centralization of power in both the company town and the military post. The War Department through the post commander and the corporate board of directors through its local manager determined housing policies, distributed services, and otherwise controlled the daily operation of the community.

The paternalism that was inherent in such an arrangement did not discourage efforts of soldiers to improve their lives. They pooled their resources to buy books, lamp fuel, tableware, and recreational equipment. They also established social and educational organizations, among which the Tenth Cavalry's Y.M.C.A. was most significant. Life in the military version of the company town did not inhibit the exercise of initiative among the soldiers.

Conditions on post may have been somewhat better for privates than they were for civilian laborers in company towns or elsewhere. Surgeon Jefferson Kean believed the rate of sickness among the families of enlisted men was "certainly much less than among the people of their station in life in the small frontier towns, as for example Crawford near this post." Kean's colleague, Doctor George Adair, added that soldiers were also "financially superior to the civil laborer who receives a dollar and a quarter a day," probably because the private could use the facilities and services on post. This was surely true for the blacks: Chaplain George Prioleau of the Ninth Cavalry said that few black school teachers made as much money as the soldiers. In addition, the military diet was probably superior to that available to civilians. According to the post surgeon's 1893 "just presentation of the ordinary fare of the soldier," each man consumed approximately 400 pounds of meat a year, as well as the grains and dried vegetables in the ration, produce from the post garden, and locally purchased fresh milk. While Department of Agriculture data on per capita food consumption only goes back to 1899 and does not cover all dietary components, in that year meat consumption averaged 150 pounds, which was less than half the amount eaten by soldiers in the Robinson dining halls during 1893.[55]

Housing was one area where Fort Robinson conspicuously lagged behind civilian company towns. There were certain similarities. The size and elaborateness of quarters varied with the status of the occupant, and members of the community were assigned residences by the post commander. However, some enlisted families resided in extreme congestion and squalor on Laundresses Row or in abandoned buildings. Surgeon Kean acknowledged that these conditions caused numerous morale and sanitation problems. He advocated the erection of small tenements or cottages, similar to the rows of neat, plain homes in western company towns, for re-enlisted soldiers and their families. Had his suggestion for improvement been adopted, it would have made the resemblance between the post and a company town even clearer.[56]

The basic difference between the military post and company town was functional. The privately owned town was designed to generate profits, usually for absentee owners. Fort Robinson, on the other hand, was a public institution which represented a complex investment in the area in which it was located. Fort Robinson and the soldiers and officers of its garrison cleared the Pine Ridge for settlement, then protected residents and provided them employment, important services, and economic support. In many ways, Fort Robinson provided the strong and stable base for Anglo-American society on the Pine Ridge.

Table 1. The Whore Tax, 1888-1907. Figures in ( ) indicate number of months for which data is available.[57]

Year	Amount
1888	$ 90 (4)
1890	50 (2)
1897	102 (5)
1899	32 (2)
1902	226 (unk)
1903	326 (unk)
1904	425 (12)
1905	772 (6)
1906	1,633 (11)
1907	1,038 (6)

Table 2. Military Expenditures Available for Local Consumption, 1886-1911
(in thousands of dollars).

Year	Military Pay[58]	Civilian Pay[59]	Local Contracts[60]	Construction Contracts	Total
1886	41	4	0	3	48
1887	72	4	6	55	137
1888	90	4	3	1	98
1889	94	6	23	12	135
1890	83	8	20	3	114
1891	94	9	27	78	208
1892	82	7	18	1	108
1893	112	6	17	1	136
1894	107	6	29	0	142
1895	94	7	22	3	126
1896	84	6	7	2	99
1897	92	6	10	7	115
1898	42	6	5	0	53
1899	39	10	7	0	56
1900	28	9	11	11	59
1901	31	9	3	26	69
1902	100	9	18	9	136
1903	112	9	17	22	161
1904	119	6	27	24	176
1905	109	NA	23	9	141
1906	86	NA	48	8	142
1907	67	NA	11	194	272
1908	104	NA	14	221	339
1909	157	NA	69	15	241
1910	119	NA	25	12	156
1911	130	NA	34	4	168

Table 3. Military Expenditures, 1886-1911 (in thousands of dollars).

Year Total	Local[61]	Dawes County	Three-[62] County	NWern[63] Neb.	Nebraska	Other	Total
1886	48	6	0	0	16	1	71
1887	137	20	0	2	14	0	173
1888	98	12	0	0	0	23	133
1889	135	2	0	0	2	12	151
1890	114	0	0	0	15	6	135
1891	208	4	0	0	8	12	232
1892	108	2	0	18	10	20	158
1893	136	0	0	5	22	11	174
1894	142	1	2	0	7	10	162
1895	126	6	0	0	16	0	148
1896	99	0	0	15	6	1	121
1897	115	1	0	3	24	3	146
1898	53	5	0	2	3	3	66
1899	56	0	1	5	17	12	91
1900	59	0	1	0	25	0	85
1901	69	0	0	0	9	0	78
1902	136	0	0	2	54	7	199
1903	161	0	0	9	59	3	232
1904	176	0	2	0	53	0	231
1905	141	0	0	10	32	0	183
1906	142	0	1	7	31	0	181
1907	272	0	1	7	35	0	315
1908	339	0	0	0	72	0	411
1909	241	0	0	4	77	0	322
1910	156	0	1	21	63	0	241
1911	168	0	2	17	11	0	198

Table 4. The Size of the Garrison and Saloon Revenues.[64]

Year	Mean Garrison Size	License Fees	Occupation Taxes	Total Revenues
1887	321	$ 0	$ 115.00	$ 115.00
1888	401	1,833.00	110.00	1,943.00
1889	430	3,416.70	207.50	3,624.30
1890	381	3,000.00	180.00	3,180.00
1891	452	3,000.00	144.00	3,144.00
1892	353	2,684.00	140.00	2,824.00
1893	517	2,000.00	2,000.00	4,000.00
1894	476	2,500.00	1,250.00	3,750.00
1895	412	2,000.00	500.00	2,500.00
1896	367	2,500.00	625.00	3,125.00
1897	421	2,335.00	586.75	2,921.25
1898	205	2,000.00	500.00	2,500.00
1899	212	2,000.00	500.00	2,500.00
1900	155	1,500.00	375.00	1,875.00
1901	159	1,200.00	682.50	1,882.50
1902	495	2,500.00	1,375.00	3,875.00
1903	537	2,000.00	1,400.00	3,400.00
1904	563	2,000.00	1,400.00	3,400.00
1905	508	2,000.00	1,400.00	3,400.00
1906	408	2,500.00	1,750.00	4,250.00
1907	302	3,000.00	2,100.00	5,100.00
1908	411	2,605.49	2,605.49	5,210.98
1909	568	2,416.67	2,416.67	4,833.34
1910	425	2,000.00	4,000.00	6,000.00
1911	487	2,000.00	4,000.00	6,000.00
1912	567	1,500.00	3,000.00	4,500.00

EPILOGUE

FORT ROBINSON AFTER 1916

Fort Robinson remained an active installation until 1948. However, it clearly entered a new era after the departure of the garrison for duty on the Mexican border in 1916. World War I itself brought no new mission to the post. It was slated to serve as a Signal Corps training center, but the war did not last long enough for plans to materialize.[1] Afterward, the post performed a number of logistical and support functions but never again housed a substantial community of combat troops and their families.

For the two decades after World War I, Fort Robinson was known more for its animals than its people. In 1919, the post started a two-decade career centered on horses. Known officially as Robinson Quartermaster Intermediate Depot, it was larger than the other two Army remount stations at Fort Reno, Oklahoma, and Front Royal, Virginia. Once the home of large cavalry garrisons, the old Indian-fighting fort was on its way to becoming the world's largest cavalry remount station. In its new role, Robinson also became the training site for the American equestrians who competed in the 1936 Berlin Olympics and who later trained for the 1940 Helsinki games that were canceled after war broke out in Europe.[2]

The Indian War days were far from forgotten. On September 5, 1934, twin monuments in memory of Lieutenant Levi H. Robinson, the post's namesake, and the Oglala chief Crazy Horse were dedicated. Many living symbols of Robinson's rich history attended, among them a former Fifth Cavalry Trumpeter, James Alldridge, who had served on post in 1882. Two buffalo soldiers, former Sergeants Caleb Benson and William Beckett of the Tenth Cavalry, both of whom had retired and remained in Crawford, were there, and so was buckskin-clad rancher James H. Cook, who had employed several of their comrades at his ranch near Agate Springs. Dr. B. F. Richards, now president of the local chamber of commerce but formerly city physician during the heyday of prostitution in Crawford, also attended and listened as local newspaper publisher Karl Spence read from John Neihardt's poem, "The Death of Crazy Horse." "Whoever spoke of Crazy Horse," Neihardt had written, "still heard ten thousand hoofs," and it may be that some who listened to Spence that day thought they heard the faint drumming sound of Indian ponies in the distance. The local paper, which a generation previously had promoted July 4th extravaganzas that featured cavalry troops and the post band, now boasted of "the biggest historical celebration ever held in this section."[3]

The memories lingered, some of them written on the land within sight of the post. North of Fort Robinson stood Red Cloud Buttes and Chaffee Butte, again pairing an Oglala leader with an officer of the Indian-fighting Army. South of the White River three terrain features bore the names of former commanders of the Ninth Cavalry. To the west were Biddle Heights and Tilford Heights; to the southeast stood Mount Hatch. North of Soldiers Creek, a butte carried the name of Walter Reed, the renowned surgeon who saved the life of Jules Sandoz and was one of Crawford's early slumlords.[4]

Eight years after dedication of the Robinson and Crazy Horse monuments, another wave of nostalgia swept over the Pine Ridge. In 1942, a squadron of the Fourth Cavalry, Mackenzie's regiment which had come to Fort Robinson in the days after the Custer fight while Crazy Horse still lived, came down from Fort Meade. They paraded on horseback for the last time, then turned in their mounts at the Robinson remount depot. The cavalry days were over.[5]

Robinson remained involved with the supply of animals, but this was the twentieth century Army. The emphasis had shifted completely from mounts to pack animals. Robinson continued to train and supply mules and horses through World War II but not for riders.

During the war against the Axis powers, other functions were added and overall activity at the fort increased. Still under the Quartermaster Department, the post became a reception and training center for war dogs. The Fort Robinson War Dog Reception and Training Center, activated on October 3, 1942, became the nation's largest K-9 reception and training center, where, as Thomas Buecker noted, "thousands of dogs, not cavalrymen, were trained for war." As one of the two active Quartermaster remount depots with plenty of condemned cavalry horses available as dog food, Robinson was a natural for this new mission.[6]

The kennels had room for 2,000 dogs, and the veterinary hospital that remained open throughout the war treated over 6,000 animals. The dogs themselves were all volunteers, or at any rate were volunteered by their owners. The government never had to resort to purchase.[7]

As many as 400 soldiers again garrisoned the fort, and once again there was dancing, fishing, and horseback riding in the hills. Fort Robinson was acquiring a reputation as "the Country Club of the Army," although it was surely among the most isolated of such resorts. The 1926 "Baedeker of the Army" had warned of "no good shopping district within 50 miles," and noted the existence of but one hotel in Crawford. Little had changed since then.[8]

At the peak of operations, after all of the Army's K-9 training was consolidated on post late in 1944, over 1,800 dogs were at Robinson at one time. Dog handlers as well as the dogs themselves underwent training on post. For the dogs, basic training lasted two weeks and emphasized obedience. The advanced course lasted from eight to thirteen additional weeks, and prepared the canine trainees for sentry duty or for tactical use as attack dogs, messengers, scouts, or sled dogs. Still others learned to assist Army medics in locating casualties. Handlers went through two-week programs before actually dealing with dogs.[9]

In addition, a prisoner-of-war camp was constructed in 1943 at the base of the hill on which Red Cloud's White River agency had stood. The camp, activated on March 15, had room for about 3,000 inmates. For most of the war, the camp population fluctuated between 600 and 700, mostly from Field Marshal Erwin Rommel's Afrika Corps. Early in 1945, the Army also brought 1,600 men from the German Navy, raising the prisoner population to over 2,000.[10]

It all ended for Fort Robinson on July 1, 1948, when the Army transferred the installation to the Department of Agriculture. But, although the post remained open until 1948, in a fitting way Fort Robinson completed its cycle of development with the prisoner-of-war camp. The post had its beginnings in the effort to control and restrict the Sioux and their movements and activities. Over seventy years later, after a varied career in the Indian wars, border troubles, and industrial disputes, one of its last functions approximated its first—confinement and control of a dangerous enemy.

ABBREVIATIONS

AAAG .... Acting Assistant Adjutant General
AAG .... Assistant Adjutant General
ADC .... Aide-de-Camp
AG .... Adjutant General
AGO .... Adjutant General's Office
ANJ .... *Army and Navy Journal*
BG .... Brigadier General
CG .... Commanding General
CO .... Commanding Officer
DeptDak .... Department of Dakota
DeptMo .... Department of the Missouri
DivMo .... Military Division of the Missouri
DP .... Department of the Platte
DPL .... Denver Public Library
GCM .... General Court Martial
HQ .... Headquarters
IG .... Inspector General
LC .... Library of Congress
LR .... Letters Received
LS .... Letters Sent
MG .... Major General
MH .... Medical History
NA .... National Archives
NSHS .... Nebraska State Historical Society
QM .... Quartermaster
QMG .... Quartermaster General
RBHML .... Rutherford B. Hayes Memorial Library
RG .... Record Group

SG	Surgeon General
TR	Telegrams Received
TS	Telegrams Sent
TWX	Telegram
USA	United States Army
USAMHI	United States Army Military History Institute
USMA	United States Military Academy
VA	Veterans Administration
WHC	Western History Collection
WSA	Wyoming State Archives

ENDNOTES

NOTES FOR PREFACE

1. Some examples of the literature on trans-Mississippi posts are: Dee A. Brown, *Fort Phil Kearny, An American Saga* (New York, 1962); Robert C. Carriker, *Fort Supply, Indian Territory: Frontier Outpost on the Plains* (Norman, Oklahoma, 1970); Chris Emmett, *Fort Union and the Winning of the Southwest* (Norman, 1965); Leroy R. Hafen and Francis M. Young, *Fort Laramie and the Pageant of the West, 1834-1890* (Glendale, California, 1938); J. Evetts Haley, *Fort Concho and the Texas Frontier* (San Angelo, Texas, 1952); Remi Nadeau, *Fort Laramie and the Sioux Indians* (Englewood Cliffs, New Jersey, 1967); Wilbur S. Nye, *Carbine and Lance: the Story of Old Fort Sill* (Norman, 1935); Carl Coke Rister, *Fort Griffin on the Texas Frontier* (Norman, 1956); David K. Strate, *Sentinel to the Cimarron: the Frontier Experience of Fort Dodge, Kansas* (Dodge City, Kansas, 1970).

2. For the combat history of these regiments, see William H. Leckie, *The Buffalo Soldiers, A Narrative of the Negro Cavalry in the West* (Norman, 1967).

3. Crawford (Nebraska) *Tribune*, March 31, 1911.

NOTES FOR CHAPTER 1

1. James C. Olson, *Red Cloud and the Sioux Problem* (Lincoln, 1965), pp. 158, 163.

2. *Ibid.*, p. 164; Roger T. Grange, Jr., "Fort Robinson, Outpost on the Plains," *Nebraska History*, 39 (September 1959), pp. 195-197; Report, CG, DivMo, *Annual Report of the Department of War, 1874*, I, p. 25.

3. *Ibid.*, I, p. 23; CG, DP, to CO, Sioux Expedition, February 19 and 24, and May 19, 1874, LR, Sioux Expedition (NA, RG 393).

4. Paul A. Hutton, *Phil Sheridan and his Army* (Lincoln, 1985), pp. 290-291.

5. Grange, "Fort Robinson," pp. 197-198; Olson, *Red Cloud and the Sioux Problem*, p. 166; Special Order 2, February 28, 1874, Special and Special Field Orders, Sioux Expedition (NA, RG 393); Report, CG, DP, *Annual Report of the Department of War, 1874*, I, p. 32.

6. Grange, "Fort Robinson," pp. 198-199; Special Order 4, March 8, 1874, and Special Order 5, March 12, 1874, Special and Special Field Orders, Sioux Expedition; CO, Sioux Expedition, to CO, Camp at Red Cloud, March 8, 1874, LS, Sioux Expedition (NA, RG 393); Report, CG, DivMo, Annual Report of the Department of War, 1874, I, p. 25; Report, CG, DP, *Ibid.*, I., p. 32.

7. CO, Camp at Spotted Tail, to CO, Sioux Expedition, March 15, 1874, Retained Records, Sioux Expedition (NA, RG 393); CO, Sioux Expedition, to AAG, DP, April 6 and May 5, 1874, LS, Sioux Expedition; Grange, "Fort Robinson," p. 200.

8. CO, Sioux Expedition, to Dr. J. J. Saville, March 8, 1874, and to AAG, DP, May 1, 1874, LS, Sioux Expedition; General Order 4, March 29, 1874, General Orders, Sioux Expedition (NA, RG 393); Post Returns, Camp Robinson, April 1874 (NA, RG 94); Report of the Secretary of War, *Annual Report of the Department of War, 1875*, I, p. 9; AAG, DivMo, to AAG, USA, May 20, 1874, Retained Records, Sioux Expedition; Thomas W. Dunlay, *Wolves for the Blue Soldiers: Indian Scouts and Auxiliaries with the United States Army, 1860-90* (Lincoln, 1987), p. 71; "Map of Reconnaissance," 1874, Civil Works Map File, #Rds 216, Records of the Office of the Chief of Engineers (NA, RG 77); "Reconnaissance of Freight Route or Indian Supplies between Cheyenne, Wyoming, and the Red Cloud Agency, Nebraska," Central Map File, #1103, Records of the Bureau of Indian Affairs (NA, RG 75).

9. CO, Sioux Expedition, to AAG, DP, June 22, 1874, LS, Sioux Expedition; George E. Hyde, *Red Cloud's Folk, a History of the Oglala Sioux* (Norman, 1967), p. 221; Grange, "Fort Robinson," pp. 202-204.

10. Donald D. Jackson, *Custer's Gold: The United States Cavalry Expedition of 1874* (New Haven, 1966), pp. 2, 81-85, 87-89, 104; CO, Fort Lincoln, to AAG, DeptDak, September 2, 1874, and TWX, Lieutenant Marcy Lynde, to CG, DeptDak, September [2?], 1874, DivMo Special File: Black Hills Expedition, 1874 (NA, RG 393); Hutton, *Phil Sheridan and his Army*, pp. 290-291. For a copy of the treaty, see Charles J. Kappler, *Indian Affairs, Laws, and Treaties*. Vol II (Washington, D.C., 1903), pp. 770-775.

11. TWX, CG, DeptDak, to AAG, DivMo, October 13, 1874, and CO, Camp Sheridan, to AAG, DP, October 26, 1874, DivMo Special File: Black Hills Expedition, 1874; TWX, CG, DP, to CO, District of the Black Hills, October 14, 1874, and Endorsement to CO, Camp Sheridan, October 16, 1874, Endorsements Sent, District of the Black Hills (NA, RG 393).

12. O. W. Coursey, *Beautiful Black Hills* (Mitchell, South Dakota, 1925), pp. 39-42; Special Order 10, December 23, 1874, Special Orders, District of the Black Hills (NA, RG 393); Post Returns, January 1875; MG Guy V. Henry, Jr., to Vance E. Nelson, June 10, 1967, Fort Robinson File (NSHS, Lincoln); Guy V. Henry, "Adventures of American Army and Navy Officers. II. A Winter March to the Black Hills," *Harper's Weekly*, 39 (July 27, 1895), p. 700; Guy V. Henry, Jr., "Brief Narrative of the Life of Guy V. Henry, Jr." typescript, Box 2, Guy V. Henry, Jr., papers, USAMHI.

13. Special Order 13, December 31, 1874, and Special Order 3, March 26, 1875, Special Orders, District of the Black Hills.

14. Lewis F. Crawford, *Rekindling Camp Fires: The Exploits of Ben Arnold* (Bismarck, North Dakota, 1926), pp. 209-212; TWX, AG, USA, to CG, DivMo, March 17, 1875, DivMo Special File: Black Hills, 1875 (NA, RG 393); Report, AG, DP, September 16, 1875, and CG, DP, to AAG, DivMo, September 15, 1875, Crook Letterbooks, I (RBHML, Fremont, Ohio).

15. Special Order 14, June 30, 1875, Special Order 17, August 3, 1875, and Special Order 18, August 5, 1875, Special Orders, District of the Black Hills; Post Returns, July-September 1875; TWX, CO, Camp Robinson, to CO, District of the Black Hills, May 10, 1875, Endorsement, CO, District of the Black Hills, to CO, Camp Sheridan, May 11, 1875, and CO, Camp Sheridan, to CO, District of the Black Hills, June 5, 1875, and Endorsement, CO, District of the Black Hills, to CO, Camp Robinson, July 22, 1875, Endorsements Sent, District of the Black Hills.

16. TWX, CG, USA, to CG, DivMo, July 13, 1875, DivMo Special File: Black Hills, 1875; CO, Camp Sheridan, to CO, District of the Black Hills, July 15, 1875, and CG, DP, to CO, District of the Black Hills, November 8, 1875, Endorsements Sent, District of the Black Hills; Grange, "Fort Robinson," p. 206; Post Returns, August 1875; Special Order 19, August 9, 1875, Special Orders, District of the Black Hills.

17. TWX, CG, DP, to CO, District of the Black Hills, May 3 and 4, 1875, and Endorsement to CO, Camp Robinson, May 4, 1875, Endorsements Sent, District of the Black Hills; Post Returns, May-July and December 1875.

18. Report, AG, DP, September 16, 1875, Crook Letterbooks, I; CO, Camp Robinson, to CO, District of the Black Hills, October 16, 1875, Endorsements Sent, District of the Black Hills.

19. Report, CG, USA, *Annual Report of the Department of War, 1875*, I, p. 34, Olson, *Red Cloud and the Sioux Problem*, pp. 215-216.

20. CG, DP, to AAG, DivMo, January 28, 1876, and AAG, DP, to CO, Forts McPherson, Laramie, Fetterman, North Platte, and Sidney Barracks, March 11, 1876, Crook Letterbooks, I; Olson, *Red Cloud and the Sioux Problem*, pp. 216-217; Robert Wooster, *The Military and United States Indian Policy 1865-1903* (New Haven, 1988), p. 148; Jerome A. Greene, "George Crook," in Paul A. Hutton, ed., *Soldiers West: Biographies from the Military Frontier* (Lincoln, 1987), pp. 117-118, 131; Dunlay, *Wolves for the Blue Soldiers*, pp. 46, 77.

21. Post Returns, June-July 1876; TWX, CG, DP, to AG, DivMo, July 12, 1876, Crook Letterbooks, I; Military Division of the Missouri, *Record of Engagements with Hostile Indians within the Military Division of the Missouri, 1868 to 1882, Lieutenant General P. H. Sheridan, Commanding* (Washington, D.C.; 1882) p. 59; Olson, *Red Cloud and the Sioux Problem*, p. 223; Report, CG, USA, *Annual Report of the Department of War, 1876*, I, p. 35; Grange, "Fort Robinson," p. 210; Hutton, *Phil Sheridan and his Army*, p. 313.

22. TWX, AAG, DP, to AAG, DivMo, July 27 and 31, and August 4, 1876, DivMo Special File; Sioux War, 1876 (NA, RG 393).

23. *Ibid.*, July 29 and August 3, 1876.

24. *Ibid.*, August 11, 1876; Post Returns, August 1876; J'Nell L. Pate, "Ranald S. Mackenzie," in Hutton, ed., *Soldiers West*, pp. 178, 187-189; Hutton, "Preface," in Hutton, ed., *Soldiers West*, pp. x-xi.

25. *Ibid.*; CO, District of the Black Hills, to CG, DivMo, September 2, 1876, DivMo Special File: Sioux War, 1876; Grange, "Fort Robinson," p. 212.

26. Post Returns, September 1876; Grange, "Fort Robinson," p. 211; AAG, DP, to AAG, DivMo, September 7, 1876, DivMo Special File: Sioux War, 1876, CG, DP to CO, 5th Cavalry, September 25, 1876, and to CO, District of the Black Hills, September 25, 1876, Crook Letterbooks, I; Hutton, *Phil Sheridan and his Army*, p. 322.

27. *Ibid.*, October 1, 1876; Charles King, *Campaigning with Crook and Stories of Army Life* (Ann Arbor, 1960), pp. 160, 165-166; Dunlay, *Wolves for the Blue Soldiers*, pp. 133, 161.

28. Olson, *Red Cloud and the Sioux Problem*, p. 232; Military Division of the Missouri, *Record of Engagements*, p. 64; TWX, CG, DP, to CG, DivMo, October 23, 1876, Crook Letterbooks, I.

29. TWX, CG, DP, to CG, DivMo, October 24, 1876, DivMo Special File: Sioux War, 1876; Report, CG, USA, *Annual Report of the Department of War, 1876*, I, p. 37; Earle R. Forrest and Joe E. Milner, *California Joe* (Caldwell, Idaho, 1935), p. 275.

30. TWX, E. B. Farnum to CG, DP, February 15 and 19, 1877, and to CG, DivMo, February 15, 1877, and Matthewson and Jones to CG, DP, February 20, 1877, and TWX, Lieutenant Cummings, to CG, DP, February 2, 25, and 28, 1877, TR, General Crook's ADC, I (NA, RG 393); Post Returns, February 1877; Division of the Missouri, *Record of Engagements*, p. 67.

31. Post Returns, March-August 1877; CO, District of the Black Hills, to ADC, DP, March 17, 1877, DivMo Special File: Sioux War, 1877 (NA, RG 393); TWX, E. B. Farnum and others to CG, DP, March 23, 1877, and Captain Peter Vroom to ADC, DP, March 27, and April 9, 1877, TR, General Crook's ADC; TWX, ADC, DP, to Captain Vroom, April 8, 1877, TS, General Crook's ADC (NA, RG 393).

32. CG, DP, to CG, DivMo, March 15, 1877, Crook Letterbooks, I; TWX, ADC, DP, to CO, Cantonment Reno, March 21, 1877, and to CO, Fort Fetterman, April 8, 1877, and CG, DP, to CG, DivMo, April 16, 1877, TS, General Crook's ADC.

33. Post Returns, April 1877; TWX, CG, DP, to CG, DivMo, April 13, and 21, 1877, TS, General Crook's ADC; Thomas B. Marquis, *A Warrior Who Fought Custer* (Minneapolis, 1931), p. 304.

34. TWX, AAG, USA, to CG, DP, January 8, 1877, TR, General Crook's ADC; TWX, CG, DP, to CG, DivMo, April 13, 1877, DivMo Special File: Sioux War, 1877. Also see Oliver Knight, "War or Peace, the Anxious Wait for Crazy Horse," *Nebraska History*, 43 (Winter 1973), pp. 521-544.

35. Post Returns, April 1877; TWX, CG, DP, to CG, DivMo, April 16 and 27, 1877, TS, General Crook's ADC; TWX, AAG, DP, to AAG, DivMo, May 7, 1877, DivMo Special File: Sioux War, 1877; Hutton, *Phil Sheridan and his Army*, p. 326; Report, CG, DP, *Annual Report of the Department of War, 1877*, I, p. 85.

36. Luther P. Bradley, Private Journal, January 1867-December 1880, entry for May 26, 1877, Box 1, Luther P. Bradley papers, USAMHI; Luther P. Bradley to Mrs. Bradley, 26 May, 1877, Box 2, Bradley papers, USAMHI.

37. Bradley, private journal, entries for June 12, 22, 26, and 30, July 23 and 24, and August 5, 1877.

38. TWX, AAG, DP, to CG, DP, August 31, 1877, TR, General Crook's ADC; CG, DP, to CO, Camp Robinson, September 1, 1877, TS, General Crook's ADC; Bradley to Mrs. Bradley, 5 September, 1877, Box 2, Bradley papers.

39. TWX, CO, Camp Robinson, to CG, DP, September 4, 1877, TR, General Crook's ADC; TWX, CG, DP, to CO, Camp Robinson, September 4, 1877, TS, General Crook's ADC.

40. TWX, CO, Camp Robinson, to Major Gilliss, Cheyenne Depot, September 5, 1877, Lieutenant Clark to CG, DP, September 5, 1877, and CG, DivMo, to Major Gilliss, September 5, 1877, TR, General Crook's ADC; TWX, CG, DP, to CO, Camp Robinson, September 5, 1877, TS, General Crook's ADC.

41. Mari Sandoz, *Crazy Horse, The Strange Man of the Oglalas* (Lincoln, 1961), pp. 407-409, 413. Also see Paul D. Riley, ed., "Oglala Sources on the Life of Crazy Horse, Interviews Given to Eleanor H. Hinman," *Nebraska History*, 57 (Spring 1976), pp. 21, 28-29, 43; Robert A. Clark, ed., *The Killing of Chief Crazy Horse: three eyewitness views by the Indian, Chief He Dog; the Indian-white, William Garnett; the White doctor, Valentine McGillycuddy* (Lincoln, 1988).

42. Bradley to his wife, September 5, 1877, folder f, box 2, Bradley papers.

43. TWX, Lieutenant Clark, to CG, DP, September 6, 1877, TR, General Crook's ADC; AAG, DP, to AAG, DivMo, September 6, and 8, 1877, DivMo Special File: Sioux War, 1877; Bradley to his wife, September 9 and 11, 1877, folder f, box 2, Bradley papers.

44. Bradley to his wife, September 23, October 5 and 25, 1877, folder f, box 2, Bradley papers; Lieutenant Jesse M. Lee to Bradley, September 10, 1877, folder a, box 5, Bradley papers.

45. TWX, CG, DP, to CG, DivMo, October 15, 1877, TS, General Crook's ADC; Olson, *Red Cloud and the Sioux Problem*, pp. 254, 262.

NOTES FOR CHAPTER 2

1. TWX, AAG, DP, to AAG, DivMo, May 14, 1877, DivMo Special File: Sioux War, 1877; Fred M. Hans, *The Great Sioux Nation* (Chicago, 1907), p. 542; Sandoz, *Cheyenne Autumn* (New York, 1964), pp. 18-19.

2. *Ibid., passim*; Post Returns, October 1878; TWX, CG, DP, to CG, DivMo, October 28, 1878, DivMo Special File: Cheyenne Outbreak (NA, RG 393).

3. TWX, CG, DP, to CG, DivMo, October 28, and 31, 1878, *Ibid.*

4. Post Returns, November-December 1878; CG, DP, to AAG, DivMo, December 12, 1878, Crook Letterbooks, I. During the winter Little Wolf evaded the Army and completed the trek to Montana, only to be captured near Fort Keogh in March. For correspondence relating to this epilogue, see the Division of the Missouri Special Files on the Cheyenne Outbreak and Little Wolf Papers.

5. Secretary of the Interior to Secretary of War, November 22, 1878, DivMo Special File: Cheyenne Outbreak.

6. In accordance with Special Order 8, Department of the Platte, January 21, 1879, a board of officers convened at Fort Robinson on January 25, took testimony on the escape, the skirmishes that followed, and the final clash on Warbonnet Creek. The testimony and findings, which form the basis of the short narrative which follows, are in NA, RG 393.

7. Findings, *Ibid.*

8. Testimony of Captains Henry Wessells and Peter Vroom, *Ibid.*

9. Testimony of Captains Henry Wessels and Joseph Lawton, and Lieutenant J. F. Cummings, *Ibid.*

10. Post Returns, January 1879 and December 1880.

11. Findings, Investigation of Cheyenne Outbreak; TWX, CG, USA, to CG, DivMo, January 21, 1879, DivMo Special File: Cheyenne Outbreak.

12. After some were tried for murder in Kansas but released for lack of evidence, all were allowed to live out their days on the Tongue River Reservation in Montana. Dull Knife died there in 1883. Sandoz, *Cheyenne Autumn*, pp. 324-325.

13. Robert P. Burleigh, "Range Cattle Industry in Nebraska to 1890," (Unpublished M.A. Thesis, University of Nebraska, 1937), p. 122; Carl Lockmon, *The Years of Promise* (n. p., 1971), p. 126; Nellie Snyder Yost, ed., *Boss Cowman: The Recollections of Ed Lemmons, 1857-1946* (Lincoln, 1969), p. 113; O. B. Waddill to Lawrence Bixby, February 17, 1964, *The Nebraska Cattleman*, 20 (April 1964), p. 30; Edgar Beecher Bronson. *Reminiscences of a Ranchman* (Lincoln, 1962), pp. 130-131.

14. CG, DP, to AAG, DivMo, December 4, 1878, Crook Letterbooks, I; Post Returns, June-October 1879.

15. *Ibid.*, January 1879.

16. CG, DP, to CG, DivMo, April 23, 1878, and August 8, 1880, Crook Letterbooks, I.

17. Report, CG, DivMo, *Annual Report of the Department of War, 1880*, I, p. 55; *Ibid., 1883*, p. 140; Omaha *Bee*, September 19, 1883; CG, DP, to CG, DivMo, August 29, 1882, Crook Letterbooks, I; Edward M. Coffman, *The Old Army, A Portrait of the American Army in Peacetime, 1784-1898* (New York, 1986), p. 282; Wooster, *The Military and United States Indian Policy*, pp. 183-184.

18. Report, CG, DP, *Annual Report of the Department of War, 1884*, I, p. 84; Report, CG, DivMo, *Ibid., 1888*, I, p. 69.

19. Report, CG, DP, *Ibid., 1885*, I, pp. 142, 146; Post Returns, October 1885. The only real depredation was not the work of Indians. A gang of road agents took the Robinson payroll from a stagecoach in January 1886. The robbers were never found, and the theft remains a part of local folklore. See Mabel Kendrick, "Whitney History," Crazy Horse Cultural Center, ed., *Old Timers Tales*, I (Chadron, 1971), p. 115, and Kendrick, "The Hold-up," *Ibid.*, II, pt. 2 (Chadron, 1972), p. 211.

20. Order 51, March 13, 1890, Post Orders, Fort Robinson (NA, RG 393); Post Returns, Aril-July 1890; Grange, "Fort Robinson," p. 226; Report, CG, DeptMo, *Annual Report of the Department of War, 1886*, I, p. 119.

21. (Buffalo) *Big Horn Sentinel*, March 20, 1886; Crawford *Crescent*, quoted in *ANJ*, 25 (November 19, 1887), p. 322; Chadron *Democrat*, March 18, 1886; Coffman, *The Old Army*, p. 282.

22. CO, Fort Robinson, to AAG, DP, August 11, 1887, LS, Fort Robinson (NA, RG 393); *ANJ*, 24 (May 28, 1887), p. 875; *Ibid.*, 25 (October 22, 1887), p. 242.

23. TWX, CO, Fort Robinson, to AAG, DivMo, May 26, 1888, and to AAG, DP, May 29, 1888, LS, Fort Robinson; Captain A. W. Corliss, Diary, II, May 30, 1888 (WHC, DPL).

24. CO, Fort Robinson, to AAG, DP, May 29, 1888, LS, Fort Robinson; Post Returns, May 1888.

25. Corliss, Diary, II, February 27, 1889; CO, Fort Robinson, to AAG, DP, April 10, 1889, LS, Fort Robinson; Order 109, May 10, 1889, and Order 134, June 8, 1889, Post Orders, Fort Robinson.

26. Post Returns, April-June 1890; CO, Fort Robinson, to AAG, DP, April 23 and 24, and June 20, 1890, and to Agent Hugh Gallagher, April 24, 1890, LS, Fort Robinson; Order 88, April 26, 1890, Order 176, August 19, 1890, Order 182, August 25, 1890, Order 216, October 9, 1890, Order 222, October 20, 1890, Order 236, November 4, 1890, Post Orders, Fort Robinson; Corliss, Diary, III, June 18, 1890.

27. Robert M. Utley, *The Last Days of the Sioux Nation* (New Haven, 1963), p. 103. On the Ghost Dance theology, see James Mooney, *The Ghost Dance Religion and the Sioux Outbreak of 1890* (Washington, D.C., 1896).

28. TWX, CO, Fort Robinson, to D. F. Royer, October 17, 1890, LS, Fort Robinson.

29. Utley, *The Last Days of the Sioux Nation*, pp. 108-109. The unfortunate Royer has received a very bad press. Scholars place much of the blame for the failure to control the situation on him. For example, see Utley, *The Last Days of the Sioux Nation*, p. 112, and Olson, *Red Cloud and the Sioux Problem*, p. 325. A contemporary journalist, William F. Kelley, sensibly concluded that Royer had inherited a situation so badly deteriorated that he could do nothing. Alexander Kelley and Pierre Bovis, eds., *Pine Ridge 1890* (San Francisco, 1971), p. 68.

30. CO, Fort Robinson, to AAG, DP, November 14, 1890, LS, Fort Robinson; Leckie, *The Buffalo Soldiers*, p. 253.

31. Order 247, November 17, 1890, and Order 248, November 18, 1890, Post Orders, Fort Robinson; Post Returns, November 1890; Chadron *Democrat*, November 20, 1890; Ruth Van Ackeren, ed., *Sioux County: Memories of its Pioneers* (Harrison, 1967), p. 119; L. W. Colby, "The Sioux Indian War of 1890-'91," *Transactions and Reports, Nebraska State Historical Society*, 3 (1892), p. 147; CO, Fort Robinson, to L. C. Shane, December 15, 1890, LS, Fort Robinson.

32. *ANJ*, 28 (December 6, 1890), p. 243; *Ibid.*, 28 (December 13, 1890), p. 267; Alexander Perry, "The Ninth U.S. Cavalry in the Sioux Campaign of 1890," *Journal of the United States Cavalry Association*, 4 (March 1891), p. 38; TWX, CG, DP, to Colonels Sanford and Carr, December 13, 1890, to CG, DeptDak, December 14, 1890, and to CG, DivMo, December 16, 1890, TS, CG, DP, Pine Ridge, 1890, II (NA, RG 393).

33. Kelley and Bovis, eds., *Pine Ridge 1890*, pp. 145, 148.

34. *Ibid.*, p. 192; TWX, CG, DP, to CG, DivMo, December 29, 1890 and to Colonel Sanford, December 29, 1890, TS, CG, DP, Pine Ridge, IV; Utley, *The Last Days of the Sioux Nation*, pp. 235-236; *ANJ*, 28 (January 10, 1891), p. 331; *Ibid.*, 28 (January 17, 1891), p. 355; Perry, "The Ninth U.S. Cavalry in the Sioux Campaign of 1890," p. 39.

35. Utley, *The Last Days of the Sioux Nation*, pp. 239-240; Report, CG, DivMo, *Annual Report of the Department of War, 1891*, I, p. 151; Virginia W. Johnson, *The Unregimented General: A Biography of Nelson A. Miles* (Boston, 1962), pp. 294-295.

36. TWX, CG, DP, to CO, Fort Robinson, December 31, 1890, TS, CG, DP, Pine Ridge, IV; Kelley and Bovis, eds., *Pine Ridge 1890*, p. 219; Post Returns, January-February 1891; TWX, CO, Fort Robinson, to ADC, CG, DP, January 5, 1891, LS, Fort Robinson; Order 2, January 3, 1891, Order 4, January 7, 1891, and Order 6, January 9, 1891, Post Orders, Fort Robinson; Helen Ring, "The Story of a Nebraska Pioneer," typescript, Everett Pitt Wilson MSS (NSHS, Lincoln).

37. *ANJ*, 28 (January 3, 1891), p. 319; Post Returns, January 1891; Colby "The Sioux Indian War of 1890-'91," pp. 159-162, 166.

38. Utley, *The Last Days of the Sioux Nation*, pp. 252, 259-260; James T. King, *War Eagle: A Life of General Eugene A. Carr* (Lincoln, 1963), p. 245; Post Returns, January-March 1891; Lieutenant Grote Hutcheson, "The Ninth Regiment of Cavalry," Theodore F. Rodenbaugh and William L. Haskin, eds., *The Army of the United States* (New York, 1896), p. 287.

39. Quoted in Jack D. Foner, *The United States Soldier Between Two Wars* (New York, 1970), p. 135.

40. *ANJ*, 28 (March 14, 1891), p. 491; *Ibid.*, 28 (March 28, 1891), p. 534; *Ibid.*, 28 (April 4, 1891), p. 546. Sanitary Report, March 1891, MH, Fort Robinson (NA, RG 393).

41. *ANJ*, 28 (December 27, 1890), p. 298; *Ibid.*, 28 (January 10, 1891), p. 331; *Ibid.*, 28 (May 2, 1891), p. 620; Post Returns, May, July, and November 1891.

NOTES FOR CHAPTER 3

1. CO, Fort Robinson, to AAG, DP, November 13, 1894, LS, Fort Robinson (NA, RG 393); Report of the Secretary of War, *Annual Report of the Department of War, 1894*, I, p. 10.

2. Frank N. Schubert, "The Suggs Affray: The Black Cavalry in the Johnson County War," *Western Historical Quarterly*, 4 (January 1973), pp. 58-62; Post Returns, June-August 1892 (NA, RG 94); Crawford *Tribune*, June 24, 1892; Grange, "Fort Robinson," p. 229.

3. Schubert, "The Suggs Affray," pp. 63-68; Post Returns, November 1892. Privates Abraham Champ and Emile Smith, the principals in the barroom brawl that preceded the affray and the alleged leaders of the raiders, apparently were not convicted of any wrongdoing. Neither was listed on later returns as discharged or sentenced by military courts. Smith even continued to teach school at Robinson after the Suggs incident.

4. Post Returns, June-July 1894.

5. *Ibid.*, July 1894.

6. *Ibid.*, August 1894; *ANJ*, 31 (August 11, 1894), p. 874; T. A. Larson, *History of Wyoming* (Lincoln, 1965), p. 298.

7. Schubert, "The Black Regular Army Regiments in Wyoming, 1885-1912," Unpublished M.A. Thesis, University of Wyoming, 1970, pp. 45-46.

8. Post Returns, July 1895; *ANJ*, 33 (September 7, 1895), p. 41. Notes accompanying a Roster of Troops serving in the Department of the Platte, August 29, 1895, Miscellaneous Records, DeptMo (NA, RG 393).

9. *ANJ*, 32 (August 24, 1895), p. 855; Post Returns, July-October 1895; Schubert, "Black Soldiers on the White Frontier: Some Factors Influencing Race Relations," *Phylon*, 33 (Winter 1972), p. 414.

10. Post Returns, June-July 1897; Crawford *Tribune*, July 2, 1897; CO, Fort Robinson, to AG, DP, August 10, 1897, LS, Fort Robinson; Report, CG, DP, *Annual Report of the Department of War, 1897*, I, pp. 175-176.

11. Post Returns, February and April 1898; Special Order 71, April 16, 1898, Post Orders, Fort Robinson (NA RG 393); Crawford *Tribune*, April 22, 1898.

12. *Ibid.*

13. Post Returns, April 1898; Report, CG, DP, *Annual Report of the Department of War, 1898*, I, p. 194.

14. Melvyn Dubofsky, *We Shall Be All: A History of the Industrial Workers of the World* (Chicago, 1969), p. 37.

15. CO, Fort Robinson, to AG, DeptMo, February 28, 1899, LS, Fort Robinson; Post Returns, May-November 1899; Regimental Returns, 1st Cavalry, May-September 1899 (NA, RG 94); Crawford *Tribune*, May 5, 1899; Report, CG, DeptMo, *Annual Report of the Department of War, 1899*, I, pt. 3, p. 15.

16. For a summary of the specific problems faced by White River Utes, see Floyd A. O'Neil, "An Anguished Odyssey: The Flight of the Utes, 1906-1908," *Utah Historical Quarterly*, 36 (Fall 1968), pp. 315-327. Estimates of the number of migrants range between 200 and 700. There were only 1,250 Utes on the Uintah reservation, so the group that left was a large but indefinite portion of the residents. *Annual Report of the Department of the Interior, 1907*, II, p. 175.

17. *Ibid.*, p. 122; Governor Brooks to E. A. Hitchcock, Secretary of the Interior, September 17, 1906, and TWX, to President Theodore Roosevelt, October 18, 1906, Brooks MSS (WSA, Cheyenne).

18. Brooks to Hitchcock, September 17, 1906, Brooks MSS; *Annual Report of the Department of the Interior, 1907*, II, pp. 122-123.

19. See, for example, Sheridan *Post*, September 25, October 16, and October 26, 1906; (Cheyenne) *Wyoming Tribune*, October 17, 1906; Cheyenne *Daily Leader*, October 16, 1906.

20. New York *Times*, October 19, 1906; Crawford *Tribune*, October 19, 1906.

21. *Annual Report of the Department of the Interior, 1907*, II, p. 125; O'Neil, "An Anguished Odyssey," p. 323; Sheridan *Post*, November 1, 1906.

22. Post Returns, October 1906; Report, CG, DeptMo, *Annual Report of the Department of War, 1907*, III, p. 123.

23. Post Returns, October 1906; Crawford *Tribune*, November 2, 1906; Regimental Returns, 10th Cavalry, October 1906 (NA, RG 94); *Annual Report of the Department of the Interior, 1907*, II, p. 124; Report, CG, DeptMo, *Annual Report of the Department of War, 1907*, III, pp. 123-124; Thomas R. Buecker, "An Excellent Soldier and an Efficient Officer," *Nebraskaland*, 67 (June 1989), pp. 13-17.

24. Regimental Returns, 10th Cavalry, October-November 1906; Cheyenne *Daily Leader*, October 27 and 31, 1906; New York *Times*, October 31, 1906.

25. *Ibid.*, Regimental Returns, 10th Cavalry, October-November 1906.

26. New York *Times*, November 1, 1906.

27. *Ibid.*, November 1 and 4, 1906; Regimental Returns, 10th Cavalry, October 1906; Post Returns, November-December 1906; *Annual Report of the Department of the Interior, 1907*, II, p. 125; Report, CG, DeptMo, *Annual Report of the Department of War, 1907*, III, pp. 124-125. The Utes won their point in Washington, but were not welcomed as friends by the Sioux. Disgusted and defeated, they returned to Utah in 1908.

28. Regimental Returns, 10th Cavalry, November 1906; Crawford *Tribune*, November 16, 1906.

29. Post Returns, February-May 1907; Crawford *Tribune*, May 24, 1907; Private Kirtley to Post Surgeon, October 14, 1907, and Post Surgeon to Post Adjutant, October 14, 1907, Register of Correspondence, Post Surgeon (NA, RG 393).

30. Report, CG, DeptMo, *Annual Report of the Department of War, 1907*, III, p. 109; Report, CO, DeptMo, *Ibid.*, 1911, III, p. 67. For details of Warren's success in obtaining troops for his state, see Lewis L. Gould, *Wyoming, A Political History, 1868-1896* (New Haven, 1968), pp. 129, 267.

31. Post Returns, November 1910-February 1911, November 1913-May 1914. The Twelfth joined six cavalry regiments and 1.5 infantry regiments on the Rio Grande, where they enforced President Taft's embargo and patrolled the border. Report of the Secretary of War, *Annual Report of the Department of War, 1912*, I, pp. 13-14.

32. Post Returns, 1915-1916.

NOTES FOR CHAPTER 4

1. MG Guy V. Henry, Jr., to Vance E. Nelson, June 10, 1965, Fort Robinson File (NSHS, Lincoln); Grange, "Fort Robinson," p. 232; Omaha *Bee*, September 19, 1883; Post Surgeon to AG, USA, June 30, 1893, MH, Fort Robinson.

2. CO, Fort Robinson to AAG, DP, December 5, 1886, January 2, 1892, and September 25, 1894, LS, Fort Robinson; Post Surgeon to AG, USA, June 30, 1893, and Sanitary Report, September 1890, MH, Fort Robinson; Buecker, "The 1887 Expansion of Fort Robinson," *Nebraska History*, 68 (Summer 1987), pp. 83-93.

3. CO, Fort Robinson, to AAG, DP, August 11, 1887, LS, Fort Robinson; Grange, "Fort Robinson," p. 232; Post Surgeon to AG, USA, June 30, 1893, MH, Fort Robinson.

4. *Ibid.*, Ellen M. Biddle, *Reminiscences of a Soldier's Wife* (Philadelphia, 1907), p. 227.

5. Sanitary Report, April 1896, MH, Fort Robinson; Report of the SG, *Annual Report of the Department of War, 1897*, I, p. 550; Report, CG, DeptMo, *Ibid.*, 1907, III, p. 109.

6. CO, Fort Robinson, to Post QM, June 24, 1890, and to AAG, DP, April 18, 1892, LS, Fort Robinson.

7. Grange, "Fort Robinson," p. 217; Corliss, Diary, II, March 21, 1888 and III, January 20, 1889; CO, Fort Robinson, to Captain C. A. Stedman, June 7, 1891, LS, Fort Robinson.

8. CO, Fort Robinson, to AG, DeptMo, June 27, 1898, LS, Fort Robinson. This letter is lined out in the ledger, so it was probably never sent.

9. Post Surgeon to Post Adjutant, January 30, 1904, LS, Post Surgeon (NA, RG 393).

10. *ANJ*, 28 (March 23, 1891), p. 659.

11. Corliss, Diary, II, May 29 and 30, and July 8, 1888.

12. Order 257, December 31, 1891, Post Orders, Fort Robinson; CO, Fort Robinson, to Lieutenant Frank S. Armstrong, February 19, 1897, LS, Fort Robinson.

13. Fanny McGillycuddy, "Notes kept . . . at Camp Robinson, December 13, 1876-February 22, 1877, and with the Army on an expedition to the Black Hills, February 23-April 11, 1877," typescript (NSHS, Lincoln), pp. 16-22.

14. Merrill J. Mattes, *Indians, Infants, and Infantry* (Denver, 1960), p. 252; Corliss, Diary, II, February 21, 24, and 25, October 3, 1887, and February 10, 1888 and III, November 27, 1888, and November 26, 1889; *ANJ*, 32 (July 27, 1895), p. 789; *Ibid.*, 25 (June 23, 1888) p. 956; *Ibid.*, 26 (October 27, 1888), p. 102; Biddle, *Reminiscences of a Soldier's Wife*, p. 22.

15. *ANJ*, 27 (November 30, 1889), p. 271; *Ibid.*, 27 (May 17, 1890), p. 719; *Ibid.*, 28 (December 6, 1890), p. 243; *Ibid.*, 32 (February 23, 1895), p. 427.

16. *Ibid.*, 25 (June 16, 1888), p. 936; *Ibid.*, 29 (June 11, 1892), p. 737; Corliss, Diary, III, *passim*; Order 3, January 4, 1889, Post Orders, Fort Robinson.

17. *ANJ*, 30 (March 18, 1893), p. 503; *Ibid.*, 30 (June 24, 1893); p. 737; Biddle, *Reminiscences of a Soldier's Wife*, p. 222; Van Ackeren, *Sioux County*, p. 108.

18. Willard E. Wight, ed., "A Young Medical Officer's Letters From Fort Robinson and Fort Leavenworth, 1906-1907," *Nebraska History*, 37 (June 1956), pp. 141-142; Mattes, *Indians, Infants, and Infantry*, p. 251; Corliss, Diary, III, March 15, and April 11, 1889; *ANJ*, 26 (March 30, 1889), p. 625; *Ibid.*, 26 (April 20, 1889), p. 677.

19. Corliss, Diary, II, February 27, September 17, and 19, October 9, and 28, and December 16, 1887.

20. Edward N. Glass, *History of the Tenth Cavalry 1866-1921* (Fort Collins, Colorado, 1972), pp. 45-49; Post Returns, August 1904, August-September 1905, April 1906; Crawford *Tribune*, July 1, 1904, June 16, and 30, 1905, June 3, and October 28, 1910.

21. Biddle, *Reminiscences of a Soldier's Wife*, pp. 230, 233; *ANJ*, 33 (October 12, 1895), p. 92.

22. Biddle, *Reminiscences of a Soldier's Wife*, pp. 242-243.

23. Crawford *Tribune*, December 18, 1896.

24. See Chapter 5, "Enlisted Men and Their Families," regarding Biddle's relations with the enlisted community.

25. Mattes, *Indians, Infants, and Infantry*, p. 251; Wight, ed., "A Young Medical Officer's Letters," p. 138.

26. *ANJ*, 27 (January 18, 1890), p. 402.

27. Cleveland *Gazette*, March 5, 1898; Post Returns, April-September 1905; Crawford *Tribune*, April 6, 1894.

28. CO, Fort Robinson, to Lieutenant Charles Young, April 5, 1890, and to AG, USA, May 7, 1897, LS, Fort Robinson.

29. Quoted in Cleveland *Gazette*, April 7, 1894.

30. William T. Corbusier, "Camp Sheridan, Nebraska," *Nebraska History*, 42 (March 1961), p. 45; Corliss, Diary, II, June 30, 1887; *ANJ*, 24 (July 2, 1887), p. 975; Biddle, *Reminiscences of a Soldier's Wife*, p. 229.

31. Corliss, Diary, III, November 27, 1888; *ANJ*, 27 (September 7, 1889), p. 19; *Ibid.*, 32 (June 15, 1895), p. 699.

32. Harold J. Cook, *Tales of the 0-4 Ranch* (Lincoln, 1968), p. 67; Corliss, Diary, III, May 18, 1890; Crawford *Tribune*, August 19, 1904.

33. Donald Danker, Interview with Miss [Clarissa?] Lindeman (NSHS, Lincoln).

34. Don Rickey, Jr., *Forty Miles a Day on Beans and Hay, the Enlisted Soldier Fighting the Indian Wars* (Norman, 1973), pp. 66-67, Corliss, Diary, III, March 2, 1889, and July 11, 1889; *Souvenir Book: Crawford, Nebraska, 75th Year, 1886-1961*, (Crawford, 1961), p. 127; Crawford *Tribune*, November 4, 1910, and February 17, 1911.

35. Crawford *Bulletin*, February 3, 1900; Petition, Robinson Post #261, G.A.R., to the Secretary of War, May 5, 1894, AGO File 6427 ACP 81 (NA, RG 94); Richmond *Planet*, December 18, 1897.

36. *ANJ*, 25 (July 30, 1887), p. 6; Corliss, Diary, II, July 7, 1887.

37. *ANJ*, 30 (November 19, 1892), p. 213; *Ibid.*, 30 (December 10, 1892), p. 257; *Ibid.*, 30 (December 17, 1892), p. 271; CO, Fort Robinson, to Captain James A. Hutton, October 27, 1892, LS, Fort Robinson.

38. *ANJ*, 30 (May 27, 1893), p. 659; *Ibid.*, 31 (July 28, 1894), p. 842; CO, 8th Infantry, to AG, USA, LS, 8th Infantry (NA, RG 391); CO, Fort Robinson, to Captain James A. Hutton, February 21, 1894, to AG, DP, February 26, 1894, and to AAG, DP, March 8, 1894, LS, Fort Robinson; Post Returns, April-July 1894.

NOTES FOR CHAPTER 5

1. Coffman, *The Old Army*, p. 308; Miller J. Stewart, "Army Laundresses: Ladies of the 'Soap Suds Row,'" *Nebraska History*, 61 (Winter 1980), p. 434.

2. Post Surgeon to Medical Director, DP, December [?] 1889, and to Post Adjutant, August 10, 1893; Sanitary Reports, July and December 1887, February 1888, and August 1893, MH, Fort Robinson.

3. Post Adjutant to Unit Commanders, June 3, 1891, LS, Fort Robinson.

4. Post Adjutant to Post QM, June 22, 1891, LS, Fort Robinson.

5. Post Surgeon to CO, Fort Robinson, September 3, 1903, LS, Post Surgeon.

6. Post Surgeon to Medical Director, DP, December [?] 1889, MH, Fort Robinson.

7. Sanitary Report, July 1891, MH, Fort Robinson; *ANJ*, 35 (April 2, 1898), p. 590.

8. Sanitary Report, July 1891, MH, Fort Robinson.

9. *Ibid.*, August 1897.

10. *Ibid.*, July 1891.

11. CO, Fort Robinson, to AG, DeptMo, March 23, 1898, LS, Fort Robinson; Entry, March 1898, MH, Fort Robinson; *ANJ*, 35 (April 2, 1898), p. 590.

12. *Ibid.*; Crawford *Tribune*, March 25, 1898.

13. Crawford *Clipper*, January 22 and 29, 1892. Patton's punishment could not have been too severe. Less than two years later, he was promoted to sergeant in E Troop, the same unit in which Cragg served. *ANJ*, 32 (February 9, 1895), p. 390.

14. Sanitary Report, July 1891; Post Surgeon to AG, USA, June 30, 1893, MH, Fort Robinson; Orders 73, September 25, 1894, Post Orders.

15. Sanitary Report, July 1891, and Post Surgeon to AG, USA, June 30, 1893, MH, Fort Robinson.

16. Donald Danker, interviews with Miss [Clarissa?] Lindeman, and Sergeant W. F. Heck, retired (NSHS, Lincoln); CO, Fort Robinson, to AG, DeptMo, August 5, 1902, LS, Fort Robinson.

17. Omaha *Bee*, September 19, 1893.

18. CO, Fort Robinson, to AAG, DP, August 10, 1893, LS, Fort Robinson.

19. VA File XC 2648848, Rufus Slaughter; Medical Director, DP, to AAG, DP, September 29, 1893, MH, Fort Robinson. These figures include officers' families.

20. Census of Fort Robinson, Nebraska, August 5, 1893, Enclosure to Letter, Post Surgeon, to Post Adjutant, August 10, 1893, MH, Fort Robinson; VA File XC 2659372, John C. Proctor.

21. *ANJ*, 29 (July 2, 1892), p. 782.

22. *Ibid.*, 32 (March 2, 1895), p. 439; Sanitary Report, August 1893, and Entries, April and August 1904, and February 1906, MH, Fort Robinson; Crawford *Bulletin*, September 19, 1902.

23. Sanitary Reports, June 1894, March 1897, January 1899, March 1900, July 1902, and January 1904, MH, Fort Robinson.

24. Surgeon Peter Field began in 1904 to note how many previous births there had been in a family to whom an infant was born. The data that follows is taken from his entries in the post Medical History.

25. The son born to the wife of Sergeant Silas Johnson was not mentioned by the surgeon, but noted by Chaplain Anderson in his March 1906, report. AGO File 53910 (NA, RG 94).

26. Don Rickey, Jr., Interview with Simpson Mann (NSHS, Lincoln), Omaha *Bee*, November 28, 1883; Omaha *World Herald*, February 20, 1938; Crawford *Tribune*, December 5 and 22, 1899, and June 22, 1900.

27. Cleveland *Gazette*, July 24, 1886; Crawford *Tribune*, November 20, 1896, and September 18, 1903; Crawford *Bulletin*, September 19, 1902; Monthly Reports, Chaplain Anderson, December 1904, and December 1905, AGO File 53910.

28. CO, K/9th Cav., to CO, Fort Robinson, February 10, 1887, and Endorsement, CO, Fort Robinson, to CO, K/9th Cav., Register of Correspondence, Fort Robinson (NA, RG 393).

29. Private George Fredericks, K/9th Cav., to CO, K/9th Cav., March 8, 1887, and Endorsements of March 8, 9, and 10, 1887; CO, Fort Robinson, to CO, K/9th Cav., March 14, 1887; Private George Fredericks to CO, Fort Robinson, March 18, 1887, and Endorsements of March 19 and 26, 1887, Register of Correspondence, Fort Robinson.

30. Post QM to CO, Fort Robinson, March 29, 1888, Register of Correspondence, Fort Robinson; CO, Fort Robinson, to CO, G/9th Cav., July 19, 1893, and to CO, A/9th Cav., November 19, 1894, LS, Fort Robinson.

31. CO, Fort Robinson, to Lieutenant E. F. Ladd, 9th Cav., July 21, 1890, to CO, I/9th Cav., July 23, 1890, and to Lieutenant E. Hubert, 8th Inf., July 25, 1890, LS, Fort Robinson.

32. Post Adjutant to Post QM, May 28, 1891, and CO, Fort Robinson, to AAG, DP, June 11, 1891, LS, Fort Robinson.

33. CO, Fort Robinson, to Trumpeter Rogers, I/9th Cav., October 6, 1895, LS, Fort Robinson.

34. Leckie, *The Buffalo Soldiers*, p. 232.

35. CO, Fort Robinson, to CO, A/9th Cav., February 3, 1893, LS, Fort Robinson.

36. *ANJ*, 32 (February 23, 1895), p. 422; *Ibid.*, 33 (December 7, 1895), p. 236.

37. CO, Fort Robinson, to AAG, DP, August 10, 1893, and to CO, A/9th Cav., November 20, 1893, LS, Fort Robinson; Endorsement, August 8, 1894, to letter, Mrs. Bertie G. Fort to the Secretary of War, July 28, 1894, QM Consolidated File, Fort Robinson (NA, RG 92).

38. CO, Fort Robinson, to CO, I/9th Cav., December 23, 1894, LS, Fort Robinson.

39. This data was compiled from the correspondence section of Post Returns. The War Department indicated its approval of each married re-enlistee by telegram. The messages do not suggest when the marriages took place but do indicate that a growing number of men took wives.

40. Endorsement, June 22, 1902, on Lincoln Washington to CO, 10th Cav., n.d., LS, 10th Cav. (NA, RG 391); *ANJ*, 37 (September 23, 1899), p. 81; *Ibid.*, 37 (December 9, 1899), p. 344; Chief Clerk, DeptMo, to Sergeant Major Lincoln Washington, April 13, 1910, Miscellaneous Records, DeptMo (NA, RG 393).

41. Monthly Reports, Chaplain Anderson, May 1903, August 1904, and September 1904, AGO File 53910.

42. Captain J. W. Watson, 10th Cav., to Adjutant, 10th Cav., December 5, 1898, cited in Herschel Cashin, et al., *Under Fire with the Tenth Cavalry* (Huntsville, 1899), p. 186; Crawford *Bulletin*, July 29, 1904; Crawford *Tribune*, July 29, 1904; Monthly Report, Chaplain Anderson, August 1904, AGO File 53910. Mrs. Bell was taken to Omaha for trial by a federal court, according to the Crawford *Tribune*, August 5, 1904.

43. Monthly Report, Chaplain Anderson, August 1904, AGO File 53910.

44. Kean to Medical Director, DP, December [?] 1889, and Adair to Medical Director, DP, December 23, 1889, MH, Fort Robinson. Both letters responded to the Medical Director's request for an assessment of the living conditions for married soldiers and for possible solutions to a lack of coherent policy regarding them.

45. Sanitary Report, August 1893, MH, Fort Robinson.

NOTES FOR CHAPTER 6

1. Grange, "Fort Robinson," pp. 198-201; Homer W. Wheeler, *Buffalo Days; Forty Years in the Old West* (Indianapolis, n.d.), p. 123; Omaha *Bee*, September 19, 1883.

2. *Ibid.*; Post Returns, August-December 1883; Diagram of Cavalry Barracks Built By Troops, Fiscal Year Ending June 30, 1884, Miscellaneous Fortifications File, Fort Robinson #8, Records of the Office of the Chief of Engineers (NA, RG 77).

3. Post Surgeon to AG, USA, June 30, 1893, MH, Fort Robinson, CO, Fort Robinson, to AAG, DP, September 25, 1894, LS, Fort Robinson.

4. Post Surgeon to AG, USA, June 30, 1893, MH, Fort Robinson.

5. Don Rickey, Jr., Interview with Simpson Mann.

6. *ANJ*, 27 (January 11, 1890), p. 386.

7. Rickey, Interview with Simpson Mann; Sanitary Report, July 1891, MH, Fort Robinson.

8. CO, D/8th Inf., to CO, Fort Robinson, January 21, 1888, Register of Correspondence, Fort Robinson.

9. Sanitary Report, May 1887, and December 1887, MH, Fort Robinson; General Crook to the AAG, DivMo, August 27, 1887, Crook Letterbooks, I; Rickey, Interview with Simpson Mann.

10. *Ibid.*; Sanitary Report, November 1889; Post Surgeon to AG, USA, June 30, 1893, MH, Fort Robinson.

11. Post Surgeon to Post Adjutant, September 8, 1892; Sanitary Report, October 1894, and endorsement, CO, Fort Robinson, to Post Surgeon, November 8, 1894; Sanitary Report, November 1899, MH, Fort Robinson.

12. Register of Contracts, 1881-1912, Volumes 9 and 10 (NA, RG 92); Post Surgeon to Post Adjutant, May [?], and July 5, 1902, MH, Fort Robinson; Report of the SG, *Annual Report of the Department of War, 1912*, I, p. 695.

13. Sanitary Report, October 1894, and May 1895, MH, Fort Robinson; CO, Fort Robinson, to AG, DeptMo, August 5, 1902, LS, Fort Robinson.

14. Post Surgeon to Post Adjutant, May 8, 1909, MH, Fort Robinson.

15. Sanitary Report, October 1894, January 1895, and January 1897; Post Surgeon to Post Adjutant, January 17, 1895, MH, Fort Robinson; Report of CG, DeptMo, *Annual Report of the Department of War, 1910*, III, pp. 82-83.

16. Russell F. Weigley, *History of the United States Army* (New York, 1967), pp. 269-270; James A. Huston, *The Sinews of War: Army Logistics 1775-1953* (Washington, D.C., 1966), p. 268; Report of the AG, *Annual Report of the Department of War, 1887,* I, p. 84.

17. CO, Fort Robinson, to AAG, DP, August 30, 1886, LS, Fort Robinson; Rickey, Interview with Simpson Mann; Report of the Commissary General, *Annual Report of the Department of War, 1883,* I, p. 585.

18. Post Returns, August 1892; Order 142, August 27, 1892, Post Orders.

19. Corbusier, "Camp Sheridan, Nebraska," p. 33; CO, Fort Robinson, to CO, K/9th Cav., March 12, 1890, LS, Fort Robinson; Report of Inspection, Fort Robinson, August 21, 1893; Reports of Inspections, DP, II (NA, RG 393).

20. CO, C/9th Cav., to D. M. Ferry and Company, Detroit, March 15, 1886, LS, C/9th Cav. (NA, RG 391); Order 33, February 19, 1890, Order 29, February 22, 1892, and General Order 8, February 18, 1896, Post Orders.

21. Order 48, March 10, 1890, Order 241, November 9, 1890, and Order 40, March 9, 1892, Post Orders.

22. Order 236, November 11, 1889, Post Orders.

23. CO, C/9th Cav., to Post Adjutant, August 19, 1885, and to CO, M/5th Cav., September 11, 1885, LS, C/9th Cav.

24. CO, C/9th Cav., to Lieutenant C. J. Crane, August 12, September 3, and October 7, 1885, LS, C/9th Cav.

25. Order 141, August 14, 1886, Post Orders; Entry, April 1891, MH, Fort Robinson; Post Surgeon to Chief Surgeon, DeptMo, April 15, 1903, and to Post Adjutant, April 15, 1903, LS, Post Surgeon.

26. CO, Fort Robinson, to AAG, DP, April 18, 1893, and to Post Surgeon, August 3, 1899, LS, Fort Robinson; Post Returns, June 1896; Sanitary Report, March 1897, and Special Sanitary Report, December 16, 1899, MH, Fort Robinson; Report of the SG, *Annual Report of the Department of War, 1897,* I, p. 568.

27. Sanitary Report, August 1900, and June 1901, MH, Fort Robinson; Post Surgeon to SG, USA, September 8, 1900, and to Post Adjutant, January 7, 1902, LS, Post Surgeon; Post Returns, November 1900; Crawford *Tribune,* October 4, 1901.

28. Post Surgeon to AG, USA, June 30, 1893, MH, Fort Robinson.

29. *Ibid.,* Register of Beef and Vegetable Contracts, 1894-1895 (NA, RG 92).

30. Report of the Commissary General, *Annual Report of the Department of War, 1895,* I, p. 380; Sanitary Report, February 1906; Secretary of Agriculture to Secretary of War, March 3, 1906, MH, Fort Robinson.

31. Van Ackeren, *Sioux County,* pp. 148, 197; I. R. Paris, "This Land," Crazy Horse Cultural Center, ed., *Old Timers Tales,* II, pt. 1, p. 30; *Compendium of History, Reminiscence, and Biography of Western Nebraska* (Chicago, 1909), p. 537; Harrison (Nebraska) *Sun,* August 20, 1930.

32. Circular, Fort Robinson, June 11, 1886, Post Orders; CO, Fort Robinson, to CO, G/9th Cav., June 22, 1893, and to CO, D/9th Cav., June 23, 1893, LS, Fort Robinson, Crawford *Tribune*, September 2, October 14, 1910.

33. Rickey, *Forty Miles a Day on Beans and Hay*, p. 82; CO, C/9th Cav., to Miller and Stephenson China and Glass Company, August 4, 1885, LS, C/9th Cav.; CO, H/9th Cav., to QMG, USA, February 23, 1898, LS, H/9th Cav. (NA, RG 391).

34. Order 255, December 30, 1888, Post Orders.

35. Special Order 51, May 17, 1897, Special Order 69, July 5, 1897, and Special Order 78, July 20, 1897, Post Orders.

36. Post Returns, June 1887.

37. Amendment to Sanitary Report of October 1888, November 19, 1888, Sanitary Report, October 1889, and Special Investigation of the Post Guard House, December 9, 1889, MH, Fort Robinson.

38. *Ibid.*; Report of Inspection, Fort Robinson, December 2, 1889, Reports of Inspection, DP, II; Order 88, May 10, 1887, and Order 238, November 14, 1889, Post Orders; CO, Fort Robinson, to AAG, DP, March 8, 1890, LS, Fort Robinson; Sanitary Report, March 1890, MH, Fort Robinson.

39. Report of the QMG, *Annual Report of the Department of War, 1891*, I, p. 511; Register of Contracts, 1881-1912, Volume 5; Post Surgeon to AG, USA, June 30, 1893, MH, Fort Robinson; CO, Fort Robinson, to AAG, DP, August 25, 1892, LS, Fort Robinson.

40. Report of the QMG, *Annual Report of the Department of War, 1897*, I, p. 343; Report of the Chief of Staff, *Ibid., 1911*, I, p. 170; Order 224, November 16, 1887, Order 241, December 6, 1887, Order 129, June 2, 1889, and Order 12, February 17, 1904, Post Orders; Post Surgeon to AG, USA, June 30, 1893, MH, Fort Robinson; Lieutenant A. C. Hart to CO, Fort Robinson, April 19, 1903, Register of LR, Fort Robinson (NA, RG 393).

41. CO, Fort Robinson, to AAG, DP, June 19, 1887, and to the Officer of the Day, May 15, and June 15, 1902, LS, Fort Robinson; Rickey, Interview with Simpson Mann; General Order 155, September 25, 1908, quoted in *Annual Report of the Department of War, 1911*, I, p. 170.

42. Order 48, March 10, 1886, Post Orders; CO, Fort Robinson, to Officer of the Guard, May 18, 1893, and to AG, USA, January 31, 1895, LS, Fort Robinson.

43. *ANJ*, 28 (November 8, 1890), p. 170; CO, Fort Robinson, to AAG, DP, October 16 and 19, 1891, LS, Fort Robinson.

44. Order 182, September 12, 1887, Post Orders.

45. CO, Fort Robinson, to CO, K/9th Cav., January 25, 1887, to the Chief QM, DP, September 26, 1888, and to Sergeant William A. Vrooman, G/9th Cav., June 25, 1894, LS, Fort Robinson; Order 77, May 7, 1892, Post Orders.

46. Post Returns, 1874-1913, record these escapes.

47. Monthly Reports, Chaplain Alexander P. Landry, May 1911, to March 1915, AGO Files 1603701, 1879923, 2006526, and 2130171 (NA, RG 94).

NOTES FOR CHAPTER 7

1. Byron Price, "Mutiny at San Pedro Springs," *By Valor & Arms*, 1 (Spring 1975), pp. 31-34; Robert V. Haynes, "The Houston Mutiny and Riot of 1917," *Southwestern Historical Quarterly*, 74 (April 1973), pp. 418-439. Haynes lists most of the incidents which took place in 1885-1916 in footnote 74 on p. 437. Some others are mentioned in Michael C. Robinson and Frank N. Schubert, "David Fagen: An Afro-American Rebel in the Philippines, 1899-1901," *Pacific Historical Review*, 44 (February 1975), p. 70. Also see Leckie, *The Buffalo Soldiers*, pp. 235-236; Schubert, "The Suggs Affray," pp. 57-68.

2. Proceedings of GCM, Sergeant Emanuel Stance, Fort McKavett, Texas, January 3, 1873 (NA, RG 153). For a summary of Stance's career up to 1887, see Schubert, "The Violent World of Emanuel Stance, Fort Robinson, 1887," *Nebraska History*, 55 (Summer 1974), pp. 203-207.

3. Order 123, June 20, 1887, Post Orders, Fort Robinson.

4. Order 126, June 25, 1887, Post Orders.

5. Order 130, July 4, 1887, Post Orders.

6. Order 225, November 17, 1887, and Orders 226, November 18, 1887, Post Orders.

7. Order 188, September 23, 1887, Post Orders.

8. Order 140, July 13, 1887, Post Orders.

9. Order 241, December 6, 1887, Post Orders.

10. Order 238, December 3, 1887, Post Orders.

11. Rickey, Interview with Simpson Mann.

12. Entry for December 1887, MH, Fort Robinson; CO, Fort Robinson, to AAG, DP, February 5, 1888, LS, Fort Robinson.

13. CO, Fort Robinson, to Honorable Judge Dandy, United States Circuit Court, Omaha, January 4, 1888, LS, Fort Robinson.

14. CO, Fort Robinson, to Governor Thayer, January 4, 1888, and to AAG, DP, March 4, 1888, LS, Fort Robinson; Post Returns, September and December 1886.

15. CO, Fort Robinson, to AAG, DP, February 5, 1888, LS, Fort Robinson.

16. *Ibid.*, March 4, 1888.

17. CO, Fort Robinson, to AAG, DP, March 13, 1888, and December 24, 1888, LS, Fort Robinson.

18. *Ibid.*; Regimental Returns, 9th Cavalry, January 1889 (NA, RG 94).

19. Corliss, Diary, II, December 25, 1887; Rickey, Interview with Simpson Mann.

20. *Ibid.*

21. *ANJ*, 24 (June 18, 1887), p. 936; Record of Summary Court Martials, Fort Robinson (NA, RG 393).

22. *ANJ*, 25 (December 31, 1887), p. 442; *Ibid.*, 25 (January 15, 1888), p. 482.

23. CO, Fort Robinson, to AAG, DP, December 24, 1892, and May 1, 1891, LS, Fort Robinson; *ANJ*, 30 (April 25, 1891), p. 600; *Ibid.*, 30 (May 30, 1891), p. 683.

24. CO, Fort Robinson, to AAG, DP, May 1, 1891, LS, Fort Robinson.

25. *Ibid.*

26. CO, Fort Robinson, to CO, I/9th Cav., May 8, 1891, and to AAG, DP, May 20, 1891, LS, Fort Robinson.

27. Order 40, 9th Cavalry, May 20, 1891, Regimental Orders (NA, RG 391).

28. CO, Fort Robinson, to AAG, DP, June 26, 1891, LS, Fort Robinson; *ANJ*, 32 (May 31, 1895), p. 871.

29. Anonymous Pamphlet, appended to GCMO 41, DP, July 10, 1893, AGO File PRD 13194, Barney McKay (NA, RG 94).

30. CO, Fort Robinson, to AAG, DP, April 29, 1893, LS, Fort Robinson; Omaha *Progress*, April 22, 1893. The broadside was also published in the Omaha *Bee*, May 4, 1893.

31. Order 33, April 29, 1893, Post Orders; Chadron *Citizen*, quoted in Crawford *Tribune*, April 28, 1893.

32. GCMO 41, DP, July 10, 1893, AGO File PRD 13194.

33. Application of Attorney Alphonso C. Hart for Removal of Disability from Barney McKay, n.d., AGO File PRD 13194; CO, Fort Robinson, to Officers of the Guard, May 18, 1893, LS, Fort Robinson.

34. Application of Attorney Alphonso C. Hart for Removal of Disability from Barney McKay, n.d., AGO File PRD 13194.

35. *Ibid.*; GCMO 41, DP, July 10, 1893, AGO File PRD 13194.

36. Proceedings of GCM, Sergeant Barney McKay, Fort Robinson, June 1-21, 1893 (NA, RG 153); GCMO 41, DP, September 4, 1893.

37. Proceedings of GCM, Sergeant Barney McKay.

38. Lieutenant Montgomery D. Parker to Honorable John M. Langston, July 22, 1893, appended to *Ibid.*

39. Proceedings of GCM, Sergeant Barney McKay.

40. Barney McKay to J. Addison Porter, Secretary to the President, Washington, D.C., October 6, 1897, AGO File PRD 13194.

41. Confidential Letter, CO, Fort Robinson, to CG, DP, May 6, 1893, appended to Proceedings of GCM, Sergeant Barney McKay. The letter was not entered in the Department's ledger of letters received. The evidence against Plummer is carefully examined in Earl F. Stover, "Chaplain Henry V. Plummer, His Ministry and His Court-Martial," *Nebraska History*, 56 (Spring 1975), pp. 29-32. Also see Crawford *Tribune*, May 5, 1893.

42. *Ibid.*; VA File XC 2659455, Barney McKay; Nellie Arnold Plummer, *Out of the Depths or the Triumph of the Cross* (Hyattsville, Maryland, 1927), p. 138. Bernard probably drew some satisfaction from his role in forcing Plummer out of the service during the following year. See Chapter 10.

43. AG, USA, to the Secretary of War, May 7, 1894, Barney McKay to the Secretary of War, July 7, 1897, and House Bill 4900, 56th Cong., 1st Sess., December 19, 1899, AGO File PRD 13194.

44. Schubert, "The Suggs Affray," p. 64.

NOTES FOR CHAPTER 8

1. Cleveland *Gazette*, March 5, 1898; Indianapolis *Freeman*, February 25, 1905.

2. Richmond *Planet*, December 18, 1897; *ANJ*, 28 (May 2, 1891), p. 620; Proceedings of GCM, Sergeant Barney McKay.

3. Crawford *Tribune*, October 15 and 29, 1897, January 7, 1898, November 27, 1908, November 5, 1909, December 13 and 20, 1912, and January 13, 1913.

4. Cleveland *Gazette*, May 4, 1895; Crawford *Tribune*, December 18, 1908.

5. Grange, "Fort Robinson," p. 193; Henry G. Waltmann, "The Subsistence Policy with Special Reference to the Red Cloud and Spotted Tail Agencies," unpublished M.A. thesis, University of Nebraska, 1959, p. 91; Sutlers and Traders File, Fort Robinson (NA, RG 94); Fanny McGillycuddy, "Notes kept . . . at Camp Robinson," p. 18; Norbert R. Mahnken, "The Sidney-Black Hills Trails," *Nebraska History*, 30 (September 1948), p. 213.

6. Special Order 6, March 17, 1874, Special Orders, Sioux Expedition; CO, Camp Robinson, to CO, Sioux Expedition, September 7, 1874, Endorsements Sent, Sioux Expedition; Sutlers and Traders File, Fort Robinson.

7. Grange, "Fort Robinson," p. 209; Agnes W. Spring, *The Cheyenne and Black Hills Stage and Express Routes* (Lincoln, n.d.), pp. 55, 81.

8. Sutlers and Traders File, Fort Robinson; C. F. Gund, "Notes on Early History of Crawford," typescript (NSHS, Lincoln); Omaha *Bee*, September 19, 1883; *Reminiscences of a Ranchman*, pp. 156, 165; "Fort Robinson, Neb." 1882, Real Estate Division Map File, Records of the Office of the Chief of Engineers (NA, RG 77).

9. Grange, "Fort Robinson," pp. 217, 219.

10. Order 198, October 11, 1887, and Order 238, December 2, 1887, Post Orders, Fort Robinson.

11. Reminiscence of Charles and Mary Hansen, *Souvenir Book: Crawford, Nebraska, 75th Year, 1886-1961*, p. 49; CO, Fort Robinson, to AAG, DP, May 16, 1890, LS, Fort Robinson; B. S. Paddock to CO, Fort Robinson, December 26, 1886, with two endorsements, Register of Correspondence, Fort Robinson; Report of Inspection, Fort Robinson, December 2, 1889, Reports of Inspection, DP, I.

12. Corliss, Diary, I, June 30, 1887, and III, August 1, 1889; *ANJ*, 27 (September 7, 1889), p. 19; *Ibid.*, 30 (June 24, 1893), p. 737; *Ibid.*, 30 (November 19, 1892), p. 213; *Ibid.*, 30 (December 17, 1892), p. 271.

13. *Ibid.* 25 (June 16, 1888), p. 936; *Ibid.*, 25 (June 30, 1888), p. 975; *Ibid.*, 26 (December 22, 1888), p. 321.

14. AG, USA, to CG, DivMo, February 5, 1889, QM Consolidated File, Fort Robinson, Report of the AG, *Annual Report of the Department of War, 1889*, I, p. 86; Order 70, March 25, 1889, Order 221, October 26, 1889, Order 226, October 31, 1889, Post Orders. Fort Robinson; CO, Fort Robinson, to Post Exchange Officer, April 21, 1893, LS, Fort Robinson.

15. QMG to Chief QM, DivMo, January 10, 1890, QM Consolidated File, Fort Robinson; CO, Fort Robinson, to AAG, DP, May 4, 1890, May 16, 1890, and December 2[?] 1892, LS, Fort Robinson.

16. CO, Fort Robinson, to B. S. Paddock, December 3, 1893, and June 6, 1894, LS, Fort Robinson.

17. *ANJ*, 27 (January 4, 1890), p. 369; Crawford *Tribune*, March 8, 1901, June 26, 1903, January 12, 1906, and February 12, 1915.

18. Omaha *Bee*, December 6, 1888. Real estate tax records for Crawford support the author of the *Bee* article, who signed himself "WDE."

19. Beatrice Coffee, "My Grandfather's Pioneer Days in Sioux County," typescript, Everett Pitt Wilson MSS (NSHS, Lincoln); Rhoda Pederson, "A Western Nebraska Pioneer," Wilson MSS; "Charles William Percy," "C. G. Hollibaugh," and "James English Family," *Souvenir Book*, pp. 41, 87, 120.

20. Biddle, *Reminiscences of a Soldier's Wife* , p. 224; Crawford *Gazette*, December 15, 1893; CO, Fort Robinson, to Post Exchange Officer, April 23, 1893, and to AG, USA, February 27, 1893, LS, Fort Robinson; Order 57, July 11, 1893, Post Orders, Fort Robinson.

21. Report of the AG, *Annual Report of the Department of War, 1892*, I, p. 57; Order 136, July 1, 1890, Post Orders, Fort Robinson; CO, Fort Robinson, to AAG, DP, January 20, 1892, LS, Fort Robinson; Report of Inspection, Fort Robinson, August 21, 1893, Reports of Inspection, DP, II.

22. This summary is compiled from data in post orders for 1889-1892.

23. Post Returns, January 1893; CO, Fort Robinson, to AG, USA, February 27, 1893, and to AAG, DP, December 31, 1894, LS, Fort Robinson; Order 11, February 29, 1895, Post Orders, Fort Robinson; Report of Inspection, Fort Robinson, September 3, 1894, Reports of Inspections, DP, II.

24. CO, Fort Robinson to AG, USA, June 30, 1892, and September 5, 1894; LS, Fort Robinson; Statement of Financial Operations of Post Exchange, at Fort Robinson, Nebraska, for six months ending June 30, 1899, QM Consolidated File, Fort Robinson.

25. CO, Fort Robinson, to AG, USA, January 18, 1893, and to Post Exchange Officer, May 13, 1898, LS, Fort Robinson; Lincoln *State Journal*, January 25, 1896.

26. Order 199, September 17, 1890, Order 33, May 21, 1894, and Special Order 100, August 31, 1897, Post Orders, Fort Robinson.

27. Statements of QM Sergeant M. E. Drew, Commissary Sergeant Karl J. Thompson, Ordnance Sergeant W. B. Rose, and Hospital Steward Oscar F. Temple, Report of the AG on Canteens, *Annual Report of the Department of War, 1899*, I, pt. 1, pp. 206, 228, 245, 269.

28. CO, Fort Robinson, to AG, DeptMo, August 22, 1902, and to AG, USA, January 18, 1893, and to AG, USA, January 15, 1894, LS, Fort Robinson.

29. Report of BG John Coppinger, CG, DP, *Annual Report of the Department of War, 1896*, p. 175; Police Court Docket, Crawford, Nebraska (Municipal Records, Crawford, Nebraska); Post Returns, April 1896; *ANJ*, 33 (April 25, 1896), p. 614; *Ibid.*, 33 (May 9, 1896), p. 658; *Ibid.*, 33 (May 23, 1896), p. 695.

30. *ANJ*, 33 (May 9, 1896), p. 658; *Ibid.*, 33 (April 11, 1896), p. 577.

31. CO, Fort Robinson, to AG, DP, June 23, 1897, and to Dawes County Board of Commissioners, June 30, 1893, LS, Fort Robinson.

32. Crawford *Tribune*, June 18, 1896.

33. Statements of First Lieutenant M. F. Davis and Captain J. G. Galbraith, Report of the AG on Canteens, *Annual Report of the Department of War, 1899*, I., pt. 1, p. 105.

34. Post Returns, February 1902; Report of the Secretary of War, and the IG, USA, *Annual Report of the Department of War, 1902*, I, pp. 42, 404; CO, Fort Robinson, to AG, DeptMo, August 22, 1902, LS, Fort Robinson.

35. Grange, "Fort Robinson," p. 233; *Annual Report of the Department of War, 1905*, I, p. 286.

36. *ANJ*, 38 (July 8, 1901), p. 998.

37. Rickey, *Forty Miles a Day on Beans and Hay*, p. 187; Rickey, Interview with Simpson Mann; Merrill J. Mattes, *Indians, Infants, and Infantry, The Story of Andrew and Elizabeth Burt* (Denver, 1960), p. 252; Corliss, Diary, II, June 7, 1887, and III, June 29, 1888; Post Surgeon to AG, USA, June 30, 1893, MH, Fort Robinson.

38. Cleveland *Gazette*, June 26, 1886.

39. *Ibid.*, July 24, 1886.

40. Crawford *Tribune*, June 4 and 18, 1897.

41. *Ibid.*, June 25, 1897.

42. Schubert, "The Black Regular Army Regiments in Wyoming, 1885-1912," pp. 57-61, 101.

43. Crawford *Tribune*, September 1, 1899, and May 30, 1902.

44. Thomas J. Clement, "Athletics in the American Army," *Colored American Magazine*, 8 (January 1905), p. 25; Albert S. Lowe, "Camp Life of the Tenth U.S. Cavalry," *Ibid.*, 7 (March 1904), pp. 205-206; CO, 10th Cavalry, to [?], February 11, 1903, LS, 10th Cavalry.

45. Clement, "Athletics in the American Army," p. 25; Crawford *Tribune*, May 19, 1905.

46. *Ibid.*, April 20, 1906; Crawford *Bulletin*, July 11, 1902; William W. Hay, interview with Chaplain Earl F. Stover, San Antonio, 1967, Marvin Fletcher collection, USAMHI archives.

47. Crawford *Tribune*, October 25, 1907, November 1, 15, and 22, 1907, and November 20, 1908.

48. *Ibid.*, November 15, 1905, January 10, February 23, and April 5, 1912.

49. General Order 12, May 26, 1897, Post Orders, Fort Robinson.

50. CO, Fort Robinson, to AG, USA, November 4, 1902, LS, Fort Robinson; Clement, "Athletics in the American Army," p. 25; R. R. Wright, ed., *Encyclopedia of the African Methodist Episcopal Church* (Philadelphia, 1947), p. 67.

51. Crawford *Tribune*, July 10, 1903; Reminiscence of Howard Dodd, typescript (Vertical File, Fort Robinson Museum).

52. Crawford *Clipper*, January 8 and 15, 1892; Crawford *Tribune*, May 18, 1904.

53. *Ibid.*, December 29, 1905, March 2, April 13 and 20, 1906.

54. General Order 9, DivMo, August 27, 1880; Post Returns, September 1880.

55. CO, C/8th Infantry, to CO, Fort Robinson, December 6, 1886, and CO, Fort Robinson, to CO, C/8th Infantry, December 6, 1886, Register of Correspondence, Fort Robinson.

56. *ANJ*, 25 (December 31, 1887), p. 443; Order 216, October 9, 1890, Post Orders, Fort Robinson.

57. Armstrong family history, Marvin Fletcher Collection, USAMHI archives.

58. Order 185, September 20, 1887, Post Orders, Fort Robinson.

59. Corliss, Diary, II, December 1, 5, and 8, 1886, and August 31, September 24, October 12, and December 11, 1887; Order 220 and 221, November 12, 1887, Post Orders, Fort Robinson.

60. J. S. Collins to Webb Hayes, October 9, 1888, and March 14, 1890, R. B. Hayes MSS (RBHML, Fremont, Ohio); *ANJ*, 35 (September 18, 1897), p. 38; VA File C 2441072, George Byers.

61. Post Returns, August 1886; CO, Fort Robinson, to Chief Signal Officer, USA, September 23, and October 12, 1886, LS, Fort Robinson.

62. *Winners of the West*, 9 (June 30, 1934), p. 4.

63. Cleveland *Gazette*, November 27, 1886, and January 12, 1889.

64. Lowe, "Camp Life of the Tenth U.S. Cavalry," p. 206; Charlie Simmons, "Thanksgiving Day in the Tenth Cavalry," *The Voice of the Negro*, 2 (January 1905), p. 663; Indianapolis *Freeman*, December 3, 1904.

65. Simmons, "Thanksgiving Day," pp. 663-664; Crawford *Tribune*, May 5, 1905; Chaplain William T. Anderson, Monthly Report, May 1904, AGO File 53910.

66. Simmons, "Thanksgiving Day," p. 664; Indianapolis *Freeman*, December 3, 1904.

67. Monthly Report, Chaplain Anderson, January 1905, AGO File 53910; Stephen B. Barrow, "Christmas in the United States Army," *Colored American Magazine*, 8 (February 1905), p. 96; Corliss, Diary, II, December 24, 1887.

68. Barrow, "Christmas in the United States Army," pp. 96-97.

69. *Ibid.*

70. *ANJ*, 27 (November 30, 1889), p. 271; Biddle, *Reminiscences of a Soldier's Wife*, p. 242; Crawford *Tribune*, April 4, December 8, and 15, 1905, and January 19, 1906.

71. Crawford *Tribune*, March 3, and 31, May 12, June 16, and December 29, 1905.

72. Crawford *Tribune*, March 3 and 31, May 12, June 16, and December 29, 1905, and April 13, 1906.

73. Crawford *Tribune*, August 4 and 18, 1905; Lowe, "Camp Life of the Tenth U.S. Cavalry," pp. 205-206.

74. Crawford *Tribune*, May 9, 1902, January 5 and December 9, 1904, February 17, 1905, April 27, 1906, and February 8, 1907; Van Ackeren, *Sioux County*, p. 209.

75. *ANJ*, 25 (July 2, 1888), p. 1040; Order 155, July 2, 1889, Post Orders, Fort Robinson; CO, Fort Robinson, to Committee on Arrangements for July 4, 1893, June 29, 1893, LS, Fort Robinson.

76. "Gibbons Family History," Crazy Horse Cultural Center, *Old Timers Tales*, I, p. 142; Crawford *Bulletin*, July 9, 1900; Crawford *Tribune*, July 2 and 9, 1897, June 6 and 27, 1902, July 5, 1907, and July 7, 1911.

77. *Ibid.*, July 10, 1908. The town paid $50 for the band in 1890. A year earlier, four special policemen cost $5 each. CO, Fort Robinson, to A. O. Cheney, May 21, 1889, LS, Fort Robinson; Crawford City Council, Minutes, I, August 7, 1889 (Municipal Records, Crawford, Nebraska).

78. Crawford *Tribune*, June 27, 1902, and May 17, 1907.

79. *Ibid.*, July 11, 1902.

80. Crawford City Council, Minutes, II, July 5, 1907; Crawford *Tribune*, July 5, 1907.

81. *Ibid.*, July 11th, 1902, July 10, 1903, July 14, 1905, September 23, 1910, and September 5 and 22, 1913; Regimental Returns, 8th Cavalry, August 1908 (NA, RG 94).

NOTES FOR CHAPTER 9

1. Order 168, October 3, 1886, Order 232, October 31, 1890, and Order 151, September 12, 1892, Post Orders, Fort Robinson; CO, Fort Robinson, to Sgt. Ingoman, D/9 Cav., Blacksmith Walker, I/9 Cav., Trumpr. Rogers, G/9 Cav., and Pvt. J. Davis, G/9 Cav., March 22, 1893, LS, Fort Robinson.

2. CO, Fort Robinson, to AG, USA, July 17, 1891, LS, Fort Robinson; Report of Post Schools, April 30, 1892, School Reports, DP (NA, RG 393).

3. Report of CG, DeptMo, *Annual Report of the Department of War, 1912*, III, p. 44.

4. Corliss, Diary, II, March 28 and 31, 1887, January 23 and 28, 1888, III, July 5, August 1, September 2, and November 19, 1889, May 3 and 12, July 12 and 14, and August 12, 1890; Crawford *Tribune*, December 18, 1905.

5. *Ibid.*, November 6, 1896, June 4, 1897, November 16, 1906, April 10, May 22, and December 4, 1908.

6. Anthony J. Hytrek, "The History of Fort Robinson, Nebraska, from 1900 to the Present" (Unpublished N.A. Thesis, Chadron State College, 1971), p. 16; Hay interview, Marvin Fletcher collection.

7. Crawford *Tribune*, September 9 and October 20, 1910, January 10, 1912, and February 14, 1913; R. E. Hageman, ed., *Fighting Rebels and Redskins; Experiences in Army Life of Colonel George B. Sanford 1861-1892* (Norman, 1969), p. 95.

8. Hay interview.

9. *Annual Report of the Department of·War, 1878*, p. v: *Ibid.*, 1880, p. ix; *Ibid.*, 1883, p. 21; *Ibid.*, 1884, p. 878; *Ibid.*, 1891, p. 70.

10. CO, Fort Robinson, to AG, USA, October 30, 1890, LS, Fort Robinson.

11. CO, F/9 Cav., to CO, Fort Robinson, March 13, 1897, Register of Correspondence, Fort Robinson; CO, Fort Robinson, to AAG, DP, November 28, 1892, LS, Fort Robinson.

12. Cleveland *Gazette*, August 9, 1890, and May 4, 1895; VA File XC 2659455, Barney McKay).

13. Theophilus G. Steward, *The Colored Regulars in the United States Army* (New York, 1969), p. 281; Voucher, Fort Robinson, 9 December, 1902, 10th Cavalry papers, USAMHI archives.

14. CO, Fort Robinson, to AAG, DP, January 24, 1894, LS, Fort Robinson; Report of Post Schools, April 30, 1892, School Reports, DP; Monthly Report, Chaplain Plummer, April 1893, AGO File 6474 ACP 81.

15. CO, Fort Robinson, to CO, F/9 Cav., March 30, 1889, and to CO, L/8 Inf., March 30, 1889, LS, Fort Robinson; Order 211, October 31, 1891, Order 186, October 31, 1892, and Order 15, February 17, 1893, Post Orders, Fort Robinson; Cleveland *Gazette*, March 5, 1898.

16. Report of the IG, *Annual Report of the Department of War, 1894*, p. 94; Order 77, October 22, 1895, Post Orders, Fort Robinson. The advanced course prescribed by the Army for post schools included elementary algebra, geometry, plane trigonometry, grammar, geography, descriptive astronomy, history, anatomy, composition, and elocution. *Annual Report of the Department of War, 1893*, IV, p. 10.

17. Chaplain Anderson to CO, Fort Robinson, April 25, 1903, and Endorsement, CO, Fort Robinson, to Post QM, April 25, 1903, Register of LR, Fort Robinson; Cleveland *Gazette*, March 5, 1898.

18. Indianapolis *Freeman*. July 19, 1902.

19. Monthly Reports, Chaplain Anderson, October 1902, February and April, 1904, AGO File 53910.

20. B. F. Thornton, "Economy," *Colored American Magazine*, 9 (March 1905), pp. 150-151. This paper and Corporal Joseph Wheelock's essay are reprinted in Schubert, "The Fort Robinson Y.M.C.A., 1902-1907; A Social Organization in a Black Regiment," *Nebraska History*, 55 (Summer 1974), pp. 175-178.

21. Joseph M. Wheelock, "Our Own Editors and Publishers," *Colored American Magazine*, 8 (January 1905), p. 29.

22. Monthly Reports, Chaplain Anderson, February 1903, September 1904, February 1905, and November 1906, AGO File 53910.

23. *Ibid.*, July 1904; Crawford *Bulletin*, July 24, 1903.

24. Rickey, *Forty Miles a Day on Beans and Hay*, p. viii, asserted that the regulars endured such isolation. The comment was deleted from the 1972 printing of Rickey's book.

25. Order 169, October 3, 1886, Order 62, March 31, 1888, Order 254, December 28, 1888, Order 259, December 9, 1899, and Order 1, January 1, 1892, Post Orders, Fort Robinson; CO, Fort Robinson, to AAG, DP, March 31, 1897, LS, Fort Robinson.

26. Order 15, January 23, 1888, and Order 254, December 28, 1888, Post Orders, Fort Robinson; Report of the AG, *Annual Report of the Department of War, 1892*, I, p. 56; Report of the AG, *Ibid., 1897*, pp. 100-101; Corliss, Diary, II, January 25, 1888; Coffman, *The Old Army*, pp. 276-277, 286.

27. Order 15, January 23, 1888, Post Orders, Fort Robinson; CO, Fort Robinson, to AAG, DP, November 30, 1893, LS, Fort Robinson; *ANJ*, 33 (March 14, 1896), p. 499; CO, Fort Robinson, to Lieutenant John Ryan, Ninth Cavalry, n. d., 1899, and to AG, USA, January 7, 1900, LS, Fort Robinson.

28. Corliss, Diary, II, February 3, 1888; CO, Fort Robinson, to AAG, DP, January 31, 1893, November 30, 1893, and October 23, 1897, LS, Fort Robinson; *ANJ*, 33 (March 14, 1896), p. 499.

29. Omaha *Bee*, September 19, 1883.

30. CO, Fort Robinson, to AG, USA, July 17, 1891, LS, Fort Robinson; Chaplain George C. Mullins, Report on Education, *Annual Report of the Department of War, 1883*, p. 715.

31. CO, Fort Robinson, to AG, USA, July 17, 1891, August 26, 1891, and February 2, 1892, and to AAG, DP, July 17, 1891, LS, Fort Robinson.

32. CO, Fort Robinson, to AAG, DP, February 15, 1893, August 21, 1890, and November 26, 1894, LS, Fort Robinson.

33. Corliss, Diary, II, December 27, 1886, April 3 and 17, May 29, 1887, January 2 and 14, 1888.

34. CO, Fort Robinson, to QMC, USA, May 12, 1886, and to AAG, DP, February 15, 1893, LS, Fort Robinson; Report of Post Schools, January 31, 1892, School Reports, DP; Post Surgeon to Editor, New York *Times*, August 10, 1903, and to Editor, *Leslie's Weekly*, August 20, 1903, LS, Post Surgeon.

35. Biddle, *Reminiscences of a Soldier's Wife* , p. 224; Cleveland *Gazette*, March 5, 1898, *ANJ*, 35 (December 31, 1897), p. 443.

36. Omaha *Bee*, September 19, 1883; Lieutenant E. S. Wright to CO, Fort Robinson, December 30, 1887; AAG, DP, to CO, Fort Robinson, February 10, 1888, Register of Correspondence, Fort Robinson; Order 8, January 16, 1889, and Orders 210, October 10, 1889, Post Orders, Fort Robinson; *ANJ*, 30 (October 22, 1892), p. 15.

37. Monthly Reports, Chaplain Plummer, February 1892, April and June 1893, AGO File 6474 ACP 81.

38. Cleveland *Gazette*, August 14, 1886, and January 1, 1887; *ANJ*, 29 (July 2, 1892), p. 782; Richmond *Planet*, December 18, 1897. A copy of the April 22, 1893, *Progress*, is appended to Proceedings of GCM, Sergeant Barney McKay.

39. Indianapolis *Freeman*, September 27, 1902; Wheelock, "Our Own Editors and Publishers," p. 30; *The Voice of the Negro*, I (December 1904), pp. 606-607.

40. Wheelock, "Our Own Editors and Publishers," p. 30.

NOTES FOR CHAPTER 10

1. Post Returns, May 1880-October 1882, and May-December 1890; Omaha *Bee*, November 28, 1883; Report of CG, DP, *Annual Report of the Department of War, 1883*, I, p. 128.

2. *Ibid.*, 1887, p. 428; Omaha *Bee*, December 6, 1888; Crawford *Clipper*, January 8, 1892.

3. Henry V. Plummer to Secretary of War Robert T. Lincoln, n. d. [1881]; Commission, Henry V. Plummer, July 8, 1884, AGO File 6474 ACP 81.

4. Allen Allensworth, another former slave, was commissioned chaplain of the Twenty-Fourth Infantry shortly after Plummer joined the Army. The only black officer to precede Plummer into the service was Lieutenant Henry O. Flipper of the Tenth Cavalry.

5. Testimonial of Mrs. J. Garrard, Enclosure to John C. Langston and Alain Rutherford to the President of the United States, October 27, 1894, AGO File 6474 ACP 81; Monthly Reports, Chaplain Plummer, January 1892, February and October 1893, AGO File 6474 ACP 81. These figures understate the importance of the school for enlisted men's families since officers probably did not send their offspring to mingle with those of black privates.

6. Monthly Reports, Chaplain Plummer, July-October 1892, and April 1893, AGO File 6474 ACP 81.

7. CO, Fort Robinson, to AAG, DP, May 3, 1892, LS, Fort Robinson; Efficiency Reports, Henry V. Plummer, May 17, 1890, and December 15, 1891, AGO File 6474 ACP 81.

8. Monthly Reports, Chaplain Plummer, September 1891, January and February 1892, AGO File 6474 ACP 81; CO, Fort Robinson, to AAG, DP, May 3, 1892, LS, Fort Robinson.

9. CO, Fort Robinson, to Post Chaplain, January 19, 1892, and to AAG, DP, February 16, 1892, LS, Fort Robinson; Sanitary Report, March 31, 1894, MH, Fort Robinson.

10. CO, Fort Robinson, to Post Chaplain, n. d. (November 1892) and to AAG, DP, February 3, 1893, LS, Fort Robinson.

11. CO, Fort Robinson, to AAG, DP, May 1 and July 8, 1891, and February 17, 1892, LS, Fort Robinson.

12. Monthly Report, Chaplain Plummer, March 1892, AGO File 6474 ACP 81.

13. CO, Fort Robinson, to AAG, DP, April 25 and May 3, 1892, and to Chaplain Plummer, May 2, 1892, LS, Fort Robinson.

14. CO, Fort Robinson, to Chaplain Plummer, June 28, 1893, and July 5, 1893, and Endorsement, Bernard to Biddle, July 1, 1893, LS, Fort Robinson.

15. Efficiency Reports, Chaplain Plummer, December 15, 1892, and January 14, 1894, AGO File 6474 ACP 81; CO, Fort Robinson, to AAG, DP, July 29, 1893, LS, Fort Robinson.

16. Chaplain Plummer to AG, USA, April 20, 1894, AGO File 6474 ACP 81.

17. Bishop Henry M. Turner and others to the Secretary of War, April 25, 1894; Petition, Allegheny, Pennsylvania, to the Secretary of War, April 27, 1894, AGO File 6474 ACP 81. These petitions came so soon after Plummer himself wrote to Washington that he must have solicited the endorsements prior to making the proposal to the government.

18. Bishop Turner to the Secretary of War, April 23, 1894, Petition, Robinson Post #261, Grand Army of the Republic, to the Secretary of War, May 5, 1894, and AG, USA, to Chaplain Plummer, n. d., AGO File 6474 ACP 81.

19. Post Returns, June 1894; CO, Fort Robinson, to AAG, DP, June 9, 1894, LS, Fort Robinson.

20. Chaplain Plummer to AG, USA, September 11, 1894, and Endorsements, AGO File 6474 ACP 81.

21. Affidavits, L. N. Freeman, Albert Whipple, C. E. Wilson, and T. G. Harris, October 18, 1894, appended to John M. Langston and Alain Rutherford to the President of the United States, October 21, 1894, AGO File 6474 ACP 81.

22. Affidavit, Mrs. Mary Biddle Lane Garrard, October 18, 1894, appended to *Ibid.*

23. *Ibid.*; Bishop Turner to President Grover Cleveland, October 18, 1894, AGO File 64 74 ACP 81.

24. Record of Admissions, Fort Robinson Hospital, Chaplain Henry V. Plummer, AGO File 6474 ACP 81; CO, Fort Robinson, to AAG, DP, August 9, 1894, LS, Fort Robinson.

25. General Order 56, Headquarters, USA, November 2, 1894; Affidavits, John and Lizzie Miller, October 22, 1894, appended to Langston and Rutherford to the President of the United States, October 27, 1894, AGO File 6474 ACP 81; Proceedings of GCM, Chaplain Henry V. Plummer, August 27-September 7, 1894, Fort Robinson (NA, RG 153).

26. Chaplain Plummer to AG, USA, November 9, 1894, AGO File 6474 ACP 81.

27. Langston and Rutherford to the President, October 27, 1894, AGO File 6474 ACP 81.

28. Cleveland *Gazette*, July 14, 1894.

29. Report of Captain E. H. Crowder to CG, DP, June 28, 1894, LR, DP (NA, RG 393); Proceedings of GCM, Chaplain Henry V. Plummer.

30. *ANJ*, 32 (October 27, 1894), p. 141; Proceedings of GCM, Sergeant David Dillon, September 24, 1894, Fort Robinson (NA, RG 153).

31. *Ibid.*

32. *Ibid.*

33. Delilah L. Beasley, *Negro Trailblazers of California* (Los Angeles, 1919), pp. 292-293.

34. George W. Prioleau, "Is the Chaplain's Work in the Army a Necessity?" Theophilus G. Steward, ed., *Active Service or Gospel Work Among the U.S. Soldiers* (New York, 1897), p. 28.

35. Crawford *Tribune*, January 29 and November 12, 1897, and March 11, 1898.

36. Cleveland *Gazette*, February 20, 1897, and April 9, 1898; Crawford *Tribune*, March 4, 1898.

37. *Ibid.*, May 4, 1898; *Souvenir Book: Crawford, Nebraska, 75th Year, 1886-1961*, pp. 108-112; Crawford *Bulletin*, July 7, 1900.

38. CO, Fort Robinson, to AG, DeptMo, August 5, 1902, LS, Fort Robinson; Monthly Reports, Chaplain Anderson, September and October 1902, and May 1904, AGO File 53910; Sanitary Report, March 1904, MH, Fort Robinson.

39. Crawford *Tribune*, November 27, 1908; Monthly Report, Chaplain Anderson, March 1905, AGO File 53910.

40. *Ibid.*, December 1902.

41. Endorsement, CO, Fort Robinson, January 3, 1903, on *Ibid.*, January 1903; Samuel B. McPheeters to William M. McPheeters, March 15, 1907, quoted in Wight, "A Young Medical Officer's Letters from Fort Robinson and Fort Leavenworth, 1906-1907," p. 146.

42. Monthly Reports, Chaplain Anderson, October 1902, December 1902, December 1904, February 1905, April 1905; Monthly Report, Chaplain Neil P. Brennan, January 1908, AGO File 1311782 (NA, RG 94); David M. Reimers, *White Protestantism and the Negro* (New York, 1965), p. 83.

43. Monthly Reports, Chaplain Brennan, January 1908, and January 1910, AGO Files 1338059 and 1617194; Crawford *Tribune*, April 22, 1901; Monthly Reports, Chaplain Alexander Landry, August 1911, and May 1912, AGO Files 1603701 and 1879823 (NA, RG 94).

NOTES FOR CHAPTER 11

1. Huston, *The Sinews of War*, p. 255; Grange, "Fort Robinson," pp. 232-233; Omaha *Bee*, September 26, 1883; Report, CG, DeptMo *Annual Report of the Department of War, 1902*, IX, p. 54.

2. Percy M. Ashburn, *A History of the Medical Department of the United States Army* (Boston, 1929), pp. 149-150, *Annual Report of the Department of War, 1916*, I, p. 470.

3. Ashburn, *History of the Medical Department*, p. 89; Samuel B. McPheeters to William B. McPheeters, October 11, 1906, Wight, ed., "A Young Medical Officer's Letters from Fort Robinson and Fort Leavenworth, 1906-1907," p. 137.

4. Ashburn, *History of the Medical Department*, pp. 108, 140, 209; Coffman, *The Old Army*, p. 383; *Annual Report of the Department of War, 1901*, I, pt. 2, p. 574.

5. Private Walter Pulpress to the Post Surgeon, April 5, 1899, Register of Correspondence, Post Surgeon.

6. Mrs. Glen Kremen, "Early Days in and Around Glen," *Old Timers Tales*, I, p. 182; I. R. Paris, "This Land," *Ibid.*, II, pt. 1, p. 25; Harold J. Cook, *Tales of the 0-4 Ranch* (Lincoln, 1968), p. 10; *Souvenir Book, Crawford, Nebraska, 75th Year, 1886-1961*, p. 35.

7. CO, Fort Robinson, to Post Surgeon, February 5, 1886, LS, Fort Robinson; Mari Sandoz, *Old Jules* (Lincoln, 1971), pp. 43-53.

8. C. F. Gund, "Notes on Early History of Crawford," typescript (NSHS, Lincoln); *Souvenir Book*, p. 29.

9. Cook, *Tales of the 0-4 Ranch*, pp. 37, 68.

10. Crawford *Tribune*, January 15 and 29, 1897, and January 14, 1898.

11. Grange, "Fort Robinson," p. 219; Captain A. W. Corliss, Diary, II, December 17, 1886; Sanitary Report, March 1888, and January 1890, MH, Fort Robinson.

12. *Ibid.*, October 1894, and January 1899; Report of the SG, *Annual Report of the Department of War, 1884*, p. 724; Post Surgeon to CO, Fort Robinson, September 28, 1903, and December 8, 1908, LS, Post Surgeon; Post Surgeon to CO, Fort Robinson, December 6, 1903, and April 26, 1904, CO, Fort Robinson, to Troop Commanders, December 6, 1903, Register of LR, Fort Robinson.

13. Crawford City Council, Minutes, II, December 19, 1900 (Municipal Records, Crawford, Nebraska); Entries for December 1900, January 1901, and January 1902, MH, Fort Robinson; Crawford *Tribune*, December 18, 1900, February 1, April 26, October 18, and November 29, 1901, and January 31, 1902.

14. Post Surgeon to CO, Fort Robinson, January 31, 1902, LS, Post Surgeon; CO, Fort Robinson, to President, Crawford Town Council, February 1, 1902, LS, Fort Robinson; Dr. A. M. Cross to Post Surgeon, August 7, 1902, Register of Correspondence, Post Surgeon.

15. Post Surgeon to President, Crawford Town Council, July 20, 1903, and to SG, USA, July 22, 1903, LS, Post Surgeon; Dr. G. A. Meredith to Post Surgeon, July 27, 1903, Register of Correspondence, Post Surgeon; Entries for July and August 1903, MH, Fort Robinson.

16. Dr. G. A. Meredith to Post Surgeon, August 10, 1904, Register of Correspondence, Post Surgeon; CO, Fort Robinson, to Dr. Sanderson, June 12, 1898, and to AG, DeptMo, June 16, 1898, LS, Fort Robinson.

17. Post Returns, January 1910; Crawford *Tribune*, January 14, 21, and 28, 1910.

18. Certificates of Disability, Fort Robinson, 1875-1905 (NA, RG 393); Post Surgeon to Post Adjutant, January 16, 1904, LS, Post Surgeon. Data on 1903 cases comes from a series of letters Surgeon Field wrote unit commanders when he released soldiers to duty after treatment (LS, Post Surgeon).

19. General Order 9, February 18, 1898, Post Orders, Fort Robinson. Regarding Army attitudes toward prostitution, see Anne M. Butler, *Daughters of Joy, Sisters of Misery: Prostitutes in the American West, 1865-1890* (Urbana, 1985), pp. 122-146, 153.

20. City Council Minutes, II, January 12, 1898.

21. CO, Fort Robinson, to Chairman, Village Board of Trustees, June [?] 1902, LS, Fort Robinson; Chairman, Village Board of Trustees, to Captain Charles H. Grierson, July 17, 1902, Register of Correspondence, Post Surgeon; City Council Minutes, II, April 3, 1902.

22. On the St. Louis experiment and the political and medical debates that swirled around it, see John C. Burnham, "Medical Inspection of Prostitutes in America in the Nineteenth Century: the St. Louis Experiment and its Sequel," *Bulletin of the History of Medicine*, 45 (May-June 1971), pp. 203-218; Burnham, "The Social Evil Ordinance—A Social Experiment in Nineteenth Century St. Louis," *Bulletin of the Missouri Historical Society*, 27 (April 1971) pp. 203-217.

23. City Council Minutes, II, July 23, 1902; Crawford *Tribune*, August 1, 1902; Burnham, "The Social Evil Ordinance," p. 205.

24. Post Surgeon to Post Adjutant, January 16, 1904, LS, Post Surgeon.

25. Crawford *Tribune*, May 6, 1904.

26. Monthly Report, Chaplain Anderson, December 1902, AGO File 53910; CO, Fort Robinson, to Post Chaplain, December 3, 1902, LS, Fort Robinson; David F. Musto, *The American Disease: Origins of Narcotics Control* (New Haven, 1973), p. 20; Butler, *Daughters of Joy, Sisters of Misery*, p. 67; Mary Murphy, "The Private Lives of Public Women: Prostitution in Butte, Montana, 1878-1917," Susan Armitage and Elizabeth Jameson, eds., *The Women's West* (Norman, 1982), p. 200.

27. Monthly Report, Chaplain Anderson, March 1903, and Endorsement, CO, Fort Robinson, n. d., AGO File 53910; Post Surgeon to Post Adjutant, January 16 and 30, 1904, LS, Post Surgeon; Sanitary Report, March 1905, MH, Fort Robinson.

28. Musto, *The American Disease*, pp. 3, 7.

29. Entries for August 6 and 8, 1912, Police Court Docket (Municipal Records, Crawford, Nebraska).

NOTES FOR CHAPTER 12

1. Van Ackeren, *Sioux County*, pp. 54, 100-101; Crawford *Tribune*, April 18, 1919; Mrs. Glen Kremen, "Early Days Around Glen," p. 181.

2. Rickey, *Forty Miles a Day on Beans and Hay*, p. 232; *Compendium of History, Reminiscence, and Biography of Western Nebraska*, p. 320.

3. Mrs. Glen Kremen, "Early Days Around Glen," p. 181.

4. Newspapers for Crawford are scarce for the early years. No papers are available until 1892, with the exception of infrequent reprints in the *Army and Navy Journal*. Some of the papers published in the first few years, such as the *Crescent*, have disappeared entirely. For later years, for which newspaper runs are nearly complete, it is easier to get an accurate picture of veterans who remained in town.

5. VA File C 2555351, James F. Jackson.

6. Crawford *Bulletin*, February 17, 1900; *Annual Report of the Department of War, 1907*, I, p. 71; CO H/9th Cavalry, to Chief QM, DP, August 3, 1897, LS, H/9th Cavalry.

7. Report of Inspection, Fort Robinson, September 3, 1894, Reports of Inspection, DP, II; Statement of Financial Operations of Post Exchange, at Fort Robinson, Nebraska, for six months ending June 30, 1899, QM Consolidated File, Fort Robinson.

8. Crawford *Tribune*, May 27 and August 18, 1904; Crawford *Bulletin*, May 27, 1904; Post QM to CO, Fort Robinson, May 13, 1904, and Chief QM, DeptMo, to CO, Fort Robinson, Register of LR, Fort Robinson, July 16, 1904.

9. *Souvenir Book: Crawford, Nebraska, 75th Year, 1886-1961*, p. 59; VA File XC 2499129, Caleb Benson.

10. Cook, *Tales of the 0-4 Ranch*, pp. 60-61, 93, 98-100; Crawford *Tribune*, February 23, 1917.

11. Cook, *Tales of the 0-4 Ranch*, pp. 101-102; VA Pension File SC 874522, Alex Stepney; List of Interments, Fort Robinson (Vertical File, Fort Robinson Museum).

12. Cook, *Tales of the 0-4 Ranch*, pp. 60, 67-68; Regimental Returns, 10th Cavalry, July 1904.

13. Crawford *Tribune*, May 14 and 21, 1897, October 6, 1905, November 22, 1907, July 5, 1918, and April 2, 1920; Cleveland *Gazette*, January 1, 1887.

14. C. F. Gund, "Notes on Early History of Crawford," typescript; Crawford *Tribune*, December 6, 1907; VA File XC 2705872, Henry McClain.

15. This data is taken from Dawes County tax lists, filed with the county treasurer in Chadron. The lists were examined at five year intervals, starting in 1887, Crawford's first full year of existence. The 1916 list was used instead of 1917 because World War I brought a large number of new residents to northwestern Nebraska. The influx may have affected real estate values and the total amount of taxable personal property. During the entire period, all property other than real estate, including savings accounts and negotiable instruments, was taxed as personal property.

16. Dawes County Tax lists, 1902, 1907, 1912, 1916.

17. Crawford *Tribune*, September 23, 1904; Donald Danker, Interview with Joe Hand (NSHS, Lincoln); Police Court Docket (Municipal Records, Crawford, Nebraska).

18. This section on residential patterns was developed from the property tax lists, used in conjunction with the 1955 edition of the Crawford plat map.

19. Gund, "Notes on Early History of Crawford."

20. VA File XC 2648848, Rufus Slaughter; Crawford *Tribune*, April 7, 1899.

21. VA File XC 2648848, Rufus Slaughter.

22. VA File XC 2499129, Caleb Benson.

23. VA File C 2567358, Benjamin Hartwell; VA File SC 2705872, Henry McClain; Crawford *Tribune*, November 22, 1907.

24. Petition, Robinson Post 261, Grand Army of the Republic, to the Secretary of War, May 5, 1894, AGO File 6474 ACP 81. The letter on behalf of Chaplain Plummer's colonization proposal was signed by twenty-five members, including two veterans of the Ninth Cavalry.

25. *ANJ*, 32 (April 13, 1895), p. 536; Cleveland *Gazette*, February 27, 1892; Crawford *Tribune*, May 14, 1897.

26. *Ibid.*, February 20, 1903, July 29, 1904, and January 19, 1906.

27. *Ibid.*, May 31, 1912, and September 13, 1913.

28. Crawford *Tribune*, November 15, 1912, and September 5, 1913; *Northwestern Nebraska News*, September 3, 1931.

29. Crawford *Tribune*, November 15, 1912, January 30, 1914, November 3, 10, and 24, 1916, August 24 and 31, 1917.

30. Rickey, *Forty Miles a Day on Beans and Hay*, p. 337.

31. Mae Manion, *"Prairie Pioneers" of Box Butte County* (Alliance, 1970), pp. 142-143; Crawford *Tribune*, February 24 and August 18, 1911.

32. *Ibid.*, December 15, 1899, March 22, 1901, August 1, 1902, July 31, 1903, August 29 and September 22, 1905, March 23, 1906, and December 4, 1914.

33. *Ibid.*, January 22, 1909, June 3, 1910, February 17, April 21, and October 20, 1911, August 16, 1912, July 12, 1914, July 27, 1917; Dawes County Tax List, 1916; *Northwestern Nebraska News*, September 18, 1930.

34. *Souvenir Book*, p. 42; Dorothy Meredith, "My Most Unforgettable Character," Crazy Horse Cultural Center, *Old Timers Tales*, III, p. 13.

35. Post Returns, April 1891, and January-February, 1896; Crawford *Tribune*, June 7, and 14, 1901, and May 1, 1903.

36. Joy Buckley, "Notes on Some Early Settlers of the Upper White River Area," Crazy Horse Cultural Center, *Old Timers Tales*, 1, pp. 146, 148; *Annual Report of the Department of the Interior, 1906*, pp. 20-21; Arthur R. Reynolds, "Land Frauds and Illegal Fencing in Western Nebraska," *Agricultural History*, 23 (1949), p. 174; Addison E. Sheldon, *Land Systems and Land Policies in Nebraska* (Lincoln, 1936), pp. 182, 185.

37. Crawford *Tribune*, August 25, and November 16, 1905; Buckley, "Notes on Some Early Settlers," p. 148; Johnson to CO, Fort Robinson, November 16, 1903, Register of LR, Fort Robinson; CO, 10th Cavalry to Johnson, May 4, 1904, LS, 10th Cavalry.

38. Crawford *Tribune*, April 24, 1914, and May 5, 1916; Crawford *Courier*, September 11, 1914.

39. Dawes County Tax Lists, 1892-1916.

NOTES FOR CHAPTER 13

1. Contemporary citizens, postmasters general as well as local boosters, considered postal receipts an important economic indicator. In 1883 postmasters' salaries were tied to postal revenue by law, and Postmaster General William Gresham observed

that pay in his department would therefore depend "largely upon the condition of the business interests of the country." The data in table R139-145 of *The Statistical History of the United States from Colonial Times to 1957* (Stamford, 1957), pp. 496-497, shows that receipts throughout the nation did react to overall economic change. There is some danger in using postal receipts as an economic indicator since postal officials and the businessmen they served were not above padding receipts by minor frauds and overpurchase of stamps. However, all distortion was probably upward, so changes in receipts probably still indicate the direction of shifts in economic activity. Report of the Postmaster General, *Annual Report of the Post Office Department, 1883*, p. 10; Report of the Postmaster General, *Ibid.*, 1902; Report of the First Assistant Postmaster General, *Ibid.*, 1893, p. 84; Crawford *Tribune*, March 28, August 1, and October 3, 1902.

2. See, for example, Crawford *Tribune*, June 28, 1901, and June 26, 1903.

3. *The Corn Belt*, 2 (July 1896), p. 14, and 6 (April 1898), p. 5. Also see *The Great Northwest, its Marvelous Growth and Wealth* (Omaha, 1889), pp. 3, 14.

4. Transportation contracts are not considered because the arrival of the railroad in 1886 eliminated this once-lucrative source of income. Previously Army freighting was a profitable enterprise for Sidney businessmen. Cornelius Ferris, J. A. Pratt, and George Jewitt, who formed the Sidney and Black Hills Transportation Company, dominated Fort Robinson shipping. William E. Lass, *From the Missouri to the Great Salt Lake, an Account of Overland Freighting* (Lincoln, 1972), pp. 203, 206; Transportation Contracts, Edward Fenlon, Cornelius Ferris, George Berry, David Brown, J. A. Pratt, and John Hindry (NA, RG 92).

5. Prior to 1891 Fort Robinson had the only postal facility. After the Crawford office opened, the one on post continued in operation. In 1906 the Post Office Department changed the basis for calculating postmasters' salaries. Post offices were grouped into several classes, based on ranges of revenue. At the same time, the Department discontinued publication of receipts for each post office.

6. Data for this summary comes from the minutes of the Crawford City Council (Municipal Records, Crawford, Nebraska), which announced election results each year, and the Register of Contracts, 1871-1912, 21 Volumes (NA, RG 92).

7. Crawford *Tribune*, August 19, 1904.

8. Occupational data for this summary comes from the following sources: local newspapers; *Compendium of History, Reminiscence, and Biography of Western Nebraska; Souvenir Book; Crawford, Nebraska, 75th Year, 1886-1961.*

9. Crawford City Council, Minutes, I, September 15, 1886.

10. *The Compiled Statutes of the State of Nebraska, 1885* (Omaha, 1885), pp. 135, 142; J. E. Cobbey, *Consolidated Statutes of Nebraska, 1891* (Lincoln, 1891), p. 66.

11. Post Returns, March 1881; Report of the AG, *Annual Report of the Department of War, 1881*, p. 45; Report of the IG, *Ibid.*, 1882, p. 71. After the elimination of the trader's store and establishment of the canteen system, only beer sales were permitted on post.

12. Ordinance 22, June [2], 1888. In 1901 the allocation of occupation taxes on saloonmen to local schools became a state-wide practice. Crawford *Tribune*, May 24, 1901.

13. Crawford City Council, Minutes, I, December 5, 1892, April 3, 1893, March 20, 1895, and II, November 23, 1897.

14. Crawford *Tribune*, May 30 and June 6, 1902.

15. *ANJ*, 25 (June 16, 1888), p. 963; *Ibid.*, 25 (June 30, 1888), p. 975; *Ibid.*, 26 (December 22, 1888), p. 321; Crawford *Tribune*, April 6, 1906.

16. Report of the Chief Surgeon, DP, *Annual Report of the Department of War, 1896*, p. 473; Report of Inspection, Fort Robinson, August 21, 1893, Reports of Inspections, DP, II. See Schubert, "The Suggs Affray," p. 66, for court martial and desertion data and officers' comments that indicate the greater reliability and temperance of black troops.

17. *Souvenir Book*, pp. 25, 127; Crawford *Tribune*, January 17, 1913; *Compendium of History, Reminiscence, and Biography of Western Nebraska*, p. 337.

18. Mari Sandoz, *Old Jules*, p. 117; Crawford *Tribune*, April 9, 1909, November 10, 1916, and May 4, 1917. Property tax levies are specified in city ordinances passed annually in the spring.

19. "A Historical Sketch of the First Methodist Church, Crawford, Nebraska," typescript (NSHS, Lincoln), pp. 2-3; *Souvenir Book*, p. 68; Crawford *Clipper*, January 29, 1892; Crawford *Tribune*, August 4, 1905.

20. Crawford City Council, Minutes, I, May 2 and 5, 1892, II, May 4, 5 and 11, 1899; Crawford *Tribune*, March 11, 1898, May 5 and 12, 1899. There is no information regarding who closed the saloons and on what basis this decision was reached. Rominger, whom the *Tribune* identified as an outside agitator, lived in Crawford for at least two years, from 1897 to 1899, and ran for city council in April 1899, when he received one vote, presumably his own.

21. Crawford City Council, Minutes, II, December 5, 1905.

22. Four shootings in town during 1902 through 1907 involved black troopers of the Tenth Cavalry. A student of the community has correctly linked these incidents to the end of beer sales at the Post Exchange. Certainly more troops went to town after military prohibition in 1901. Racial tensions could have played parts in only two of the incidents. The others involved no whites. Simple numbers were as significant as other factors in causing the increased violence: in May 1902, the garrison grew from 147 to 602. Hytrek, "The History of Fort Robinson from 1900 to the present," pp. 14, 16-17; Crawford *Tribune*, September 18, 1903, and May 18, 1906; Crawford *Bulletin*, September 18, 1903, and June 4, 1904; Post Surgeon to CO, Fort Robinson, December 26, 1903, Register of LR, Fort Robinson.

23. Donald Danker, Interview with Joe Hand; Arthur P. Howe, quoted in Hytrek, "The History of Fort Robinson," p. 16.

24. Crawford *Tribune*, June 14, 1907, and June 24, 1910; Police Court Docket; Crawford City Council, Minutes, II, July 10 and 16, 1907; Ordinance 114, July 16, 1907.

25. Butler, *Daughters of Joy, Sisters of Misery*, p. 100.

26. Ordinance 6, December 6, 1886; Crawford City Council, Minutes, I, March 7 and May 2, 1887. Other towns near military posts put prostitution to similar uses. Rister, *Fort Griffin on the Texas Frontier*, p. 134; Strate, *Sentinel to the Cimarron*, p. 99; Butler, *Daughters of Joy, Sisters of Misery*, pp. 60-61, 96, 100.

27. The list of euphemisms for prostitutes is extensive. For a wide sample, see Butler, *Daughters of Joy, Sisters of Misery*, p. 82, and Glenda Riley, *The Female Frontier: A Comparative View of Women on the Prairie and the Plains* (Lawrence, 1988), p. 131.

28. Crawford *Tribune*, April 29, 1904.

29. Crawford City Council, Minutes, I, January 8, 1894, December 17, 1895, and January 6, 1896.

30. *Ibid.*, II, May [?], 1907. Total city expenditures and revenues were reported as erratically as the whore tax, so a systematic summary of their relationship is impossible.

31. Crawford City Council, Minutes, I, May 9, 1887, January 2, 1888, June 11, and September 2, 1889, May 2, 1894, II, July 27, 1899.

32. Clarissa Lindemann Marrall, "The Night Three Men Were Shot," Crazy Horse Cultural Center, *Old Timers Tales*, II, pt. 1, p. 171.

33. Crawford *Tribune*, October 4, 1907; Police Court Docket.

34. Crawford *Tribune*, June 18, 1909, April 21, 1911; Sanitary Report, April 1910, MH, Fort Robinson.

35. Crawford City Council, Minutes, I, April 2, 1894; Crawford *Tribune*, April 9 and 30, 1897, March 25 and April 8, 1898, April 7, 1899, and April 6, 1900.

36. *The Corn Belt*, 2 (July 1896), p. 14; C. F. Gund, "Notes on Early History of Crawford," typescript, pp. 11-12; Crawford *Tribune*, March 5, 1897, and February 4 and 25, 1898.

37. L. N. Freeman, Chairman, Crawford Board of Village Trustees, to CO, Fort Robinson, February 16, 1903, Register of LR, Fort Robinson; Monthly Report, Chaplain Anderson, March 1903, AGO File 53910; Crawford *Tribune*, March 20, 1903.

38. Minnie Alice Rhoads, *A Stream Called Deadhorse* (Chadron, 1957), pp. 50-51; Crawford *Tribune*, February 12, March 5, April 6 and 23, September 3, and December 24, 1909.

39. *Ibid.*, January 14, 1910; *Souvenir Book*, p. 12; Donald Danker, Interview with Miss [Clarissa?] Lindeman.

40. Crawford *Tribune*, January 28, and February 11, 1910. Files of the *Courier* are available only for 1914, so the *Tribune* is the only source for the views of the opposing paper.

41. Crawford *Tribune*, February 18, and 25, 1910, and August 2, 1912. One of the six windows in the 1917 building of the Methodist church was purchased and dedicated to the memory of the president of the Civic League. "A Historical Sketch of the First Methodist Church," p. 5.

42. Crawford *Tribune*, March 4, 1910; Crawford City Council, Minutes, II, March 10, 1910.

43. Crawford *Tribune*, March 25, April 1, 8, 15, and 22, 1910; Crawford City Council, Minutes, II, April 8, and May 3, 1910. Crawford's decisions regarding vice and the town's relationship to the post parallels developments in Kansas cattle towns in several ways. See Robert F. Dykstra, *The Cattle Towns* (New York, 1968), pp. 74, 85, 100-105, 125-126, 239. The most interesting similarity occurred in the area of political participation. In the cattle towns, numerous factional splits stimulated wide-spread involvement in public issues. In Crawford, which maintained at least the appearance of a broad consensus for many years, the normal school disaster and related disputes over vice generated the factions that made public policy and councilmanic elections matters of general concern.

44. Crawford City Council, Minutes, II, May 3, 6, and 27, 1910.

45. *Ibid.*, May 23, 1910; Crawford *Tribune*, May 27, 1910.

46. *Ibid.*, March 10, 1911; Crawford City Council, Minutes, II, April 8, 1911.

47. *Ibid.*, April 8, and May 2, 1911; Crawford *Tribune*, March 10, 17, 24, and 31, and April 7, 1911.

48. Mae Manion, *"Prairie Pioneers" of Box Butte County*, p. 65; Van Ackeren, *Sioux County*, p. 99; *Souvenir Book: Crawford, Nebraska, 75th Year, 1886-1961*, pp. 39, 55, 70-71, Omaha *World Herald*, February 20, 1933.

49. Gene M. Gressley, *Bankers and Cattlemen* (New York, 1966), p. x.

50. For the impact of one federal agency on another portion of the West, see Michael E. Welsh, *U.S. Army Corps of Engineers: Albuquerque District, 1935-1985* (Albuquerque, 1987). Also see Gerald D. Nash, *The American West in the Twentieth Century: A Short History of an Urban Oasis* (Englewood Cliffs, New Jersey, 1973), pp. 106-107, 201-202, 233-240.

51. Nash, *The American West in the Twentieth Century*, p. 107.

52. Cheyenne *Daily Leader*, April 10, 1909.

53. Data on marriages and the destinations of the couples involved comes from local newspapers.

54. James B. Allen, *The Company Town in the American West* (Norman, 1966), p. 3.

55. Post Surgeon to Medical Director, DP, December [?], and December 23, 1889, and to AG, USA, June 30, 1893, MH, Fort Robinson; Cleveland *Gazette*, March 5, 1898; *The Statistical History of the United States from Colonial Times to the Present*, pp. 185-186.

56. Post Surgeon to Medical Director, DP, December 23, 1889, MH, Fort Robinson.

57. Data for this table comes from reports of collections in City Council minutes and local newspapers.

58. No actual payrolls are available. Estimated annual totals have been developed by multiplying the mean number of officers and enlisted men by the yearly pay of second lieutenants ($1,400) and privates ($156), respectively. The 1908 increases, which averaged 20 percent for officers and 40 percent for enlisted men, raised the figures to $1,680 and $218. The raise went into effect in May, and the mid-year change was taken into consideration in estimating the 1908 payroll. This method significantly understates the size of the military payroll and to a lesser degree the importance of all military outlays. However, the method probably yields figures that reflect changes in the actual payroll satisfactorily.

59. Civilian payrolls are based on data in post monthly returns, which reported the number of employees, their occupations, and their wages. A revised report form, which went into use in September 1904, did not include this information.

60. Contract data is derived from the twenty-one volumes of Registers of Contracts, 1871-1912 (NA, RG 92). All civilian contractors with post office addresses of Crawford or Fort Robinson are considered "local." Locally let construction contracts are included with "Local Contracts," and not "Construction Contracts."

61. "Local" expenditures are defined just as they are for Table 1: military payroll, civilian payroll, local contracts, and all construction contracts.

62. "Three-County" area is the northwestern corner of the state: Box Butte, Sheridan, and Sioux counties. Dawes County is listed separately.

63. "Northwestern Nebraska" is roughly the northwestern quarter of the state minus the four counties in the corner. Counties included in this column are Cherry, Thomas, Hooker, Grant, Logan, McPherson, Arthur, Garden, Morrill, Scottsbluff, and Banner.

64. Data for this table comes from city ordinances and city council minutes.

NOTES FOR EPILOGUE

1. Grange, "Fort Robinson," p. 230.

2. Miller J. Stewart, "Fort Robinson, Nebraska, Army Remount Depot, 1919-1945," *Nebraska History*, 70 (Winter 1989), p. 274.

3. *Northwestern Nebraska News*, September 6, 1934; "Souvenir Program: Dedication of Twin Monuments in Honor of Lieut. Levi H. Robinson . . . [and] Crazy Horse," Fort Robinson, Nebraska, September 5, 1834, File C-31, Order of Indian Wars collection, MHI. "The Death of Crazy Horse" is chapter XIV of John G. Neihardt *The Twilight of the Sioux: the Song of the Indian Wars* (Lincoln, 1971), pp. 169-179.

4. Map #629-US, sheet 7, 1929, War Department Map Collection (NA, RG 77).

5. Buecker, "The Dismounting of the 4th Cavalry," *Rural Electric Nebraskan*, 43 (February 1989), pp. 12-14.

6. Buecker, "War Dogs," *Nebraskaland* (December 1988), p. 36.

7. Buecker, "War Dogs," pp. 36, 47.

8. Buecker, "Mules, Horses and Dogs—Fort Robinson in World War II," *Periodical, Journal of the Council on America's Military Past*, XVI (April 1989), p. 35; Charles J. Sullivan, *Army Posts & Towns: the Baedeker of the Army* (Burlington, 1926), p. 180.

9. Grange, "Fort Robinson, pp. 230-231; Buecker, "War Dogs," pp. 34, 36-37.

10. Grange, "Fort Robinson," pp. 230-231; Buecker, "Mules, Horses and Dogs," pp. 44, 46.

BIBLIOGRAPHY

BOOKS

Allen, James B. *The Company Town in the American West.* Norman: University of Oklahoma Press, 1966.

Armitage, Susan, and Elizabeth Jameson, eds. *The Women's West.* Norman: University of Oklahoma Press, 1987.

Ashburn, Percy M. *A History of the Medical Department of the United States Army.* Boston: Houghton, Mifflin, 1929.

Beasley, Delilah L. *Negro Trailblazers of California.* Los Angeles: Mirror Printing, 1919.

Biddle, Ellen McGown. *Reminiscences of a Soldier's Wife.* Philadelphia: J. B. Lippincott, 1907.

Bronson, Edgar Beecher. *Reminiscences of a Ranchman.* Lincoln: University of Nebraska Press, 1962.

Butler, Anne M. *Daughters of Joy, Sisters of Misery: Prostitutes in the American West, 1865-90.* Urbana: University of Illinois Press, 1985.

Cashin, Herschel V., Charles Alexander, William T. Anderson, Arthur M. Brown, and Horace W. Bivins. *Under Fire with the Tenth U.S. Cavalry.* New York: F. Tennyson Neely, 1899.

Clark, Robert A., ed., *The Killing of Chief Crazy Horse: three eyewitness views by the Indian, Chief He Dog; the Indian-white, William Garnett; the White doctor, Valentine McGillycuddy* (Lincoln: University of Nebraska Press, 1988).

Coffman, Edward M. *The Old Army: A Portrait of the American Army in Peacetime, 1784-1898*. New York: Oxford University Press, 1986.

Cook, Harold J. *Tales of the 0-4 Ranch: Recollections of Harold J. Cook, 1887-1909*. Introduction by Agnes Wright Spring. Lincoln: University of Nebraska Press, 1968.

Compendium of History, Reminiscence and Biography of Western Nebraska. Chicago: Alden Publishing Company, 1909.

Coursey, O. W. *Beautiful Black Hills*. Mitchell, South Dakota: 1925.

Crawford, Lewis F. *Rekindling Camp Fires: the Exploits of Ben Arnold*. Bismarck: Capital Book Co., 1926.

Crazy Horse Cultural Center. *Old Timers Tales*. 3 Vols. Chadron, Nebraska: Dawes County Circulating Library, 1971-1972.

Dubofsky, Melvyn. *We Shall Be All: A History of the Industrial Workers of the World*. Chicago: Quadrangle Books, 1969.

Dunlay, Thomas W. *Wolves for the Blue Soldiers: Indian Scouts and Auxiliaries with the United States Army, 1860-90*. Lincoln: University of Nebraska Press, 1987.

Dykstra, Robert F. *The Cattle Towns*. New York: Alfred A. Knopf, 1968.

Foner, Jack D. *The United States Soldier Between Two Wars*. New York: Humanities Press, 1970.

Forrest, Earle R. and Joe E. Milner. *California Joe*. Caldwell, Idaho: Caxton Printers, 1935.

Glass, Edward L. N. *The History of the Tenth Cavalry, 1866-1921*. Tucson: Acme Printing Company, 1921.

Gould, Lewis L. *Wyoming, A Political History, 1868-1896*. New Haven: Yale University Press, 1968.

Gressley, Gene M. *Bankers and Cattlemen*. New York: Alfred A. Knopf, 1966.

Hageman, R. E., ed. *Fighting Rebels and Redskins: Experiences in Army Life of Colonel George B. Sanford 1861-1892*. Norman: University of Oklahoma Press, 1969.

Hans, Fred M. *The Great Sioux Nation*. Chicago: M. A. Donohue, 1907.

Huston, James A. *The Sinews of War: Army Logistics 1775-1955.* Washington, D.C.: Office of the Chief of Military History, 1966.

Hutton, Paul A. *Phil Sheridan and his Army.* Lincoln: University of Nebraska Press, 1985.

_____, ed. *Soldiers West: Biographies from the Military Frontier.* Lincoln: University of Nebraska Press, 1987.

Hyde, George E. *Red Cloud's Folk. A History of the Oglala Sioux Indians.* Norman: University of Oklahoma Press, 1937.

Jackson, Donald. *Custer's Gold: The United States Cavalry Expedition of 1874.* New Haven: Yale University Press, 1966.

Johnson, Virginia W. *The Unregimented General: A Biography of Nelson A. Miles.* Boston: Houghton, Mifflin, 1962.

Kappler, Charles J. *Indian Affairs, Laws and Treaties.* 2 Vols. Washington, D.C.: Government Printing Office, 1903.

Kelley, Alexander, and Pierre Bovis, eds. *Pine Ridge, 1890. An Eye Witness Account of the Events Surrounding the Fighting at Wounded Knee.* San Francisco: Pierre Bovis, 1971.

King, Charles. *Campaigning with Crook and Stories of Army Life.* Ann Arbor: University Microfilms, 1966.

King, James T. *War Eagle: A Life of General Eugene A. Carr.* Lincoln: University of Nebraska Press, 1963.

Larson, T. A. *History of Wyoming.* Lincoln: University of Nebraska Press, 1965.

Lass, William E. *From the Missouri to the Great Salt Lake: An Account of Overland Freighting.* Lincoln: Nebraska State Historical Society, 1972.

Leckie, William H. *The Buffalo Soldiers, a Narrative of the Negro Cavalry in the West.* Norman: University of Oklahoma Press, 1967.

Lockmon, Carl. *The Years of Promise.* 1971.

Manion, Mae. *"Prairie Pioneers" of Box Butte County.* Alliance: Iron Man Industries, 1970.

Marquis, Thomas B. *A Warrior Who Fought Custer.* Minneapolis: The Midwest Company, 1931.

Mattes, Merrill J. *Indians, Infants, and Infantry: The Story of Andrew and Elizabeth Burt*. Denver: Old West Publishing Company, 1960.

Mooney, James. *The Ghost Dance Religion and the Sioux Outbreak of 1890*. Fourteenth Annual Report, Bureau of American Ethnology. Washington, D.C.: Government Printing Office, 1896.

Musto, David F. *The American Disease: Origins of Narcotics Control*. New Haven: Yale University Press, 1973.

Nash, Gerald D. *The American West in the Twentieth Century: A Short History of an Urban Oasis*. Englewood Cliffs, New Jersey: Prentice-Hall, Inc., 1973.

Olson, James C. *Red Cloud and the Sioux Problem*. Lincoln: University of Nebraska Press, 1965.

Plummer, Nellie Arnold. *Out of the Depths, or the Triumph of the Cross*. Hyattsville: 1927.

Reimers, David M. *White Protestantism and the Negro*. New York: Oxford University Press, 1965.

Rhoads, Minnie Alice. *A Stream Called Deadhorse*. Chadron: Chadron Printing Company, 1957.

Rickey, Don Jr. *Forty Miles a Day on Beans and Hay: The Enlisted Soldier Fighting the Indian Wars*. Norman: University of Oklahoma Press, 1963.

Riley, Glenda. *The Female Frontier: A Comparative View of Women on the Prairie and the Plains*. Lawrence: University Press of Kansas, 1988.

Rister, Carl Coke. *Fort Griffin on the Texas Frontier*. Norman: University of Oklahoma Press, 1956.

Rodenbaugh, Theodore F., and William J. Haskin, eds. *The Army of the United States*. New York: Maynard, Merrill, and Co., 1896.

Sandoz, Mari. *Cheyenne Autumn*. New York: Hastings House, 1953.

——————————. *Crazy Horse, the Strange Man of the Oglalas*. Lincoln: University of Nebraska Press, 1961.

——————————. *Old Jules*. Boston: Little, Brown, 1935.

Sheldon, Addison E. *Land Systems and Land Policies in Nebraska*. Lincoln: Nebraska State Historical Society, 1936.

Souvenir Book: Crawford, Nebraska. 75th Year. 1886-1961. Crawford: 1961.

Spring, Agnes Wright. *The Cheyenne and Black Hills Stage and Express Routes.* Lincoln: University of Nebraska Press, n. d.

Steward, Theophilus G., ed. *Active Service, or Gospel Work Among the U.S. Soldiers.* New York: U.S. Army Aid Association, 1897.

_____. *The Colored Regulars in the United States Army.* New York: The Arno Press, 1969.

Strate, David K. *Sentinel to the Cimarron: The Frontier Experience of Fort Dodge, Kansas.* Dodge City: Cultural Heritage and Arts Center, 1970.

Sullivan, Charles J. *Army Posts & Towns: the Baedeker of the Army.* Burlington: Free Press Printing Company, 1926.

The Great North-west, its Marvelous Growth and Wealth. Omaha: Herald, 1889.

The Statistical History of the United States From Colonial Times to the Present. Stamford: Fairfield Publishers, 1965.

Utley, Robert M. *The Last Days of the Sioux Nation.* New Haven: Yale University Press, 1963.

Van Ackeren, Ruth, ed. *Sioux County, Memoirs of its Pioneers.* Harrison: Sun-News, 1967.

Weigley, Russell F. *History of the United States Army.* New York: The Macmillan Company, 1967.

Welsh, Michael E. *U.S. Army Corps of Engineers: Albuquerque District, 1935-1985.* Albuquerque: University of New Mexico Press, 1987.

Wheeler, Homer W. *Buffalo Days: Forty Years in the Old West.* Indianapolis: Bobbs-Merrill, 1925.

White, Howard A. *The Freedmen's Bureau in Louisiana.* Baton Rouge: Louisiana State University Press, 1970.

Wooster, Robert. *The Military and United States Indian Policy 1865-1903.* New Haven: Yale University Press, 1988.

Wright, R. R., ed. *Encyclopedia of the African Methodist Episcopal Church.* Philadelphia: A.M.E. Book Concern, 1947.

Yost, Nellie Snyder, ed. *Boss Cowman: The Recollections of Ed Lemmons, 1857-1946.* Lincoln: University of Nebraska Press, 1969.

PERIODICALS

Army and Navy Journal, 1887-1902.

Barrow, Stephen B. "Christmas in the United States Army," *Colored American Magazine*, 8 (February 1905).

Buecker, Thomas R. " 'An Excellent Soldier and an Efficient Officer,' " *Nebraskaland*, 67 (June 1989).

——————————. "Mules, Horses and Dogs—Fort Robinson in World War II," *Periodical*, 16 (April 1989).

——————————. "The Dismounting of the Fourth Cavalry at Fort Robinson, 1942," *Rural Electric Nebraskan*, 43 (February 1989).

——————————. "The 1887 Expansion of Fort Robinson," *Nebraska History*, 68 (Summer 1987).

——————————. "War Dogs," *Nebraskaland* (December 1988).

Burnham, John C. "Medical Inspection of Prostitutes in America in the Nineteenth Century: the St. Louis Experiment and its Sequel," *Bulletin of the History of Medicine*, 45 (May-June 1971).

——————————. "The Social Evil Ordinance—A Social Experiment in Nineteenth Century St. Louis," *Bulletin of the Missouri Historical Society*, 27 (April 1971).

Clement, Thomas J. "Athletics in the American Army," *Colored American Magazine*, 8 (January 1905).

Colby, L. W. "The Sioux Indian War of 1890-'91," *Transactions and Reports, Nebraska State Historical Society*, 3 (1892).

Corbusier, William T. "Camp Sheridan, Nebraska," *Nebraska History*, 42 (March 1961).

Grange, Roger T., Jr. "Fort Robinson, Outpost on the Plains," *Nebraska History*, 39 (September 1958).

Haynes, Robert V. "The Houston Mutiny and Riot of 1917," *Southwestern Historical Quarterly*, 74 (April 1973).

Henry, Guy V. "Adventures of American Army and Navy Officers. II. A Winter March to the Black Hills," *Harper's Weekly*, 39 (July 27, 1895).

Knight, Oliver. "War or Peace, the Anxious Wait for Crazy Horse," *Nebraska History*, 54 (Winter 1974).

Lowe, Albert S. "Camp Life of the Tenth U.S. Cavalry," *Colored American Magazine*, 7 (March 1904).

Mahnken, Norbert R. "The Sidney-Black Hills Trail," *Nebraska History*, 30 (September 1948).

Murray, Robert A. "The United States Army in the Aftermath of the Johnson County War," *Annals of Wyoming*, 38 (April 1966).

O'Neil, Floyd A. "An Anguished Odyssey: The Flight of the Utes, 1906-1908," *Utah Historical Quarterly*, 36 (Fall 1968).

Perry, Alexander. "The Ninth U.S. Cavalry in the Sioux Expedition of 1890," *Journal of the United States Cavalry Association*, 4 (March 1891).

Price, Byron. "Mutiny at San Pedro Springs," *By Valor and Arms*, 1 (Spring 1975).

Reynolds, Arthur R. "Land Frauds and Illegal Fencing in Western Nebraska," *Agricultural History*, 23 (July 1949).

Riley, Paul D., ed. "Oglala Sources on the Life of Crazy Horse, Interviews given to Eleanor H. Hinman," *Nebraska History*, 57 (Spring 1976).

Robinson, Michael C., and Frank N. Schubert. "David Fagen: An Afro-American Rebel in the Philippines, 1899-1901," *Pacific Historical Review*, 44 (February 1975).

Schubert, Frank N. "Black Soldiers on the White Frontier: Some Factors Influencing Race Relations," *Phylon*, 32 (Winter 1971).

_____. "The Fort Robinson Y.M.C.A., 1902-1907: A Social Organization in a Black Regiment," *Nebraska History*, 55 (Summer 1974).

_____. "The Suggs Affray: The Black Cavalry in the Johnson County War," *Western Historical Quarterly*, 4 (January 1973).

_____. "The Violent World of Emanuel Stance, Fort Robinson, 1887," *Nebraska History*, 55 (Summer 1974).

Simmons, Charlie. "Thanksgiving Day in the Tenth Cavalry," *The Voice of the Negro*, 2 (January 1905).

Stewart, Miller J. "Army Laundresses: Ladies of the 'Soap Suds Row,'" *Nebraska History*, 61 (Winter 1980).

_____."Fort Robinson, Nebraska, Army Remount Depot, 1919-1945," *Nebraska History*, 70 (Winter 1989).

Stover, Earl F. "Chaplain Henry V. Plummer, His Ministry and His Court Martial," *Nebraska History*, 56 (Spring 1975).

The Corn Belt, 1895-1902.

Thornton, Beverly F. "Economy," *Colored American Magazine*, 9 (March 1905).

Waddill, O. B. "Letter to Lawrence Bixby," *The Nebraska Cattleman*, 20 (April 1964).

Wheelock, Joseph M. "Our Own Editors and Publishers," *Colored American Magazine*, 8 (January 1905).

Wight, Willard E., ed. "A Young Medical Officer's Letters from Fort Robinson and Fort Leavenworth, 1906-1907," *Nebraska History*, 37 (June 1956).

Winners of the West, 1922-1941.

NEWSPAPERS

(Buffalo, Wyoming) *Big Horn Sentinel*, 1886.

Chadron (Nebraska) *Democrat*, 1886, 1888-1890.

Cheyenne (Wyoming) *Daily Leader*, 1906, 1909.

(Cheyenne) *Wyoming Tribune*, 1906.

Cleveland (Ohio) *Gazette*, 1885-1898.

Crawford (Nebraska) *Bulletin*, 1897, 1899-1904.

Crawford (Nebraska) *Clipper*, 1892.

Crawford (Nebraska) *Courier*, 1914.

Crawford (Nebraska) *Gazette*, 1893-1895, 1902.

Crawford (Nebraska) *Tribune*, 1892-1920.

Harrison (Nebraska) *Sun*, 1930.

Indianapolis (Indiana) *Freeman*, 1897-1907.

Lincoln (Nebraska) *State Journal*, 1896.

New York *Times*, 1906.

Northwestern Nebraska (Crawford) *News*, 1929-1934.

Omaha *Progress*, 1893.

Omaha *Daily Bee*, 1888, 1893.

Omaha *Weekly Bee*, 1883.

Omaha *World Herald*, 1938.

Richmond (Virginia) *Planet*, 1895-1898.

Sheridan (Wyoming) *Post*, 1906.

GOVERNMENT PUBLICATIONS, NEBRASKA

Cobbey, J. E. *Consolidated Statutes of Nebraska, 1891*. Lincoln: State Journal Company, 1891.

The Compiled Statutes of the State of Nebraska. 1881, second edition, with Amendments Comprising all Laws of a General Nature in force July 1, 1885. Omaha: Gibson, Miller & Richardson, 1885.

GOVERNMENT PUBLICATIONS, UNITED STATES

Interior Department. Annual Reports. 1906-1907.

Post Office Department. *Annual Reports.* 1883, 1886-1905.

—————————. *The Postal Laws and Regulations of the United States of America, In Effect April 1, 1902*. Washington, D.C.: Government Printing Office, 1902.

—————————. *The Postal Laws and Regulations of the United States of America, In Effect April 1, 1913*. Washington, D.C.: Government Printing Office, 1913.

War Department. *Annual Reports.* 1874-1916.

War Department, Military Division of the Missouri. *Record of Engagements with Hostile Indians Within the Military Division of the Missouri, from 1868 to 1882, Lieutenant General P. H. Sheridan, Commanding.* Washington, D.C.: Government Printing Office, 1882.

UNPUBLISHED THESES

Burleigh, D. Robert. "Range Cattle Industry in Nebraska to 1890," M.A., University of Nebraska, 1937.

Hytrek, Anthony J. "The History of Fort Robinson, Nebraska, from 1900 to the Present," M.A., Chadron State College, 1971.

Schubert, Frank N. "The Black Regular Army Regiments in Wyoming, 1885-1912," M.A., University of Wyoming, 1970.

Waltmann, Henry G. "The Subsistence Policy with Special Reference to the Red Cloud and Spotted Tail Agencies," M.A., University of Nebraska, 1959.

MANUSCRIPT MATERIALS

Municipal Records, City Hall, Crawford, Nebraska.
    City Council Minutes, 1886-1912.
    Ordinances, 1886-1917.
    Police Court Docket, 1891-1917.

Records of the Dawes County Treasurer, Chadron, Nebraska.
    Personal Property Tax Lists, 1887, 1892, 1897, 1902, 1907, 1912, and 1916.
    Real Estate Tax Lists, 1887, 1892, 1897, 1902, 1907, 1912, and 1916.

Western History Collection, Denver Public Library.
    A. W. Corliss, Diaries, 1884-1890. 3 Vols.

Rutherford B. Hayes Memorial Library, Fremont, Ohio.
    George Crook. Letterbooks. 2 Vols.
    Rutherford B. Hayes papers.

Wyoming State Archives, Cheyenne.
    Bryant B. Brooks papers.

Nebraska State Historical Society, Lincoln.

Crawford First Methodist Church. "A Historical Sketch of the First Methodist Church, Crawford, Nebraska." Typescript.

C. F. Gund. "Notes on Early History of Crawford." Typescript.

Joseph Hand. Interview (by Donald Danker). Typescript.

W. F. Heck. Interview (by Donald Danker). Audio tape.

Major General Guy V. Henry, retired. Letter to Vance Nelson.

Miss [Clarissa?] Lindeman. Interview (by Donald Danker). Audio tape.

Fanny McGillycuddy. "Notes kept at Camp Robinson December 13, 1875-February 22, 1877 and with the Army on an Expedition to the Black Hills, February 23-April 11, 1877." Typescript.

Simpson Mann. Interview (by Don Rickey, Jr.). Typescript.

Everett Pitt Wilson papers.

Fort Robinson Museum, Fort Robinson, Nebraska.

Vertical File.

National Archives, Washington, D. C.

Records of the Bureau of Indian Affairs, RG 75.

Central Map File.

Records of the Office of the Adjutant General, Record Group 94.

Document File 6474 ACP 81, Chaplain Henry V. Plummer.

Document File PRD 13194, Barney McKay.

Document File 53910, Monthly Reports, Chaplain William T. Anderson.

Document Files 1311782, 1338059, 1488357, and 1617194, Monthly Reports, Chaplain Neil F. Brennan.

Document Files 1603701, 1879823, 2006526, 2130171, Monthly Reports, Chaplain Alexander P. Landry.

Sutlers and Traders File, Fort Robinson.

Monthly Returns, 1st Cavalry, 1898-1900.

Monthly Returns, 8th Cavalry, 1907-1911.

Monthly Returns, 9th Cavalry, 1885-1898.

Monthly Returns, 10th Cavalry, 1902-1907.

Post Returns, Fort Robinson, 1874-1916.

Records of the Office of the Chief of Engineers, Record Group 77.

Civil Works Map File.

Miscellaneous Fortifications File, Fort Robinson.

Real Estate Division Map File.

War Department Map Collection.

Records of the Office of the Commissary General, Record Group 192.

Register, Beef and Vegetable Contracts, 1894-1895.

Records of the Office of the Judge Advocate General, Record Group 153.

Proceedings of General Court Martial, Emanuel Stance, 1873.

Proceedings of General Court Martial, Barney McKay, 1893.

Proceedings of General Court Martial, Henry V. Plummer, 1894.

Proceedings of General Court Martial, David R. Dillon, 1894.

Records of the Office of the Quartermaster General, Record Group 92.

Quartermaster Consolidated File, Fort Robinson.

Register of Contracts, 1871-1912. 21 Vols.
Transportation Contracts, Fort Robinson.

Records of United States Army Continental Army Commands, Record Group 393.

Department of the Missouri.
Miscellaneous Records, 1895-1912.

Department of the Platte.

Letters Received, 1893-1894.

Monthly Reports of Post Schools, 1893-1896.

Reports of Inspections, 1885-1894.

Telegrams Received, General Crook's Aide-de-Camp, 1877-1878.

Telegrams Sent, General Crook's Aide-de-Camp, 1877-1878.

Telegrams Sent, Headquarters in the Field, 1890-1891.

District of the Black Hills.

Endorsements Sent, 1874-1876.

Special Orders, 1874-1876.

Fort Robinson.

Certificates of Disability, 1875-1905.

Letters and Endorsements Sent, Post Surgeon, 1902-1904.

Letters, Telegrams, and Endorsements Sent, 1886-1902.

Medical History, 1887-1910.

Post Orders, 1886-1898.

Register of Correspondence, Post Surgeon, 1897-1904.

Register of Correspondence, 1886-1897.

Register of Letters Received, 1903-1904.

Summary Court Record, 1891-1902.

Military Division of the Missouri.

Special Files.

Black Hills Expedition, 1874.

Black Hills, 1875.

Cheyenne Outbreak, 1878-1879.

Little Wolf papers.

Sioux War, 1876.

Sioux War, 1877.

Proceedings of a Board of Officers Convened to Investigate the Cheyenne Outbreak of 1878.

Sioux Expedition, 1874.

Endorsements Sent.

General Orders.

Letters Received.

Letters Sent.

Retained Records.

Special Orders and Special Field Orders.

Records of United States Regular Army Mobile Units, Record Group 391.

Letters Sent, 8th Infantry, 1883-1899.

Orders, 9th Cavalry, 1875-1891.

Letters Sent, C Troop, 9th Cavalry, 1883-1886.

Letters Sent, H Troop, 9th Cavalry, 1896-1899.

Letters Sent, 10th Cavalry, 1902-1904.

Records of the Veterans Administration.

Pension File XC 2499129, Caleb Benson.

Pension File C 2441072, George Byers.

Pension File C 2567358, Benjamin Hartwell.

Pension File C 2555351, James F. Jackson.

Pension File XC 2705872, Henry McClain.

Pension File XC 2659455, Barney McKay.

Pension File XC 2659372, John C. Proctor.

Pension File XC 2648848, Rufus Slaughter.

Pension File SC 874522, Alexander Stepney.

U.S. Army Military History Institute archives, Carlisle, Pennsylvania.

Luther P. Bradley papers.

Benjamin O. Davis, Sr., papers.

Marvin Fletcher collection.

Guy V. Henry, Sr., papers.

Order of the Indian Wars files.

Tenth Cavalry papers.

INDEX